WHAT MARGIE HABER'S CLIENTS ARE SAYING . . .

"There are so many acting teachers out there, and I've studied with some of the best, but for auditioning, there's only Margie."

—*HEATHER LOCKLEAR (Melrose Place, Spin City)*

"Margie understands actors and is wonderful with them. She has developed a fabulous technique for auditioning and getting the job in a limited amount of time."

—*KELLY PRESTON (Jerry Maguire, Twins, Spellbinder)*

"I wish I could say that after I saw Margie Haber, I went back and I got the job. But what I think is even funnier is that I did the worst audition of my life, came to see Margie, worked with her, got a whole bunch of great ideas and was so prepared to go back. I was going to go get this job and I was gonna knock their socks off because I was so ready . . . and then they cancelled the movie!"

—*HALLE BERRY (Bulworth, Losing Isaiah)*

"Margie met me with a big smile and wisdom in her eyes. I listened. I learned. I smiled in return. Thank you, Margie."

—*JENNIFER LEWIS (The Preacher's Wife, What's Love Got to Do With It)*

"I think that auditioning is the hardest, most nerve-wracking part of being an actor. You could have all the talent in the world, but if you don't shine in your audition, you don't get the part. Margie's class really helped me relax, be comfortable and confident about my audition process."

—*JOSIE BISSETT (Melrose Place, Book of Love)*

"Margie's class made my auditions the best they have ever been and gave me the consistency that I couldn't get from an acting class alone. Now, I just love going on auditions!"

—*MICHAEL EASTON (Total Recall, Ally McBeal)*

"Margie's technique helps you get your focus off of what you're going to say next, and onto the other person. Then, you naturally begin reacting and staying in the moment, and all the other things you've always known acting, at it's best, is about. Margie makes it fun and easy to learn with her good-hearted sense of humor and her terrific ability to clearly communicate her ideas. She's as entertaining as she is didactic."

—*CRYSTAL CARSON (General Hospital)*

"Margie Haber took me from being a poor auditioner to actually enjoying the process. Her technique is like a life raft to me."

—TRAYLOR HOWARD (Two Guys and a Girl, Boston Commons)

"Using Margie's technique for an audition gives you an edge, by giving you the license to do the material and be free."

—MICHAEL BRANDON (Presumed Dangerous, JAG)

"While doing Margie's session, I got work—using her marvelous, focused, skillfull device called 'The Margie Haber Technique.' It's foolproof and direct, especially for any type of TV/film audition, because as an actor, it grounds you. It gets the actor's mind involved in the work. Margie explains the key things one should remember and put out there to get the job. I am so grateful that she has designed this Actor's Bible."

—JODI THELEN (Staying Afloat, Duet)

"I used to go into an audition and wing it. Now I have a concrete, tried and proven method for connecting with the material and presenting myself in the best possible light. Margie's technique works. Her approach enabled me to put back the fun into auditioning. What I used to dread, I now look forward to. I can't wait to get in there and start reading."

—GARY GRAHAM (Alien Nation)

"Margie's technique gives you tools—so that instead of going into an audition and flying by the seat of your pants, you have something to rely on that you can put to work constructively. There are lots of talented actors, but sometimes skill gets the job!"

—EILEEN DAVIDSON (The Young and the Restless, One Life to Live)

"With cold script in hand and Margie's 'method' in heart and soul, you are freer to sell the only thing you got: you!"

—STEVEN MACHT (Knot's Landing, Cagney & Lacey)

"Thank you. I had a block in booking prior to your class and I fundamentally attribute what has happened to what you've taught me. I got a couple of callbacks using your technique and then I booked the lead in the play, *Ah, Wilderness.* It is actually okay to use the sides! I don't have to fully memorize and it keeps me in the moment. I beat out a whole load of people!"

—MICHAEL REISZ (Ah, Wilderness)

"Margie has a sure-fire formula for finding the core of the character you're portraying. Her technique gave me the confidence to make choices, take risks and to enjoy the process."

—RENEE JONES (Days of Our Lives, LA Law, Bodies of Evidence)

"I'm just calling to thank you and acknowledge you. I got a series. I've got the lead in a series and it's a wonderful character. All that work has paid off. I'm starting to really feel myself in auditions and get through the barrier and let the talent out. So it works. Thank you. Thanks, Margie."

—DAVID BROOKS (Crusade)

"Margie takes the fear out of the unknown and teaches a solid, timeless technique that will never go out of style. It's the most effective 'Basic Training' an actor can master."

—LAR PARK LINCOLN (Knot's Landing)

"Getting the job today in film or television most often depends on how well you read in the producer's or casting director's office. Unlike acting before a camera or on a stage, 'office acting' is a totally different animal, and Margie Haber has that particular 'animal' well under control. You might say she's the Seigfried & Roy of cold-reading technique."

—EARL HOLLIMAN (Sharky's Machine, Police Woman)

"Margie Haber has changed the way I feel about auditions. She has improved my skills and also, she smells good."

—LORRAINE NEWMAN (The Coneheads, Perfect, Saturday Night Live)

"Margie helped me tremendously with the audition/cold reading process. Much of my work had been in theatre, so Margie helped pare down my performance to fit TV and film. Since then, I have had continued success not only in theatre, but also on the screen, thanks to her wonderful training and the care she has for the artist."

—AMICK BYRAM (Sunset Boulevard, Phantom of the Opera)

"With Margie's sensitivity and positive outlook, she encourages you to take risks and learn from your mistakes, not be ashamed of them. With that in mind, she's turned this "Vanilla ice cream cone into Jamoca Almond Fudge!"

—CHERYL RICHARDSON (General Hospital, Nightmare on Elm Street IV)

HOW TO GET THE PART

... without falling apart!

HOW TO GET THE PART

...without falling apart!

By Margie Haber
with Barbara Babchick

HOW TO GET THE PART . . . without falling apart!
Copyright © 1999 by Margie Haber and Barbara Babchick

LONE EAGLE PUBLISHING COMPANY™
1024 North Orange Drive, Hollywood, California 90038
Phone 323.308.3400 or 800.815.0503
A division of IFILM® Corp., www.ifilm.com

Printed in the United States of America

Cover concept by ADVANTAGE, London, T: +44 20 7613 3933
Cover and book design by Carla Green
Edited by Janna Wong Healy

Library of Congress Cataloging-in-Publication Data

Haber, Margie.
    How to get the part, without falling apart / Margie Haber with
Barbara Babchick.
        p.   cm.
    ISBN 1-58065-014-7
    1. Acting–Auditions. I. Babchick, Barbara. II. Title.
PN2071.A92H33 1999
792'.028–dc21   99-40361
                                                                       CIP

Books may be purchased in bulk at special discounts for promotional or educational purposes. Special editions can be created to specifications. Inquiries for sales and distribution, textbook adoption, foreign language translation, editorial, and rights and permissions inquiries should be addressed to: Jeff Black, IFILM Publishing, 1024 North Orange Drive, Hollywood, California 90038 or send e-mail to: info@ifilm.com

Distributed to the trade by National Book Network, 800.462.6420

IFILM® and Lone Eagle Publishing Company™ are registered trademarks.

This book is dedicated to

Michael Haber

the most wonderful son a mother could wish for

In loving memory of

Elaine Harris

and

David Wayne

CONTENTS

· ·

PART 1
GETTING
OUT OF
YOUR
OWN WAY

CHAPTER 1 / YOU ARE YOUR OWN WORST ENEMY

CHAPTER 2 / HOW YOU PRESENT YOURSELF

CHAPTER 3 / THE INTERVIEW

FOREWORD

Okay. I've never written a foreword before, and I usually just skip them completely and jump right into the book. But for Margie . . . I'll do anything!

Picture this: You barely make it through nightmare audition number 257, what with the new character they threw at you at the last minute, then yesterday, audition number 258 reads like the performance of your life, but surprise! You don't even get a callback. Now you're thinking that maybe it's time to listen to your parents and get a REAL job. But wait! Don't give up. At least not until you've checked out this book.

I met Margie when I was between work on *Dynasty* and *Melrose Place*. This was the first time in my career that I found myself unemployed and having to (HELP!) audition again. Yech! I love acting, but the thought of going out on an audition made me panic. My manager, Joan Green, sent me over to the *Margie Haber Cold Reading Workshop* to learn her cold reading technique.

So there I was, crouched in the corner of the room with my extra large sweatshirt pulled over my knees, praying that she wouldn't call on me. No such luck! Margie refused to let me hide in fear. In fact, she encouraged me (forced is more like it!) to face my fears and just get up there and do it. I was really scared. Here were all these incredible actors in her Master Class who could pick up a script and in minutes, do a scene like they had been rehearsing it for weeks. I didn't even know where to start.

My first question was, "Do you or don't you?" (Memorize the scene, that is.) I mean, for an audition, you usually don't have time to memorize the whole thing, so you're kind of half in, half out . . . it isn't pretty. The best thing about Margie's technique is that you don't have to memorize. I could read the pages and not get all freaked out about forgetting the lines. No more pressure! The words were right there in front of me and I could use them. In fact, she WANTED me to use them—what a concept!

Margie has this magical way of taking away all the fear. I started to feel better about getting up and working. Margie gave me permission to NOT be perfect. She said it was okay to make mistakes! (If only I had her instead of Mrs. Lindberger for 9th grade algebra.) And I didn't have to apologize for my mistakes, like I always did. I could just go with them and see where they took me. (Which is a not such a bad place for actors to be!)

Most acting teachers seem to focus on the seriousness of the work. Now, I'm not saying that Margie isn't a drama queen like the rest of us. But she wants actors to enjoy the process and have fun with it. Margie has this great ability to make people laugh at themselves. (And boy, was I laughing!) As a teacher, she gives so much of herself. She's honest, loving, insightful and is not afraid to tell it like it is.

So I hope you all know how lucky you are. I only wish that I had this book when I was first starting out. I'm glad that all of Margie's wisdom is finally down on paper. Read it and re-read it and keep it nearby when you need that extra bit of inspiration. (Mine'll be on my nightstand along with my daughter's Dr. Seuss collection.)

Good luck. And remember, it's not brain surgery. So have fun.

–Heather Locklear

HEATHER LOCKLEAR / *MELROSE PLACE, SPIN CITY*

My most embarrassing audition happened a zillion years ago when *Three's Company* was replacing Suzanne Somers. I went to the audition in my father's car and I'm sweating. I'm wearing a silk blouse because they were very 'in' in those days. I may have forgotten to wear deodorant but, anyway, I'm sweating because I'm nervous and there's no air conditioning in the car and I'm in L.A. and it's hot and disgusting. I see some Kleenex on the dashboard and I put it under my arms to soak up the perspiration.

So I get there. I run up to the reception desk, sit there, wait for my turn and I go in. (I remember the blouse now—it was peach!) I do my audition but no one laughs. And it is supposed to be funny! No one laughs. And then I say, " Thank you very much," and they say, "Thank you very much. Good-bye." I walk out of the door and as soon as the door shuts, they all laugh. And I'm thinking, "Whoah, maybe it was just a slow reaction."

As I walk out by the receptionist, I notice that the Kleenex has come out of my blouse and is sneaking up around my neck and breast area. So I guess they thought I stuffed my bra, I'm not sure.

Anyway, I didn't get the job.

ACKNOWLEDGMENTS

Margie and Barbara would like to thank the following people . . .

All of the actors and actresses who have contributed their stories and quotes.

All of the agents, managers, casting directors, producers and directors who have contributed stories, quotes and advice.

Everyone involved in the seminar at Howard Fine's studio, especially Howard Fine, Fern Champion, Al Onorato, Sam Weisman, and Jeff Witjas.

All of the teachers at Margie's studio—Corey Allen, Joe Anthony, Courtney Burr, Crystal Carson, Barbara Gannen, Annie Grindlay, and all of the office managers and class managers.

Joan Singleton, Jeff Black, Carla Green, Lauren Rossini and everyone at Lone Eagle Publishing and editor Janna Wong Healy.

Special thanks to Ed Asner, Jerry Bollt, Clay Cahoon, Donna Cassell, Garrett Cunneen, Steve and Adrienne Downing, Charles Ferderber, Natalie Gluck, Jacqueline Green, Chris Hershey & Associates, Barbara Jacobs, Storm Jenkins, Jennifer Kilberg, Jonathan Kirsch, Karen Kondazian, Laurie Lang, Norman Lear, Deborah Markoe, Carla Malden, Annette Paparella, Leslie Rutledge, Joan See, Barry Segel, Rich and Joanne Sells, Scott and Lucia Sherman, Erika Sloane, David Sobel, Jim Tauber and his wife, Emily.

Margie would like to thank her mother, Ruth Haber and her sisters Lois and Joan for their love and support.

Barbara would like to thank her parents, Harriet and Jack Babchick and her sisters Susan and Debbie for their love and support.

And finally, many thanks to all of our friends and relatives who have patiently helped us throughout this project.

PROLOGUE

Throughout twenty-five years of teaching, a familiar refrain echoes among my students: "I hate auditioning!" Over and over actors complain, "If only I had three weeks to prepare," or, "You should see me on the set!" or, "I can't do this; I develop my characters slowly during rehearsals." Does this sound familiar to you? You're not alone! Most actors hate to audition.

Talented actors have come to me, trembling with fear, over an upcoming audition. "Help!" they'll cry. "I feel like I'm sinking in quicksand!" To them, the audition process feels like a life-or-death situation. But, the more they struggle, the less chance they have of getting out of the situation alive . . . or of getting the part.

> *John Corbett came in for a private session to work on his reading for an audition. John was so horrified at the upcoming audition that he was ready to quit the business. After calming him down, we broke down the scene, step-by-step. By the time we finished, John breathed a sigh of relief, giving a little wink as he left our session with confidence. He got the part, becoming a regular on the long-running, highly acclaimed series* Northern Exposure.

The truth is, unless you're Julia Roberts or Tom Cruise, chances are you'll have to audition to get your next part. It doesn't matter if you know the producer's brother or have the hottest agent in town or give a great interview, eventually it all comes down to the reading—those few precious moments when your career is on the line as you stand, panic-stricken, and face the "firing squad." And, unfortunately, you probably don't have the tools to get through it without falling apart because you've never been trained to audition.

Years ago, while I was studying acting at Ithaca College, my professor, Mr. Cornea, taught us how to project as we recited Shakespearean monologues. Later, working with the legendary Lee Strasberg, hours were spent perfecting sense memory while we sipped imaginary cups of tea and felt the sun's warmth against our faces. At Harvey Lembeck's comedy workshop, we laughed and watched comic actors such as John Ritter improvise outrageous skits. Surprisingly, although I studied acting with the greats, I never learned how to audition—when I went out on readings, I felt lost, scared and often humiliated, as if I had never studied acting before.

I soon realized that auditioning is an entirely different animal. You walk into the casting director's cramped office, where people sit in judgment of your every move, and you're asked to perform without props, a set or other actors. You rarely have any time to prepare and you may have little information about the character or the script. You feel as if you have no control over your audition and you chalk it up to luck when you *do* land a part. At best, the audition process is an intimidating one; at worst, it can be a frightening, embarrassing and even abusive experience. Certainly, this is not the most supportive environment for actors! I believe it's time for actors to get wise about the audition process!

> *When an actor walks into my class, the first thing he must do is erase the negative thoughts associated with auditioning. He must erase: "I hate auditioning;" "If I only had more time, I'd be so much better;" or any other negative thoughts. And, he must replace them with positive thoughts, such as: "I love auditioning!" " I enjoy the audition process." This may sound simplistic, but it works.*

I'm writing this book to take away the three P's—Pain, Panic and Performance anxiety—and to give you back the big P—POWER. This book will help you break through the psychological roadblocks you may have about auditioning; it will give you the freedom to express your talent rather than expose your fears. It will teach you how to quickly connect to your emotional life by offering a structure to rely on and a revolutionary phrase technique to get you through readings without stumbling over the script. No more memorizing! No more worrying about the lines! After you read this book, you'll know exactly what to do and where to begin when you look at a script.

Once you get rid of the negative thoughts ("I hate auditioning," "I can't do this," "I'm not good enough") you can then focus on the specifics. You'll go in prepared. You'll own your audition! With the tips in this book, you can afford to relax a little and enjoy the process. You really *can* have fun with auditions! I give you permission to have fun. After all, if you're not going to have fun with the process, you should find another profession.

. . . .

It's Wednesday afternoon and approximately twenty actors enter the studio, each desperate to find a miracle cure for this terrible plague they call "auditions." Most of them are at their wit's end: some arrive at the strong request of their agents or managers; others come because they've heard I can work miracles with actors preparing to audition; others may have nowhere else to turn—they've taken countless acting classes but still aren't booking jobs. One by one, I talk with them about their previous experience and select twelve students to enter my advanced class while the others are read for placement. From the day they walk into my office to the end of the eight session workshop, these actors are transformed. Come. Let us journey together.

–M. H.

PART 1
GETTING OUT
OF YOUR
OWN WAY

—

YOU ARE YOUR OWN WORST ENEMY

Whose Side Are You On, Anyway?

GABRIEL BYRNE / *End of Days, The Usual Suspects*

When I went to London to become an actor, I was out of work for a year. It was very difficult for me, during that time, to convince myself that, as an Irish actor working in London, the situation would ever change. After six months, I began to despair and I began to think that I would never ever get work. And, after nine months, I was convinced that I should never be an actor. Coming up on one year, I was thinking about all kinds of other employment. Then, one day, I walked through a door and got two jobs—two movies on the same day—because I had changed my attitude. I no longer was in awe or in fear of the audition process because I really didn't care anymore. And I had learned a very valuable lesson—I learned to separate myself from my work so that if my work was attacked, it didn't necessarily mean I was a bad person, and when it was praised it didn't necessarily mean I was a good person. I also stopped depending on my work to make me happy or sad. I tried to work on myself outside of my work and make myself a more rounded and interesting human being. And that was very important, because actors are taught that the only thing that's important is acting and getting jobs. But, life also goes on, you know . . .

GABRIEL BYRNE

YOUR FRIEND, THE CASTING DIRECTOR

As an actor, you might be under the mistaken impression that the casting world is against you. You might assume that nobody in the business wants you to succeed. You may even become paranoid at the thought. When you walk into an audition, you might feel like you're going into battle instead of a safe place to work. You may see yourself as a small, insignificant pawn tossed around at the whim of giant, inaccessible creatures.

Let me wake you from your nightmare: casting directors are human, too. They have their good days and their bad days. And they, too, get overwhelmed by their job pressures. So, why not change your image of the ferocious beast to that of a non-threatening worker bee buzzing around trying to make some honey? The truth is, casting people need you just as much as you need them.

Actor Gabriel Byrne has been on both sides of the camera, starring in such films as *The Man in the Iron Mask, The Usual Suspects, Dangerous Woman*, and producing the Academy-nominated film, *In the Name of the Father*. Gabriel had this to say about auditioning: "The audition process is really a most inadequate way to determine if an actor is right or not for a particular role. Unfortunately, it's a situation most actors have to accept. Work on developing an unshakable trust in yourself and your talent. It's important to present oneself as relaxed and confident even when you don't feel it. The role will find you if you are right for it.

If you think it and feel it, the camera will capture it. Never interpret not getting a role as failure or as a reflection on yourself or your talent. It is usually a reflection of the one you are auditioning for. However, there are times when you are simply not right for the part. Be optimistic and above all try not to be emotionally invested in the outcome."

Top casting director Mike Fenton puts it this way: ". . . the casting director is your friend, hopefully. We're there to help you. When I'm reading with a room full of producers, I will do everything I can to look at you, to help you. I'm there to assist you. So make a request! I'm not going to bite your head off." This view is shared by Jessica Overwise, who has been casting and producing for many years. She says, "[Casting directors] are dying for you to be good. They want you to be good. They're your friends. So when you come in to the office, it [shouldn't be] a hostile environment. A lot of the time, you're bumping into your own fear, your own problems. It breaks my heart to see this because I love actors. I try to support them and help them as much as possible, but I think very often they are their own worst enemies."

THE SUCCESS/FAILURE SYNDROME

Your agent calls you with an appointment for the following day. You pick up the scene that afternoon, read it over a few times and then put it away. You go out for dinner and a movie, determined to work on it when you get home, but by the time you get back, it's late and you're exhausted. The next day, you figure you'll work on the scene after you get back from the gym, but then you meet a friend there and end up going to breakfast. When you get home and look at the clock, you can't believe where the time went. You rush into the shower and have just enough time to work through the scene while you're in your car on the way to the audition. Once there, you sign in and spot an old pal of yours. While you two catch up on old times, you hear your name called and you want to shout out, "But I'm not ready yet!" It's really no surprise that you fall flat on your face in the reading or that your first thought upon leaving the audition is, "God, I hate auditioning!" Anyone would feel that way after going through a scenario like that!

Oddly enough, actors are as afraid to succeed as they are to fail. I call this "The Success/Failure Syndrome." Some actors have a subconscious enemy that whispers, "If you spend time preparing but they still don't want you, then you must not be talented. You'll never make it so why not just wing it?! Then, if they don't hire you, you have a good excuse—it's because you didn't have time to prepare." In other words, secretly, an actor would rather lose the part than risk being rejected.

In my acting classes, I'll hand out a scene and give the students twenty minutes to look it over. After a few minutes, I'll see several of them goofing around instead of preparing. It shows me they are not focused and can't possibly do their best work, which may be a sign that the Success/Failure Syndrome is at work in their minds.

In my Master Class, I have a group of brilliant, talented actors who all work a lot, yet still struggle with their psychological demons. One of them, Faye Grant, who is a Broadway, TV and film actress, entered class one day. I handed her a scene from an old series called Hooperman, *in which the title character struggles to give his dog a tranquilizer. She looked at the scene and responded, "I don't want to do this. It's old material." I said, "Moonlighting has been done twenty-five times, only with different names. Now go to work."*

After all the scenes were videotaped, I critiqued each actor's performance. I noticed Faye crouching lower and lower in her chair as she watched her colleagues. Then it was her turn to be critiqued. She peeked through her fingers as she painfully watched her reading. I asked her what she thought about her performance. Faye looked at everyone in the room, sat up in her chair, and said, "I owe you all an apology. I can't believe the commitment you made with your choices while I phoned mine in. I gave myself the excuse—which I realize I do in many of my auditions—'I would never be cast for this, so why bother trying.' Well, a light bulb just went off. The reason I don't go out on half the auditions my agents set up for me and the reason I make up excuses is because I'm afraid I won't do a great job. Thank you for making me look at the truth."

Faye learned a valuable lesson that day: it's up to you. You can choose to make excuses for yourself or you can knock down that wall of fear and take a risk. Let the fear motivate you to action. Use your fear.

From the Studio

How You Sabotage Yourself

Another client, Connie, has recently become aware of how often she sabotages herself. During one class, I gave her a scene that was perfect for her abilities—a rich socialite being stalked by her psychotic brother. The character was very complex and it was one I thought Connie could really sink her teeth into. She was to work on it at home and be prepared for the next class (similar to a callback). We taped her performance and I asked her to comment on it. As she finished watching the scene, Connie looked at me, tears rolling down her cheeks.

Connie: I did it again. I knew you expected me to do great work, so I used every excuse in the book not to give it to you. I kept myself busy and successfully avoided working on this scene.

Margie: I could see you struggling from the beginning of the scene. You doubted yourself from the start and your lack of preparation during the week only made it worse. However, I did notice how well you connected emotionally towards the end.

Connie: I finally got out of my own way and allowed myself to experience the sadness that my character was feeling. I wish I could have started out that way.

Margie: You're a good actress. You deserve to be successful. Do the work and trust yourself. Keep believing in yourself and risk being seen with your work.

IT'S A NUMBERS GAME

In class, actors often ask why they should go out on a particular audition—they would never get the part, they say; it most likely will go to an actor with a high TVQ (a rating system used by broadcast television to determine a television actor's popularity and star power). Or, they'll tell me they hate the material; it's trite and superficial. Or, they can't get into the character correctly. Whenever this topic arises (and, it does, with some frequency), I always remind them that auditioning is a "numbers game." An actor who goes out on twenty-five auditions and commits to the work will eventually get a job.

Every audition you go on increases your odds of winning a part; each reading gets you closer to booking a job. Actors often ask me if they should audition for a part that is not right for them and I always tell them, "Yes!" If you understand the material and can fully connect to the character, then, by all means, go for it. Go on as many auditions as you possibly can—the more, the better. (If you are in that stage of your career when your agent is only submitting you for starring roles in major films, you can be more selective.) After all, auditioning takes practice: you constantly need to flex your audition muscles to stay limber, so when the right role comes along, you'll be primed and ready to give it your best shot.

Going on lots of auditions also gives the casting people a chance to know your work. Even if you're not right for a particular part, if you give a great audition, the casting director will likely remember you and call you in for a future project—casting directors have great memories; that's part of their job. Many actors get jobs this way: an actor may go on an audition, give a great read, get fantastic feedback but not get the job; three months later, the same casting director may call the actor on his own—without submission by the agent—for a different project.

Below is a personal account of actress Jenny Levine and how she lost the part she was originally called in to read for, but months later found herself booking another job (*Jake & The Kid*) with the same producer. It just goes to show you—when you're good, they remember you. So, if you're not right for this part, just wait . . . you could be perfect for the next. And, the only way to know if you're right for a part is to go on as many auditions as you can.

March 4	10:00 a.m.	Private w/Margie.
	3:30 p.m.	Audition #1 for *Nancy Drew*.
March 6	12:00 p.m.	Callback for *Nancy Drew*; producer Michael Klein of Nelvana Ltd. said he would like me to come screen test in Toronto.
March 20		Coaching w/Margie.

March 24   9:00 a.m.
            to 5:30 p.m.   Screen test in Toronto w/supporting characters.
                            (Everyone I tested with was cast in the show!)

(Note: the two weeks between my callback and the screen test were filled with phone calls from Production asking me about availability for scheduled shooting times, sizes for wardrobe, as well as inquiring about my driving ability, "We just want to make sure you'll be able to drive the car we just bought for the shoot!")

April 6   I'm told that two of the three networks wanted to cast me, but New Line Television (the American network with the most money of the three) actually said I was too traditional a Nancy Drew and they decided to go with a completely different look—"more like Samantha Mathis in *Pump Up the Volume.*"

June 5   Call from Michael Klein regarding a part in a new series called *Jake & the Kid.*

June 6   Call from Casting Director Leslie Swann regarding the show. I was told she would send me some scripts and the sides and I would be responsible for putting myself on tape.

June 23   10:30 a.m.   Coaching and taping w/Margie for *Jake & the Kid.*

July 6   5:00 p.m.   Taping w/Annie, Margie's associate. New scene for *Jake & the Kid.*

July 10   I was informed that the two audition tapes, along with the *Nancy Drew* screen test, would be sent to network.

July 18   10:30 a.m.   Booked the job!

August 9   In Edmonton, Alberta, filming *Jake & the Kid.*
to Dec. 15   Thanks, Margie!

IT'S OUT OF YOUR CONTROL

One of the hardest lessons to learn in life—and in auditions—is that we are not always in control of the situation. You can give the best audition of your life, you can be absolutely brilliant, but it won't guarantee you the job. There will always be reasons which prevent you from booking a job: you're too old, you're too short, you're too fat, you're too thin, you remind the producer of his ex-wife. There are countless stories of actors going on three or four call-backs—they are practically promised the role—only to have the part yanked out of their hands and placed into the lap of the season's latest starlet.

Donna Cassell has been a casting director in New York for more than twenty years; she also holds a master's degree in Drama Therapy, working as a therapist in actor support groups who share their trials and tribulations about working in the industry. Donna has come up with a list of principles that she calls the "Dynamic Laws of Casting," to which I have added some of my own. Some of the statements are humorous, some may seem rather obvious, but on the whole, an acceptance of these basic tenets will serve as a reminder that, "It's out of your control!"

THE DYNAMIC LAWS OF CASTING

- **You will not get every job for which you audition.**
- **You will get the job, but the film will fall through.**
- **You will think you've nailed it, then never hear from them again.**
- **You will have days when you are just "off."**
- **Your best reading may well occur in the elevator after the audition.**
- **You will be competing with cell phones, pagers and lunch.**
- **You will be read by people who can barely read, let alone act.**
- **You will walk in with all the confidence in the world, only to get psyched out by the gorgeous blonde in the corner.**
- **You've been told that agents and casting directors are people, too . . . but you're beginning to doubt it.**
- **YOU WILL WORK AGAIN IN THIS BUSINESS.**

COMMITMENT, COMMITMENT, COMMITMENT

As I see it, you have two choices: either go on the audition and make a full commitment to the reading or don't go at all. It's too easy to make excuses for yourself and give in to your neuroses; it's too easy to give up and wing it; it's too easy to psyche yourself out. Don't say you'll "try" to do your best— the actor who uses the word "try" always has an out. (For example, try to pick up a pencil. Don't pick it up—TRY to pick it up. You can't! Either you pick it up, or you don't.) By using the word "try," you leave room for doubt. If you eliminate the doubt, you'll become a winner. Whether you read for a part that has five lines or is a starring role, you must make the same commitment to the material and give it your all.

TIPS

- When you're feeling insecure, imagine the casting director is sitting on the toilet. After all, they're human, just like you and me.

- In the waiting room, find a private place to work and save the socializing for *after* your audition.

- You deserve to get this job, so believe in yourself. If you don't, they won't!

HOW YOU PRESENT YOURSELF

"But I was so good in the bathroom mirror . . . "

HALLE BERRY / *Bulworth, Losing Isaiah*

When I was auditioning for *Losing Isaiah*, I had to screen test with the most emotional scene of the movie—my character breaks down, sobs, weeps and is hysterical. I had to shoot that scene in the screen test about fifty times, no exaggeration. I had to shoot it so many times that, after each take, the makeup artist had to put Visine in my eyes so it wouldn't look like I had been crying at the beginning of the scene. So much Visine went into my eyes and I rubbed them so much that my corneas got scratched and after the audition, I had to be rushed to the emergency room with scratched corneas on both of my eyes. If you've ever had scratched corneas, you know they are the most painful thing in your life that you'll ever live to tell about! For forty-eight hours, I had to keep my eyes open, which was a challenge.

Ultimately, I got the job. And when we shot the movie, I had to do that scene fifty more times, but this time I didn't put Visine in my eyes and I didn't scratch my corneas!

HALLE BERRY

Karen Fineman, recently performed in a revival of the 1960s Burt Bachrach-Hal David musical, Promises, Promises, *opposite Jason Alexander (co-star of the hit series,* Seinfeld*). When I visited them after the show, Jason told me that when Karen walked into the room for her audition, he was completely knocked out by her. Not only was she beautiful, but she also possessed many of the complex qualities of the role— she was strong yet vulnerable; sexy but smart; sophisticated but naïve. Jason wondered where she came from and where she had been. (As it happens, Karen has been in the touring company of just about every major musical in the past few years.) Jason turned to the show's producer and they agreed—if she could sing a note, she would have the part. Obviously, Karen's initial impression was very strong.*

For Karen, singing wasn't the problem—she has a fabulous voice. But, as she confided to me later, she was extremely nervous at the prospect of reading with Jason Alexander. In fact, she was so nervous that, just before they began the scene, she blurted out to the director, "I just want you to know that I'm not funny. He's the funny one. Watch him." As it happened, Karen's nervous outburst was funny and it helped her win the role. But, the director later cautioned her to avoid future auditions with such negative remarks.

As strong as Karen's first impression was, she could have lost the part because of her lack of self-confidence.

FIRST IMPRESSIONS

A first impression can have a lasting effect on your audition. Your entrance can elicit a surprisingly strong reaction: either you have the auditioners on your side or, before you utter a word, they've already crossed you off their list.

Casting directors see all types of actors walk through their doors for auditions. Do you recognize yourself as any of the following types?

- The **Shy Actor** hears her name and walks down the hall as if it was Death Row and her execution is about to begin. She feels her heart palpitating. Her palms are sweaty and her mouth is dry. When the casting director greets her, she can't find her voice and asks for a drink of water. Her hand shakes as she holds the script and she prays that the casting director won't see her trembling but she is too frightened to look into his eyes.

- The **Obnoxious Actor** comes in and takes over, shaking everyone's hands with a bone-crushing grip and talking incessantly. He dominates the room, trying too hard to be friendly.

- **Ms. Attitude** walks in with a chip on her shoulder and flashing the attitude, "Who needs you? I'm better than this project." Her body language indicates that she doesn't want to be there—she's always looking for the nearest exit and never looks anyone in the eye.

- **Mr. Intense** scares the daylights out of those around him with his brooding intensity. He may be maniacally funny, or he can be someone you don't want to be left alone with.

- The **Robot Actor** has no connection to anyone in the room; it's as if he's not even present. Completely devoid of emotions, he shuts down and is emotionally unavailable.

If you were a casting director, would you want to hire any of these actors? Chances are, in those first few seconds when the first impression is made, the casting director has already crossed them off his list. Also, casting directors never forget a face (or an attitude). So, don't start your audition with the wrong impression: there are too many talented actors vying for the same part.

From the moment you walk into the room, be confident and in charge, expressing yourself through your body language and the connection you make with the casting director. Take a deep breath, make eye contact with all of your auditioners and get a feel for the room. Are they receptive and friendly? Or are they too hurried to chat? Does one person seem more approachable than the others? Give the auditioners some space so that they can objectively observe you. Then, show them you can handle the role.

If you are having a hard time focusing, ask for a moment before you read so you can center yourself into the character's being. You need to be comfortable in the room and by asking for a moment, you take charge of your own audition. This is especially valuable when your character does not have the first line of dialogue.

SHOULD YOU ENTER AS THE CHARACTER OR AS YOURSELF?

Several illustrious feature film casting directors, including Mike Fenton (*One Flew Over the Cuckoo's Nest, E.T.*), Tom McSweeney (*Dark Justice, Perfect Weapon*), Jaki Brown-Karman (*Miss Evers' Boys, Waiting to Exhale*), Carol Lefko (*Flight of Fancy, Destiny*) and Randi Hiller (*The Haunting, Peacemaker*) discussed this question at a recent Women In Film panel which I moderated. Here are the highlights of this controversial debate:

Carol Lefko: I was an assistant on *Fletch*, my first feature film, and I remember the studio guard calling to say that Joe Don Baker had arrived for his audition and he was "furious!" He went to the wrong building and we got a call from that building saying he was "crazy" and "so angry!" Then, the elevator doors opened and I heard him coming down the hall. He walks in, right past Jerry Van Dyke who was waiting for his turn to audition. Joe Don Baker shouted, "I'm ready to read now!" So I ran in and, of course, Michael Ritchie [the director] and Chevy Chase [the film's star] were already there and they took him right away. When he walked into the audition, he did his part and he was so frightening! When he finished, as he walked by me, he winked. Of course, he got the part. So sometimes, if you're like Joe Don Baker, this ploy might work. Jerry Van Dyke got up and said, "I'd like to come in tomorrow," because he didn't want to follow that performance! I didn't blame him!

Tom McSweeny: If I'm meeting you for the first time, I would like to know who you are. The casting process is not only about finding the best actor the project can afford, but also about finding the actor who has an affinity with the director—can they relate, human being to human being? I need to know who you are, because not only is it my job to bring you in, cast you and negotiate your contract, but I'm also responsible for you until the picture is completed. And, if, for some reason, you go to the set and things don't work out, I have to go back and recast. So I want to make sure that anybody I bring to the producers will behave in a professional manner, is producer-friendly, is not going to cause problems, is going to show up on time, say his lines and hit his marks without any problems. At the same time, I don't want you to take five minutes to get into character once you sit down.

Mike Fenton: I agree. For me, it depends upon where we are in the casting process. If you've had several meetings with the director and maybe you've read once and you're coming back, then it's very acceptable to come in as the character because we already know you.

Randi Hiller: I was working on a small, independent feature and there was one guy who came in three times. He was the leading contender for the producer, the director and casting. It was the final day of casting and he was going to read with the lead actress. We were all rooting for this guy. He was going to have it. When he walked in, he sat down and started to rock and mutter things about his family that we didn't want to hear. He did the scene and was brilliant, but he scared the lead actress. Since she had casting control, she didn't let us hire him.

BROOKE LANGTON / *The Net, Melrose Place*

My dog goes everywhere with me. He's an Australian shepherd and he's so smart and cute. One day, it was about 110 degrees in Hollywood. I couldn't leave him in the car and there was no where I could leave the car running so I took him in with me, figuring, I'd bring him into the room and he'd just lie there. Well, he was just lying there quietly while I auditioned. And then the scene started getting emotional. And, of course, as the character, I started getting upset. During the reading, he got up and started yelping and howling.

I knew I blew the audition. I kind of laughed and left—I was friendly about it. I could have put the dog outside the room, but they didn't give me a chance. Their reaction was more like, "Don't ever bring her in again . . . or the dog!"

PHOTOGRAPHS (HEAD SHOTS)

Every business has a calling card and ours is a picture and resumé. I receive head shots from actors all over the United States, Canada and Europe who are about to make that giant leap to Hollywood and who wish to study with me. I receive color snapshots, family photos (complete with pets) and pictures I wouldn't want my child to see.

After a teaching stint in Germany, I received an interesting array of "artsy" pictures, none of which looked anything like the actors I had just finished working with. I am sorry to say that much of the effort and money spent on these pictures was wasted. Not only were they amateurish in their presentation, but they didn't reflect the individuals.

Almost everyday, an actor comes to class with a new collection of head shots and asks me to help him choose the right one. I have looked at hundreds of proof sheets searching for the picture that captures the actor's "essence." We are all unique in some way—in the twinkle of an eye or in a smile that hides the trace of a secret or in the dimples that hint at your playfulness. Your picture doesn't need to be glamorous or sexy, it just needs to be you.

Most casting directors, managers and agents agree with me on the following basic components of a good picture:

1. **Have your photographs taken by a professional.**
   Actors don't realize how important their pictures can be. Sarah Clossy, an agent at the Writers & Artists Agency, points out that, "actors don't realize how important pictures are. They'll go to their best friend or the guy next door to get pictures taken, which is a mistake. Make sure your pictures are shot by a professional—someone who can really bring out your personality.

2. **Make sure your name and contact number are visible on the picture.**
   Often, your picture is your first introduction to casting people. Casting director Shana Landsburg underlines the importance of listing a contact number. She says, "I can't tell you how many times I'll see a great picture and want to contact the actor but there's no number, no agency name— nothing."

3. **Keep it simple. No hands. No tilt. No color.**
   Casting director Fern Champion says, "I really want a shot just of you. That's all I want. I don't want something that has been done over or some- one who is sitting with his dog or cat out in the tree. Basically, I want a natural picture."

4. **The eyes are the windows to the soul.**
   Casting director Jerry Franks says, "I go for the eyes, because I think truth comes out in them."

5. **Let your personality shine through.**
   Landsburg looks for "the light that comes out of the picture." She looks for what comes out of the face. What is the personality like? Is there light there?

RESUMÉS

Don't be embarrassed about being a novice actor, as long your resumé is presented in a professional manner.

> *You wouldn't believe how many unprofessional resumés I receive. Ac- tors will list their junior high school band recitals or walk-on parts in epic miniseries; their skills range from being double-jointed to being able to yodel. These resumés are cluttered with modeling and Extras credits and with inane hobbies that no one cares about. Either they are so jammed with information that you can't decipher them, or they're nearly empty, with one lonely credit and no acting training to back it up. I can tell immediately the caliber of actor I'm interviewing, not only by their list of credits, but also by the presentation and layout of the resumé.*

Here are some guidelines for creating a professional resumé:

1. **Make sure your name stands out.**
   Talent agent Jeff Witjas of the William Morris Agency concurs, "You may not think it's important, but your name should appear in very large letters on the top of the resumé. Some actors choose to place their names in small type, with the agency name or their credits in larger print. But your name should stand out."

2. **Theater credits are impressive.**
   New York agent Annette Paparella spends her evenings at the theater, either searching for new talent or watching her clients perform. When her New York actors come to Los Angeles, she is told that their theater backgrounds impress the casting directors.

   Feature casting director Victoria Burrows [*Contact*] stresses, "If you come from the theater, you have a good foundation. Theater is wonderful training for an actor to constantly be 'in the moment' and to live the character."

3. **Be sure to include your training.**
   Hollywood manager Sarah Schedeen always sees an actor's training as an important clue in determining how serious they are about their craft. "In Hollywood, you can't reach the real hub of activity—the top producers, agents, directors, etc.—until you have moved up the career ladder. Yet, you can get to the very best teachers in the country by taking classes. And, working with the best looks great on any resumé. It reflects a level of commitment and serious involvement that casting people want to see sitting on the other side of the desk. You may find a lesser-known teacher who can put an angle on what you're trying to accomplish in your search for inner talent. But do check out all the methods the town has to offer. Try out a few workshops and get them on your resumé."

4. **Keep your skills short and simple.**
   Retired agent Elinor Berger emphasizes, "When a resumé is sent to my office, it should include information that you would want to see if you were a casting director, such as training, experience, etc. I don't care if you're double-jointed, like to play poker or can recite the second verse of 'God Bless America' backwards."

5. **Don't lie.**
   Ours is a small world. Every week, I hold interviews at my studio and every once in awhile, when I'm reading resumés, I'll look and see the name Margie Haber under "Training!" I look up and the embarrassed

actor will mumble, "Well, I always intended to study with you." Don't lie! L.A. and New York casting directors know their business and are not stupid. If you are twenty-two years old and claim to have played Medea . . . it just doesn't fly.

RESUMÉ LAYOUT

Below is a resumé from one of my clients. It is a good sample to follow. Please note, if you have an agent, you should include the agency name and number on your resumé.

STEPHEN DOUGLAS WOOD
S.A.G.

CONTACT: 310/555-1234
HEIGHT: 6'1"
HAIR: BLOND   EYES: GREEN

FILM

LAST SON RISING	LEAD	MATTHEW CASSAVETTES, DIRECTOR
HONEY	SUPPORTING	IFANI NJOKU, DIRECTOR
THE NEXT TENANT	SUPPORTING	ROBERT WYATT, DIRECTOR
CLOSE TO	LEAD	DAVID OTTENHOUSE, DIRECTOR
(WINNER IN ITS COMPETITION AT CANNES 1997)		
GLASS HOUSES	SUPPORTING	JON JUHLIN, DIRECTOR
ST. VALENTINE (USC)	SUPPORTING	KATHRYN RICHEY, DIRECTOR
BORN ON THE FOURTH OF JULY	FEATURED	OLIVER STONE, DIRECTOR

TELEVISION

FIRST TIME FELON (HBO)	FEATURED	CHARLES DUTTON, DIRECTOR
MTV ON TEE VEE (MTV)	HOST	SUZANNE PRESTON, DIRECTOR
NIGHT FLIGHT (NBC)	SUPPORTING	TIMOTHY BOS, DIRECTOR
A KILLING IN A SMALL TOWN (CBS)	FEATURED	STEPHEN GYLLENHAAL, DIRECTOR

COMMERCIALS
LIST UPON REQUEST

THEATRE

END OF THE WORLD PARTY	PHIL	ZEPHYR THEATRE, LOS ANGELES
DAYS OF WINE AND ROSES	JOE	HUDSON BACKSTAGE, LOS ANGELES
THE LITTLE TOWN OF PRIGGET FORK	RODNEY	THE ATTIC THEATRE, LOS ANGELES
THE GLASS MENAGERIE	JIM	JEHLINGER THEATRE, NEW YORK
WHEN YA COMIN' BACK, RED RYDER?	STEPHEN	MARGO JONES THEATRE, DALLAS
HOOTERS	CLINT	MARGO JONES THEATRE, DALLAS
THE MIKADO	PISH-TUSH	CARUTH AUDITORIUM, DALLAS
NOURISH THE BEAST	BRUNO	MARGO JONES THEATRE, DALLAS
LONE STAR	RAY	GREENVILLE AVENUE POCKET SANDWICH THEATRE, DALLAS

TRAINING AND EDUCATION

LOS ANGELES
     SCENE STUDY–LARRY MOSS (CURRENTLY), IVANA CHUBBUCK
     TECHNIQUE–SANFORD MEISNER
     COLD READING–MARGIE HABER (CURRENTLY)
     VOICE–SETH RIGGS, KAREN MORROW

NEW YORK
     SCENE STUDY–UTA HAGEN
     TECHNIQUE–MADONNA YOUNG
     VOICE–LAURA GARDNER
     DANCE–AUDREY ALBERT

DALLAS
SOUTHERN METHODIST UNIVERSITY-BFA IN CINEMA AND THEATRE ARTS, CUM LAUDE
     ACTING–BOB LEONARD, KARIN RAMSEY
     VOICE–DR. THOMAS HEYWARD, RICHARD POPPINO, LUANN ARONSON

SPECIAL ABILITIES
SINGING (TENOR) · ACCOMPLISHED BACK-UP SINGER AND SESSION VOCALIST
FRENCH AND SPANISH FLUENCY, SEVERAL DIALECTS
PIANO, GUITAR, AND THE TAMBOURINE!
BASEBALL, BASKETBALL, SOCCER, VOLLEYBALL, SURFING, TENNIS, ROLLERBLADING, LONG DISTANCE RUNNING, MOUNTAIN BIKING, HIKING

THE BIG TABOO—DON'T TOUCH THE CASTING DIRECTOR!

When you audition, most likely you will be reading with the casting director. There is an unspoken law that all actors should know before they begin: Always respect a casting director's space. There is an imaginary circle around her that should stop you from approaching. This inner circle exists for two reasons:

1. It gives the reader a chance to see you with more of an objective eye; and

2. Casting directors don't like to have hundreds of hands touching them during an exhausting day of readings.

Gilda Stratten was casting the TV series *Night Court* and was in the middle of her umpteenth audition when an actor approached her: he lifted her out of her chair with his powerful grip and then plopped her back in her seat, scaring her half to death! Needless to say, Gilda has never invited that actor to audition for her again.

Even if you are reading a fight scene, you still must never touch the casting director. But, how do you compensate for this lack of physical contact? Plan to *receive* the punch rather than flail your arms about wildly in an empty space.

> *An actor in my class had a scene in which he was to be slapped. He was so nervous about how to execute this action that when it came time for it, he stopped, smiled at the video camera and started slapping his own face furiously. We all laughed, including the actor, as we watched the scene during its playback. That is the sort of funny outtake you hope will be erased when you become a star. The actor should have experienced the jolt emotionally and reacted physically. Instead of inflicting bodily harm on himself, the actor should have imagined his face being slapped, experienced that pain and reacted to it.*

IT'S NEVER HOW YOU EXPECT IT TO BE

> *At a simulated casting session for my students, each actor will come into the room to read, then stay to watch the others work. One day, when it was time for a particular actress to do her reading, she walked in, defensively, and asked, "Why are the other people here? I thought I was doing this audition by myself!" I explained that everyone was going to stay while she worked. She got very nervous and lost focus. She later*

confessed that this was a big problem for her in auditions. When things were not the way she planned, she had trouble adjusting. I told her that things are rarely the way you envision them—that's what makes the audition process challenging.

In your audition, anything can happen. The phone may ring in the middle of your dramatic moment; you don't read with the actor you were expecting to read with—instead, you may find the casting director opposite you, eating a pastrami sandwich; you're asked to read the third scene—the one you're least prepared for; you didn't know you were going to be taped. These are all scenarios actors have told me about and cried over.

When casting director Jaki Brown cast a pilot for a major studio, she remembers the producer being obnoxious and rude to the auditioning actors. Finally, she told him to stop eating and stop making phone calls while actors were in the room. Although he smiled, put his sandwich down and set his phone aside, she had the feeling that she'd never work for him again.

Hopefully, these moments are rare: if you go out on three dozen auditions, perhaps you will have one bad experience. Don't make a big deal about it or insist that your agent call and complain. It's best to let it go. However, if it is your final callback and it's the time when you need to have their attention, it's appropriate to say, "May I wait for you to finish?"

If you go into the room knowing that *anything* can happen, you will not be thrown or lose your composure. Take charge! Be flexible! Be open to change!

USE WHAT YOU'RE *NOT* GIVEN

> *"How can they expect me to audition when the casting director is buried in the script? She is completely ignoring me! How can I establish a relationship with someone who doesn't know I exist?"*

One of the most challenging aspects of auditioning is walking into the room and finding that you will not have another actor to connect with. You're stuck, staring into the glazed eyes of the exhausted reader (that is, if you're lucky enough to have him actually look at you). Or, you suffer silently through the dull drone of lines read for the hundredth time that day. Most actors try to ignore what is *not* being given to them by the reader. The problem with such a choice is that you shut down your character's emotions as well as your own.

So how do you get around this situation? Instead of lamenting over the cruel and inhumane treatment you receive, use it! Use what you are *not* getting, as long as your feelings are appropriate for the character. For example, if it's a dramatic scene, combine your feelings of rejection with the character's frustration (your thought could be, "I can't believe he doesn't care about me at all!"). If the scene is a comedy, incorporate thoughts such as, "Hey, the schmuck's not even looking at me!" If you're supposed to feel sad and alone, those feelings might translate into, "I feel so unloved. She doesn't even notice me."

Turning this negative situation to your advantage is a way to jump-start your emotions in keeping with the character's point of view. Use what is *not* given to help connect your feelings with your character's. It will help you stay emotionally available and help you get rid of your panic.

STOP APOLOGIZING FOR YOURSELF

As discussed, casting directors form an opinion of you the moment you step in the room. They can sense if you are comfortable or not; your demeanor will either be confident or apologetic. Casting directors often refer to actors as "green." This impression comes from the way you handle your reading. If you make a mistake and apologize for it, a red flag goes up. ("I'm sorry. I'm lost. Can I start again?" Or, "I'm sorry. I skipped a line. Can we back up?") These types of phrases tell the casting director that you are unprepared and feeling ill at ease.

> *This happens a lot with actors who've just begun studying with me. Soon after I start the tape and call "Action," the actor will stop the scene and ask for my forgiveness. It's extremely frustrating for all of us when this happens—something magical may have been happening. I can't help but think that the actor is unprofessional, an amateur.*

Mistakes aren't bad! They're part of the audition process and are to be expected. Actually, the smart actor will pray for mistakes. When you make a mistake, you wake up from your automatic pilot and all your systems go on alert, thereby forcing you to be present!

Never apologize! Simply recover as the character so you don't pull us out of the scene.

COMING FROM THE CHARACTER'S POINT OF VIEW (POV)

Getting lost and losing focus are part of the audition process and you can't get away from it. Sometimes an audition makes you feel like you're walking on a tightrope. It's scary knowing that you can fall off at any moment. But you do have a net. And that net is your character's thoughts. When you suddenly lose focus and you panic ("Oh my God! I don't know where I am and the casting director can sense it!") try replacing those fearful thoughts with the character's point of view. You can't imagine how safe you'll feel.

> *When I practiced transcendental meditation, I would repeat my mantra over and over again. When thoughts of the day entered my conscious- ness, I would gently push them away and slowly reintroduce my mantra. It's the same with auditioning. When your fearful thoughts start to break your concentration, push them aside and replace them with your character's thoughts.*

On the day of your audition, from the moment you wake up, think of yourself as the character. As you're brushing your teeth, getting dressed, eating breakfast, behave and react as the character would. Use the time to journey deeper into the part, cementing your character's thoughts and be- havior so that when you walk into the room, you're prepared.

From the Studio

Coming from the Character

One of my students had to perform a very difficult physical scene taking place during a hostage situation. In it, a doctor walks through a vacant lot, negotiating with criminals to let him help a bleeding man. The doctor is fright- ened but plays along, trying to befriend the bad guys. It is a tricky scene because there are certain lines that dictate physical behavior at particular times, such as, "Stop, or I'll shoot!" It's easy to get lost in all that is going on. After the actor finished his reading, we discussed it in class.

Margie: You started off well. You put a lot of humor into your open- ing. You lightened up the situation, making it less threatening to the bad guys.

Actor: I know, but then I got completely lost in the middle. I lost my place with the lines and then I wasn't walking when they told me to stop and that really threw me.

Margie: What did you say to yourself when that happened?

Actor: I kept trying to get back to the lines. I was getting really ner- vous, because I couldn't find my place. I remember thinking, "I hope nobody notices. I don't know where I am. Oh no, I should have been walking then."

Margie: And then you buried yourself.

Actor: That's exactly what it felt like.

Margie: You could have saved yourself by using the character's thoughts. What was the character feeling during that time?

Actor: He was scared out of his mind.

Margie: And so were you. If you had stayed with the character's fearful thoughts, it wouldn't have even mattered if you had gotten lost. "Oh my God, I'd better not move a muscle, or else they'll shoot. Be very careful with your next step."

Let the character's thoughts replace your fears. They'll keep you present in the scene even if you feel like you're drowning. It is the actor's thoughts that will pull you out of the moment and create fear and panic.

THE ACTOR'S BAROMETER

"Oh my God, I just had the worst audition of my life. I stunk. I was out to lunch. How embarrassing! What??!? I got a callback??!?"

"I nailed it! They loved me! I was hysterical. Look out, Friends, here I come! What??!? I didn't even get a callback??!?"

Most actors have a hard time evaluating their work after an audition. Time and again I hear statements such as, "When I watched the tape in class, I was so much better than I thought!" Actors have an image of what they think they look like and how they come across. Most of the time, this couldn't be further from the truth!

In my work with theater actors, I notice that many have been given bad advice by acting coaches or casting directors. They've been told, "Less is more." "You're too big." "Don't move at all." "Less energy!" (Whatever that means!) This bad advice forces the actors to concentrate on the negatives and, suddenly, they don't know how they are coming across.

I worked with actress Michelle Shay while she starred on Broadway in Seven Guitars. (She earned a Tony nomination for her brilliant portrayal of Louise, a sassy, outspoken woman living in Pittsburgh during the late '40s.) When Michelle began my workshop, this seasoned professional was afraid to watch herself on video. She had always been told that her performances were "too big." Trained as a theater actress, she was cautioned to bring her performances "down." Watching herself on video, Michelle cried with joy as she realized that her talent did shine through. She was not "too big"—she was just as appropriate for film and TV work as for live theater. Lou Ferguson, who also appeared in Seven Guitars, *was horrified when he watched himself perform on tape. Lou was trying so hard to be simple that he was just plain dull. Someone had told him that when performing on film, you must do nothing, and that's just what he did—nothing!*

I sometimes use a phrase with actors, **"KEEP IT SIMPLE, SWEETHEART!"** (or K.I.S.S.). But, simplicity does not mean *boring*; it means connecting to the truth of the moment and trusting that that's enough. If you are connected, the camera will pick it up. You don't have to do any more. My associate Annie Grindlay agrees, saying, "Actors are always so concerned about being interesting. But the **truth** is what is *really* interesting."

When it comes to evaluating your work, here are three very important lessons:

1. Don't take other people's advice as gospel. Sift what is given to you and trust your instincts.

2. Observe yourself on videotape whenever possible.

3. Always try to get feedback on your auditions from your agent.

TIPS

- Get to know whom you're auditioning for. What are her credits? Is she more businesslike or does she like to chat?

- When you first enter the room, use the time to get centered.

- Take advantage of your mistakes—they'll keep you spontaneous.

- Don't forget the imaginary space between you and the casting director. Respect that space!

- Don't apologize for yourself. Take your power into the audition.

- K.I.S.S. (Keep it simple, Sweetheart!)

- Listen. Take your time. Have fun.

—

THE INTERVIEW

"But . . . what are my lines?"

KELLY PRESTON / *Jerry Maguire, Addicted to Love, Twins*

My most *memorable* audition experience was meeting Diane Ladd at her home at 10 p.m. for a film she was directing and acting in, called *Miss Munck*. I felt a very strong connection to her. She was so passionate about the piece and we talked for about an hour. She told me that it was basically down to me and another actress. And I fought for it. I told her how much I wanted the role, which was playing Ladd as a younger woman. I told her that I just had to play this role!

(Kelly was in Toronto filming the movie when she called me with her story. —M.H.)

KELLY PRESTON

During your career, you will have occasion to meet casting directors—whether it's for a few minutes before a reading or for a scheduled, general interview. In any case, you must possess a presence that will make the interviewer feel comfortable and want you to get the job; you must have a certain confidence that will make the casting director believe you are the right person for the part.

Steve Downing, Executive Producer of such TV series as *MacGyver*, *Robocop* and, most recently, *F/X*, has worked extensively in Canada, so his casting directors would regularly send him audition tapes. While working on *Robocop*, Steve narrowed his selection for the lead to two men and he flew them both to Toronto. Each was talented, with equal credits and ability, but it was clear after the first interview that Steve couldn't work with the first actor. It wasn't the actor's reading that lost him the lead, it was his attitude. This is a prime reason why your presentation and attitude are critical to being hired.

STEVE DOWNING / EXECUTIVE PRODUCER—*MacGyver, Robocop, FX*

I was the executive producer of a show being shot in Toronto and was travelling to Hollywood to cast a new co-starring role, a woman, for our show. In a big hurry, and trying to keep the budget down, I rent a tiny little compact car at the airport and zoom across town to Rysher Entertainment in Santa Monica for the casting session. I hand my little car to the valet, and I notice a brand new Mustang convertible with a very, very attractive blonde woman getting out. The valet takes her car away and as they're getting ready to take my car, I notice that she gives my little rental car a sideways glance. It's a nice day, beautiful day. I walk over to the elevator where this beautiful woman is also waiting. I make a comment about what a nice day it is. I can tell by the look on her face that a guy who gets out of a little 2-door car is not worthy of her time. She literally turns her back on me without replying in any way.

So I go upstairs and into the conference room, where the casting directors are all ready for us and we begin the task at hand. The third person to enter the room is the girl from the elevator. We're introduced and she's forced to say hello to me—only she can't think of anything to say, because her jaw is sitting on the floor!

Needless to say, she didn't get the part. Not because she ignored me at the elevator, but because she wasn't right for it. I think the moral of the story is that you should be nice to everybody. And also, character fits into acting. And if you have no moral character, you're probably not going to be a very good actor.

THE INTERVIEW

There's always an element of surprise when you go into an interview. Sometimes the people are wonderful; they're on your side; they have all the time in the world and encourage you to talk and share your experiences. However, there may be times when the interviewer is in a rush; he doesn't have a second to spare; he would prefer not to be there; he'd rather have his assistant talk to you. Keep in mind that casting directors are humans, too. They have feelings; they have bad days; they have pressures; they have stress. They must find that perfect actor who keeps eluding them.

Some actors tend to go into their interviews with an agenda. They think, "This is just an interview. Let's get to the work." However, don't forget that one of the main reasons you're there is because the interviewer wants to find out who you are; he wants to see if he likes you, if you're amicable, if you're warm. (Remember, Steve Downing didn't hire the first actor he interviewed because he knew he wouldn't be able to deal with him.)

Stories are always circulating around Hollywood about how difficult this star is to work with or how terrible that one can be. Let's face it: the entertainment industry is a business of personalities. If you are to be successful in this business, you must be able to get along with people.

It all comes down to, "Know thyself." How do you come across? What feedback have you gotten from your interviews? It's important to be honest with yourself because the bottom line is: You need to be likable. People give off different attitudes; we all do. I tend to come across a little too strong so I know if I am going into an interview, I have to pull back. Others may find they are too quiet so they must train themselves to be more outgoing.

After an actor has a lukewarm interview, he may leave thinking, "I hate this damn business! I don't like to be interviewed. If you want to see my work, look at my tapes!" That kind of attitude will only put you in a negative place. You have to play the game, because that's what it is—a big game. Once you realize that, you will have some fun. If it's no longer fun, then you don't play.

TAKING IN THE ROOM

Be aware of your surroundings! What do they reveal? What's happening in the room? Remember, stay observant because you want the interviewer on your side and even the smallest observation can turn the tide of a conversation.

> *If you looked around my acting studio, you would see vintage movie posters. I also have some still photos of Judy Garland. If an actor walked into this room, she might say to the interviewer, "Judy Garland is one of my favorite people. I can't believe I'm looking at her poster right now!" All of a sudden, a conversation about Judy Garland begins and the casting director will learn more about the actor because she exposed one of her passions.*

You can go into any room and be successful. Many casting directors have told me that, after an interview, they've been won over by an actor and would love to get him a job. That's what you want, right? You want the casting directors to fight for you. But why should they fight for an actor who has an attitude or lacks warmth? By the way, warmth does not mean performing; it means being available, being open.

WHAT THEY REALLY WANT TO KNOW

The two most commonly asked questions in an interview are:

- Can you tell me a little about yourself?

- What have you been doing lately?

The first question has nothing to do with the business and everything to do with you. The second question has everything to do with the business and nothing to do with your personal life. How you answer these two simple questions will leave an indelible impression on the interviewer.

"Can you tell me a little about yourself?"

It's important to take some time before your interview to explore how you feel about yourself—how you're feeling inside. Do you feel calm? Do you feel in charge? Do you feel worthy of talking about yourself? These are hard questions to answer. But there are some tricks you can do to make answering this question a little less painful, maybe even enjoyable.

- **Tell a story**. Now, don't go on and on, beginning with the day you were born. Nobody cares about that. What interviewers care about is seeing who you are, what your personality is, whether you're likable, if you feel good about yourself. If you hem and haw, you won't get very far; in fact, you'll already have a strike against you.

Instead, pick a story to focus on. Somewhere within your struggle to sound interesting, there's a tiny seed of a story. You may not even realize you have this wonderful beginning, but start it and then let it grow into an engaging tale that tells something about you.

When I work with actors, I videotape the mock interviews so they can see how they come across. Then we discuss ways they can improve their interviews. In the excerpt below, Robert didn't know what to say, and was obviously very uncomfortable.

MH: *So, Robert, tell me about yourself.*

Robert: *Um, gee, that's a tough one. Something about me, huh? Well, I don't know. I don't have much to say. I lead a pretty boring life. What do you want to know?*

MH: *Tell me anything about yourself personally, anything you'd like to share about yourself.*

Robert: *Well, I'm really kind of a loner. I like to fish. That's about it.*

What's your impression of Robert? Are you as bored as he seems to be? If you were a casting director, would you want to hire him? It doesn't seem like Robert really wants to be in the room. Also, he comes off sounding defensive when he turns the tables on the casting director by answering their question with, "What do you want to know?"

We did learn something positive about Robert. He likes to fish. The interview would have been far more interesting if he had shared that passion with us. "Whenever I have time, I love to go up to the mountains and fish for trout. Have you ever gone trout fishing? It's so peaceful; it really helps me keep my life in perspective."

- **What turns you on**? What gets you excited will get your interviewer excited. If you're bored, he's going to be bored. On the other hand, you don't want to go overboard and give the impression of phony excitement in order to show how personable you can be. Instead, center yourself and find something that you care about.

- **Find out what's meaningful to you.** Even though this may sound serious, it doesn't have to be. (For me, my child is meaningful. I talk about him all the time and that's what I'd talk about in an interview.)

- **Don't be afraid to use adjectives**. These are some of the most creative words you can use because they carry emotion. Words like "wonderful," "bright," "darling," "clever," "enthusiastic" allow others to know who you are and how you feel about what you're saying, which is your goal. For example, if you're talking about your child, don't just dispense the facts ("I have a child and he's nine.") How much more lively it is to say, "I have the most adorable, precocious little nine-year-old boy who I am madly in love with. He is my life." You can feel the warmth in those lines; you can feel the passion and honesty.

- **Be honest!** If you have to fake caring about something, you shouldn't be talking about it. It's really no different than doing a reading. You need to own it, to know that it means something to you, to trust what you have to say for yourself and what you're feeling. As soon as you start to fake it, it's over. Then you're not doing it for yourself. Find something that you can be proud of to talk about. Remember, this is your time.

"Can you tell me about yourself?" does not mean you should give the interviewer the order in which you ate breakfast, lunch and dinner, nor should it be an almanac of your family or a recitation of boring facts (like, how old you are or where you were born). Your response should be a story, a memorable experience that means something to you.

In your interview, you always want to shift the focus toward something that's important to you.

("Speaking of *Rugrats*, I just saw the movie with my child." Boom. I brought the focus right to my child because that's a subject that excites me.) See where the conversation is going and use it to your advantage.

"What have you been doing lately?"

This is a difficult question for many actors, especially if they're not working. The first thing you should remember is that interviewers have your picture and resumé so you don't need to sit and recite your credits. And, it sounds egotistical. It's best to describe a specific situation rather than just recount a list anyone could read because what the interviewer wants to hear is what happened to you in a particular situation.

A good response to the question, "What have you been doing lately?" would be the following example, "I had the most incredible experience working with Corey Allen, who directed me in this wonderful, sympathetic movie. You know what's great about working with Corey? He's a director, not a technician. He cares about the actor. When I'm working with him I feel like he brings things out of me that another director can't. Do you know Corey?"

Let's see how well our guinea pig, Robert, did with the second most commonly-asked question:

MH: *So, what have you been doing lately?*

Robert: *Lately, I've been doing a lot of class work. I have not been working recently. I'm trying to figure out why that is . . .*

If you're not working, try to stay away from negative responses. For instance, you don't need to say that you're not working right now or that it's been slow for you. Instead, look for the positive aspects of your situation and use them in a way that makes you feel good. (Don't forget, if you feel good, the interviewer will feel good.) You could easily say, "I've been working on my career and I am really excited because I've taken some time to focus on the part of me that I thought needed work—my auditioning. I have been studying with a coach who's made me look at my work in a very different way. I actually enjoy auditioning now." Turn a negative into a positive.

Before your interview, take a moment to look at your resumé and ask yourself what you've been doing that you're proud of. It's easy to put yourself down or reduce your contribution to, "Well, I only had a few lines" or "It was just a small part." There's no such thing as a small part—there is nothing little or insignificant about it!

Scratch the words "just" and "only" from your vocabulary. Remember, how you present the information has a direct impact on how the interviewer receives it. Why not look at each job as an adventure, a process, a journey?

From the Studio

Following are some mock interviews that we did in class. Although you won't be able to get a complete picture of the actors without meeting them personally, I do think their answers to these commonly-asked questions are revealing and informative. Let's begin with an interview from an international student.

MH: Which piece of your work is your favorite?

Yen: Stagework, *The Diary of Anne Frank.* I played the mother and it played many times, 160 performances. It was a very, very, very big success in Holland and the public was completely, unbelievably emotional. It was one of my nicest ways of acting because it wasn't only being part of the play, but it was being able to say something to the world, which I find very important . . . that you say something. And in this case, history.

Comments

When Yen talked about *The Diary of Anne Frank*, she not only said it was a wonderful experience to act in, but that it was wonderful to perform in a piece that meant something to her. That was an honest, meaningful response. Doesn't her response make you want to work with her?

Now, think about the work you've done. Have you performed in anything that contains an important theme? Have you done a benefit performance for a cause or charity?

If your only credit is a small or student film, it's better to refer to this work as a "project." You don't need to emphasize that you only had three lines in it or that it was just a little student film.

. . . .

MH: Debra, tell me about yourself.

Debra: I was born in 29 Palms, California, on a Marine Base. I was a Marine brat and moved to New York. Spent a few years there. Moved back to Orange County where I grew up in Mission Viejo. Went off to college, San Diego State, to do two years of partying and a little bit of college. Decided to get serious about my studies and go up to UCSB, where the partying was just a little less intense and the studies were a little bit more intense and then I moved to L.A. I've been serious about acting since I was in second grade when I decided that I was going to become an actress. When I entered the second grade spelling bee, it came down to me and one other person and I misspelled the word "been." I spelled it "ben." It still haunts me today. But, I loved the attention I got at that spelling bee. The whole school was staring at me and applauding and I've still got the trophy, so . . . . I love all sports. I've been athletic. I've competed in a lot of things for ten to twelve years consistently and I love traveling around the world and going on wild adventures, my favorite being a safari in Africa. I'm planning my next one.

MH: So what have you been doing lately?

Debra: Well, lately I've attached myself to a couple of independent feature films, so I'll be starring in both of those whenever they get underway. That's really exciting. And my next part will be in a Movie of the Week called *Vanishing Point*, where I will play a desert woman. I guess that's back to my roots, clad in shorts and bikini top, riding a motorcycle. I run into the lead character and have a couple of really interesting encounters and conversations with him and uh, I'm looking forward to that. Shooting in January. And I just did *Babylon 5*, a two-hour special.

MH: So, the theater situation here. Tell me about that.

Debra: Well, the last play I did was an original play called *Lillith in Love* at the Richmond Shephard Theater and that was a very interesting experience. I played a person who was alive in the age of the dinosaurs; it was sort of like Adam and Eve and dinosaurs. You put the two together and make a play out of it, and it worked pretty well. It was interesting.

Comments

After viewing the videotape, Debra understood that listing things is not as important as talking about something meaningful. Later, Debra said, "It's less intimate when you're just reciting and I really saw that."

Debra's interview is different from the others—she has a lot to say, but her interview would have been more interesting had she shared just *one* of the passionate things in her life. When describing the events of your life, take the time to visualize your story first. When you have such a fabulous opportunity, don't throw it away: focus on what is interesting to you. Debra had so many things to say that when it came time to ask about her theater experience, she was no longer interesting.

. . . .

MH: Hi, Jennifer. Tell me about yourself.

Jennifer: Well, I'm an award-winning chef. I love to cook. I just won a contest for my famous Gumbo Jambalaya. I have a dog and I like to garden and I'm a pretty good golfer. Actually, I'm a very good golfer. And, uh, you know, that's life! I don't know what else to say. Those are, like, my high points and um . . .

MH: Okay, so what have you been doing lately?

Jennifer: Lately? You mean acting, right? Well, I've been working really hard. I have a showcase going up in December. I've been auditioning my butt off. All over town, you name it. This side, that side. And I love it. And, uh, let's see. I'm in class with Margie Haber. She's really wonderful. And I'm over at the Howard Fine studio and working really hard.

MH: What was your favorite acting experience?

Jennifer: Oh, probably the movie that got me my SAG card. You know, I guess everybody's pretty nostalgic about their first job, you know. But it was great. I got to work with some wonderful actors, like William Forsythe. And I worked for a month and a half. And I thought all of Hollywood was going to be like that the rest of my life, you know. And it was great!

Comments

Some of Jennifer's interview was wonderful and fun, even though she dreaded it. Having an area of expertise outside of acting is terrific—such as, being a chef—because it's boring to be around people who only think about film and television.

In the latter part of her response, Jennifer didn't have a key area to focus on. She needed to add, "I really feel good about who I am. I'm going on auditions now and it's exciting because I'm getting good feedback."

Jennifer gave a strong response when asked about her favorite acting experience because she was positive and used adjectives to describe it.

. . . .

Having a successful interview really has to do with feeling good about yourself and being centered. Allowing yourself to feel centered and self-assured in an interview will carry over into your readings.

VINCE VAUGHN / *Return to Paradise, The Lost World: Jurassic Park, Swingers*

Following is an excerpt from an article, written by Deanna Kizis, that appeared in *Buzz* Magazine (June/July 1997). It tells the story of when Vince Vaughn met with director Steven Spielberg to discuss a part in *The Lost World: Jurassic Park* ("a nature photographer who doesn't believe in dinosaurs"). I found it worthy of reprinting because it shows so clearly that, in Hollywood, even if you don't know who the players are, you'd better be on your toes.

. . . .

While waiting in the lobby of Amblin Entertainment, Vaughn, ever gregarious, unknowingly turned to *The Lost World* screenwriter David Koepp and said, "Hey, this is kind of weird, dontcha think?"

"How so?" asked Koepp.

"I'm like, 'Well, I mean, come on.'" Vince pauses. "'I'm going to see Steven Spielberg? I, like, grew up watching *Jaws*. I'm going to talk to him about playing a part in his film? I just did this little independent movie *Swingers*. I really haven't done that much. What about you?" At this point, Koepp explained that he wrote the first *Jurassic Park, Mission: Impossible* and was writing *The Lost World*.

"And I realized very quickly," says Vaughn, "that this is the guy I'm supposed to be getting over on, and I'm lettin' down my guard like, 'Who let me in the building?'"

TIPS

- It's okay to interact with your interviewer, but don't ask too many personal questions. Some actors walk into the room and try to flip the balance of power by saying, "So tell me about you." Interviewers don't want that. You're there to be interviewed, not to do the interviewing.

- Let your personality shine through. That's what makes the casting directors want to hire you.

- Never use the word "small." You know the saying, "There are no small parts, only small actors." Don't undermine yourself or undervalue your role.

- Trust that what you have to offer is enough.

—

GUIDE TO A HEALTHY INSTRUMENT

"Gotta call my therapist!"

PIERCE BROSNAN / *The Thomas Crown Affair,*
Mrs. Doubtfire

My first audition was for entrance to the Royal Academy of Dramatic Arts. Keep in mind, I wasn't interested in school—I was there to check out the babes. I walked in with hair past my shoulders, an earring and cowboy boots. I was a street performer, a big shot because I owned my own troupe and we had played in arenas. But I had never been on a proscenium stage. Then, I heard this ominous voice from the back of the theater say to me, "Okay, let's see what you can do." I was so nervous that I walked across the stage and tripped. I fell right off the stage! It was a lesson in humility. Humility, humility, humility. The following week, I went back to the Academy, humbled, but prepared.

That experience is a lesson to this day.

PIERCE BROSNAN

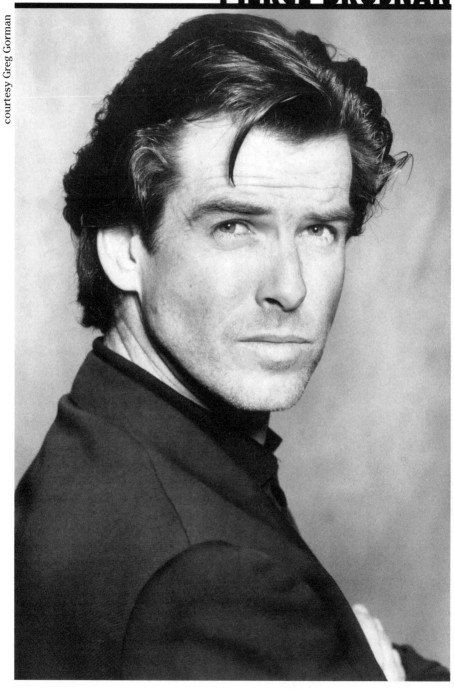

Marilyn Monroe, James Dean, Judy Garland, Montgomery Clift—what do these legends have in common? They were talented but tormented actors whose lives ended in disaster. Do you have to be a tormented soul to be a brilliant actor?

I posed this question to Corey Allen, the Emmy award-winning director who began his career in the '50s as an actor, working opposite James Dean in the classic, *Rebel Without a Cause*. Corey's response to this question was, "No. It is not necessary to be especially tormented. We all live emotional lives that swing from the bitter to the sweet. The artist needs to access and use all of it—including the torment which most of us naturally try to avoid."

COREY ALLEN / "Buzz" in *Rebel Without a Cause*

In the auditions for *Rebel Without A Cause*, the director, Nick Ray, had 500 of us seated on the bleachers out in the back lot of Warner Bros. There were all these guys in leather jackets and stomp boots being "wild ones." I was in law school—into books (in high school, I had been a "brain"). Now, I'm sitting with all these guys on the bottom rung of the bleachers, in the world of "the rumble."

Nick gave us an improvisation to do. He said, "When Perry blows the whistle, everybody get up, go to the top of the stands, turn around, come back and sit down again." I knew this was going to be a stampede. Competing with these guys seemed impossible, at best improbable.

The whistle blew and I heard myself say, "I am who I am."

Everybody stomped, shoved and scrambled for the top of the bleachers. I climbed up, bench by bench, at my own pace. By the time I got near the top, everybody was racing past me on their way back down. I stood alone up there. They had to wait on me to end the improv. I walked down, sat and thought, "This is it. This is all I've got. You can have it if you want it—all of it."

. . . .

Corey Allen is as original today as he was then. Then, he was simply an actor in search of his own truth. By doing his own thing and refusing to follow the herd, Corey stood out and therefore, got the job. Today, in addition to directing, Corey teaches an intensive workshop that helps actors connect to their emotional core. He is unlike any other teacher in his relentless, though patient, search for the truth.

During the 1950s, television was populated by one-dimensional, cardboard cut-out families like those seen on such shows as *Father Knows Best, Ozzie and Harriet* and *The Donna Reed Show*, which painted an unrealistic portrait of family life that few could live up to. I asked Corey what it was like being an actor during that time. "Well, the early '50s were a transition. Young actors had grown up watching Wayne-like heroes shooting planes out of the sky from submarine decks with a pistol. Along came Brando and Clift and Dean and, with work like theirs, came the growing realization that it was okay to be flawed and afraid. Think about *Giant*. Rock Hudson was the lead and Jimmy his antagonist, but look at the difference in styles. Hudson was a hero in broad strokes; Jimmy was the small, troubled "James Byron Dean" whom he brought into all of his performances. It took courage to share that raw, vulnerable humanness."

Today, we've come full circle. While Dean and Clift were rebelling against the machismo of the '50s, we live in a time that now more fully embraces both the lighter and darker sides of our humanity. We're no longer afraid to delve into our psyches. Therapy is no longer a forbidden subject to be treated behind closed doors.

A HEALTHY INSTRUMENT

The artist paints with a finely crafted brush and colorful palette; the pianist glides fingers across the ivory keys; and the actor . . . actors are their own instruments. The body encases a rich inner life—and this must be accessible to actors. If you are trying to paint using only a few colors or if some of the keys are broken on the piano, then you are incomplete and the audience misses out on your true talent. As an actor, it's important to have the full spectrum of your emotions available to you.

Having a healthy instrument means you recognize and accept your feelings and then you're willing to share those feelings by incorporating them into your work.

> *If I am nervous about going on an audition, first I must recognize that emotion, not shut it out and pretend it doesn't exist. Then I must accept the fact that I'm nervous and realize that it's okay to feel that way. Finally, I must be willing to share that emotion with my audience by putting it into the work, rather than hiding it or overcompensating for it.*

Don't be afraid to share the truth of who you are. That is what excites the audience—the fact that you are willing to share yourself with them. Corey Allen agrees that a healthy instrument is a self-accepted instrument. "Self-recognition, acceptance, willingness to open and then opening—those are the steps [to a healthy instrument] and the toughest part is maintaining that vigilance of acceptance."

It is so difficult for us to accept our own flaws! Sometimes, what we consider our weaknesses may actually be our strengths. And they may not be weaknesses at all, but differences. We often lose sight of the gift we were blessed with—our own, unique, individual selves.

In the late 1960s, when every young actor was trying to be another handsome leading man, like Paul Newman or Robert Redford, along came an unknown named Dustin Hoffman, who charmed us with his quirky, self-conscious star turn in *The Graduate*. In the film, Hoffman embraced his flaws and willingly shared them with the audience. In doing so, we came to know him and we felt his pain. Through his performance, he personified a lost generation.

Back-to-Back Exercise

In this class exercise, two people sit the floor, back-to-back. They are given a scene to perform but it is placed face-down on their laps and they are told, "There is no scene. There is no character. There is no story. It really is about connecting to the truth of who you are and what you're feeling at the moment. When you have some reason to pick up the paper from that truth, pick it up and express it to the person behind you."

The two actors can't see each other, but they learn that there are other things to use in life besides sight. It's kinetic; it's the heat; it's the feeling of the heart. You can feel your lungs, your breath, the way you move. And the tension in your back is amazing.

There's no masking of emotions in this exercise. If you're feeling sad, you transmit sadness. If you want to cry for ten minutes, you do. If you have a need, you come from that need. If you start to feel sensual with the other person, that's what you feel. Every emotion is permitted. What is not permitted is covering up your emotions. Any feeling that comes from your truth at that moment is acceptable.

The important thing is to avoid being self-indulgent, which actors sometimes do when they *feel* something. (All of a sudden, they get caught up in the emotion.) The point is to give your emotion to the person behind you. You experience it, feel it, give it away and see what happens next. Your partner receives it, does what he wants with it and then gives it back.

This exercise is like riding a wave. The beauty is riding the wave together rather than feeling the emotions separately. And along with that comes the realization that your feelings are valid and you can affect your partner. What is so fascinating about this "Back-to-Back Exercise" is that the actors can't see each other; they can't use the visual cues. They want to look at each other but they must experience the emotions without seeing each other.

When the exercise is over, the actors turn around and give each other a big hug. Then they face the class and describe their journeys. It's quite extraordinary to witness their breakthroughs and to see the willingness they have to share their feelings. This is the truth of the work—this is the bottom line—because, unless you come from your core, all your character work means nothing. This is the foundation of your work and our foundation as human beings.

THAT OLD BACKPACK

Our heads are filled with "tapes" that are constantly re-running home movies from our past. These tapes start rolling the moment we emerge from the womb and they get louder and longer as we become adults. It's no wonder that our reactions to certain events are loaded with past experiences. As an actor, your "tapes" can either be a valuable source of raw footage or a weighty, cumbersome piece of old baggage. The healthier you are, the easier it is to access the appropriate tapes for your work.

> I was fortunate to have had an incredible friend named Elaine Harris, who recently passed away. She was a psychotherapist who worked with many actors. Elaine used to talk about how each person carries around a backpack filled with old beliefs, old attitudes and old behaviors. "You carry your backpack into adulthood, not recognizing that it's no longer necessary. It's no longer appropriate. It may have served you well in childhood and helped you to survive, but now you have to make the transition into the world of adulthood and start emptying it. It makes it lighter for you to walk through the world. You can walk a little taller and with a little less burden. You also recognize that what you had then was necessary for then, which led to who you are now. But you don't need the same stuff anymore. So it's time to shed it."

THE FIVE EGO STATES

One way of unloading the old "stuff" is to understand the different parts of yourself. As an actor, this is particularly important because *you* are the merchandise. Elaine used a wonderful tool to help actors connect to their inner selves, called the Five Ego States; these are the internal mechanisms that make us who we are.

1. **The Critical Parent**

   This is the negative voice inside your head that finds fault in you. "You're not good enough." "You're too fat . . . too thin . . . too bald." "You're not worthy of this job." "Why bother going on the audition in the first place? You're never going to get it!"

2. **The Nurturing Parent**
   This is the part of you that protects you from your Critical Parent. It soothes your insecurities by saying, "Don't worry. You'll be fine. Everyone likes you. Take a deep breath and relax." It's the part that gives you lots of hugs. Thank God for the Nurturing Parent!

3. **The Playful Child**
   This is the part of you that doesn't care what other people think. It loves to take risks and do outrageous things. It's the part that gives you permission to play, to be free and non-judgmental, to be spontaneous. (This one is my favorite! I love to bring out my Playful Child and do crazy things.)

4. **The Fearful Child**
   Watch out for this one! This is the part of you that would like to hide under the covers and never get out of bed. It is afraid to take risks and would rather play it safe. It's the part of you that says, "I don't want to go on that audition." "It's too scary!" "They're all going to be staring at me. What if I make a mistake?!"

5. **The Adult**
   This is the responsible part of you, the part that pays the bills, picks up the script a day ahead of the audition and gets you to your audition on time. When you don't get the role, this part devises your next plan of action. "Okay. It's time to work on my audition skills, get new pictures and take my agent to lunch." Like Dr. Spock in *Star Trek*, the adult has no emotion attached to it. He just gets the job done.

TURN UP THE VOLUME!

We all contain these ego states, but sometimes one speaks louder than the other. Therefore, we need to listen to our internal voices and be aware of which voice is appropriate for a particular situation, then select that voice and turn up the volume on it while turning down the volume on the others. For example, as you enter the audition room, you may hear your Critical Parent saying, "Who are you trying to fool? You're not good enough. No one's going to like you." Your job is to turn down the volume on the Critical Parent and raise the volume of the Nurturing Parent, who'll say, "You'll do great. You are very talented. You deserve this."

A healthy instrument utilizes all five ego states. We've discussed the most common characteristics of each state and how they affect us, but don't overlook the flip side of their natures. For instance, as an actor, it's important to have a strong Playful Child, but if you lack the discipline to prepare and to get to your auditions on time, you won't be a successful actor. That's where the Adult comes in—to handle the business side. But, if you have too much Adult in you, your acting will become too intellectual and will lack emotion. Or, if you have too much of the Nurturing Parent, all you'll hear is overly supportive statements ("I'm so great; everything is fine . . . ") and this can shield you from the truth of your work and keep you from making meaningful changes.

Ego states such as the Critical Parent and the Fearful Child may appear to be completely negative but they do have positive aspects. While the Critical Parent can be a debilitating voice, it forces you to push yourself further than you might otherwise go; it does not allow you to be satisfied with mediocre work. Sometimes, the Fearful Child is correctly afraid and fear is not always a bad emotion (it makes you more alert and gives you an adrenaline rush that can keep you on your toes).

Throughout our lives, we experience changes. One ego state may be more prominent during our twenties, another during our thirties, etc. The ego states can keep us in balance and help us live a more fulfilling life.

> *My Playful Child led me on my adventure to Los Angeles; my Adult helped me open my acting studio. But when my son was born, my Fearful Child became a louder voice that I had to learn to manage. I call upon my Nurturing Parent to help keep my Fearful Child in check.*

Once you've gotten out of your own way and can move more freely through your psychological landscape, you are ready to get down to the basics of breaking down a scene.

TIPS

- **Know thyself. A healthy instrument requires the willingness to look at yourself—to recognize, accept, share.**

- **Embrace your differences. It's what makes you an individual.**

- **Come from your feelings, not just your thoughts. Feelings such as love, anger and sadness are experienced in the gut, not in the head.**

- **Be willing to let go of old baggage.**

PART 2
BREAKING DOWN THE SCENE

My theory is that auditioning is 40 percent psychological and 60 percent preparation—successful auditioning involves both a positive attitude and thorough preparation. Most actors spend too much energy trying to quiet their negative voices: "I'm not good enough." "They hate me." "I'll never get it anyway." What I have found is that when you prepare correctly, you automatically have more confidence. The more you are involved in the work, the less likely you are to succumb to your fears.

In the following chapters, you'll learn how to break down a scene; my method is divided into ten steps. Whether you have one day, one week or just twenty-five minutes to prepare for your audition, the analysis is the same. (Obviously, the more time you have, the more thorough you can be.) Each step influences the other, so it's important that you break down the scene in order. For instance, a scene may be heavier in character analysis but you must always start with the relationship to avoid omitting any vital information.

Your challenge is to break down the scene emotionally, rather than intellectually. Let's begin.

PART 2 CHAPTER 1

—

RELATIONSHIP

What do the characters mean to each other?

STEPHEN COLLINS / 7th Heaven, The First Wives Club

In the summer of 1969, I had a final callback audition in New York for the first national touring company of a Broadway hit called *40 Carats*. I was set to read for the legendary director Abe Burrows, who wrote and/or directed such shows as *Can-Can, Guys & Dolls* and *How To Succeed In Business Without Really Trying*. The producer was the even more legendary David Merrick, who at that time was the absolutely undisputed king of Broadway producers. Merrick was an incredibly feared figure, famous for feuding with the press and for his well-publicized dislike of actors.

The audition was on 45th Street at the beautiful Morosco Theatre, which, sad to say, has long since been torn down. The houselights were down and when I was called onto the stage for my reading, I couldn't see anything in the house. But I knew that David Merrick and Abe Burrows were there somewhere. The stage manager, Burrows' son Jimmy (a well-known and talented sitcom director who later directed almost every episode of *Cheers*) read with me.

I was well-prepared, on my game and I felt good. But as soon as I finished, David Merrick came bolting down the aisle toward the stage. Even though I felt I'd read well, I was terrified. He was an incredibly intimidating figure—and knew it. I was just out of college and totally green and couldn't believe this theater giant was actually going to talk directly to me.

Merrick looked me straight in the eye and, like a prosecutor who's trying to intimidate a witness, asked, "Are you a good actor?"

STEPHEN COLLINS

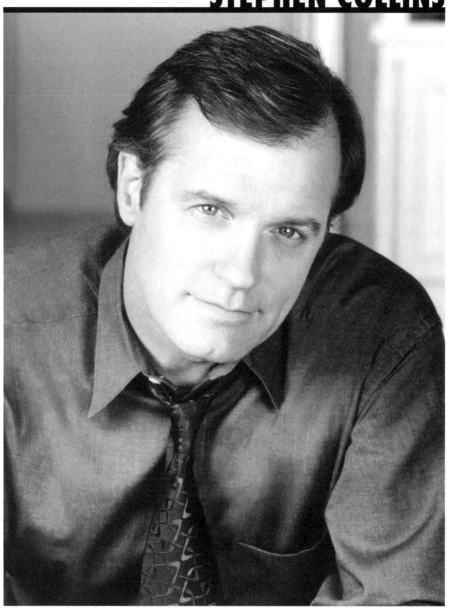

I was brought up in an old-fashioned, well-mannered home and my first thought was that I should say something falsely modest, like, "Well, uh, my friends tell me I'm good," or, "A few people I know say I have talent." But in the second or two I had to think, it occurred to me that David Merrick was no fool and maybe I should tell the truth.

"Yes," I replied, scared out of my mind.

"Fine!" he said simply. "I wouldn't want to hire someone who didn't think he was a good actor."

And that was that. He shook my hand, turned and left. I got the job, which in many ways changed my life.

. . . .

I tell this story because I believe it's essential that we actors think we're good. Otherwise, what are we doing in the game? If you don't think you're good, then do whatever it takes until you absolutely own that feeling. Because the way you feel about yourself matters—maybe as much as your talent (like it or not)—and people pick up on it right away.

You get a call from your agent to pick up the sides and you have only one hour before your audition. Panic sets in. "Where do I begin?" "How will I be able to connect to the character in such a short time?" Start from the beginning by considering the relationship between your character and the other character (or characters) in the scene. In a sea of questions and nerves, that relationship is your lifeboat; it connects you to your character's emotional life; it cements you to the role. The relationship is the glue without which the scene would just fall apart.

Buddy pictures, from *Thelma & Louise* to *Lethal Weapon*, owe much of their success to the power of the relationship between the two key characters. *Lethal Weapon* would be just another generic action picture were it not for the bond between Martin Riggs (Mel Gibson) and Roger Murtaugh (Danny Glover) and how well they play off one other. Witness the predicaments of Lucy and Ethel from *I Love Lucy*: The show was based on their zany relationship and the trouble they got into *together*. Yes, chemistry between the actors plays a part. And certainly, if you've been on a series for any length of time, you know that relationships develop. But in an audition, you don't have the luxury of time. Therefore, it is both the actor's job and his salvation to create strong relationships between the characters.

Our brain cells are filled with information; experiences shape our memories and make us who we are. However, when you first get the sides for your audition, you are an empty vessel—the character is a name on the page. Your goal is to take that which is unknown—the script—and put it in a place that you do know. It's up to you to make the choices that will fill the vessel with specific details.

TYPES OF RELATIONSHIPS

There are different types of relationships: friendship, family (including siblings) and love. In this chapter, tools are introduced that will help lead to further discovery within those relationships. To break down the relationships, excerpts from the Academy Award™-winning films, *Thelma & Louise* and *Hannah and Her Sisters* are used.

In *Thelma & Louise* (written by Callie Khouri and directed by Ridley Scott), Thelma (Geena Davis) is a repressed, dependent housewife who sneaks out on her demanding husband (Christopher McDonald) and joins her friend Louise (Susan Sarandon), a hard-as-nails waitress, for a fun-filled all-girl weekend. Their vacation takes a detour when Louise shoots and kills a local bar stud who attempts to rape Thelma in a dance hall parking lot. Shocked and scared, the women flee the scene and soon become wanted criminals. The following is an excerpt from one of the early scenes of the film: it's an exchange between Thelma and Louise as they are riding in the car. Read it through, then let's get to some key questions which are designed to flesh out the relationship between the two women.

EXT. CAR - DAY

They are driving down the interstate. Thelma reaches
for her purse and finds the gun.

>   THELMA
>   Louise, will you take care of
>   the gun?

Louise shrieks at the sight of it.

>   LOUISE
>   (startled)
>   Why in hell did you bring that?

Thelma wonders if Louise is really that naïve.

>   THELMA
>   Oh, come on, Louise...psycho
>   killers, bears...snakes! I just
>   don't know how to use it. So
>   will you take care of it?

Louise reaches over and takes the gun out of Thelma's
purse and holds it in her hand. She tests the weight
of it, and then puts it under the seat. Thelma puts
the bullets under the seat.

>   THELMA (cont'd)
>   I'm just really afraid of
>   psycho killers, I guess.

They are speeding off down the highway with the RADIO
blaring. Louise puts in a TAPE of wild R&B MUSIC.

>   THELMA (cont'd)
>   Whose place is this again?

>   LOUISE
>   It's Bob's, the day manager's.
>   He's gettin' a divorce, so his
>   wife's gettin' this place, so
>   he's just lettin' all his
>   friends use it till he has to
>   turn over the keys.

>   THELMA
> I've never been out of town
> without Darryl.
>
>   LOUISE
> How come he let you go?
>
>   THELMA
> 'Cause I didn't ask him.
>
>   LOUISE
> Aw, shit, Thelma, he's gonna
> kill you.
>
>   THELMA
> Well, he'd have never let me
> go. He never lets me do one
> goddamn thing that's any fun.
> All he wants me to do is hang
> around the house the whole time
> while he's out doing God only
> knows what.

They are both silent for a minute.

>   THELMA (cont'd)
>   (looking straight ahead)
> I left him a note. I left him
> stuff to microwave.

After a pause:

>   THELMA (cont'd)
>   (carefully)
> I guess you haven't heard
> anything from Jimmy...yet?

Louise's jaw tightens. The car speeds up.

>   THELMA (cont'd)
> ...never mind.

A huge semi-tanker carrying gas passes them on the
highway and HONKS. The mud flaps are the shiny
silhouettes of naked women. There is a bumper sticker
on the back that says: "Lick you all over—ten cents."

```
                    THELMA (cont'd)
                     (smiling)
              One of your friends?
```

Thelma is watching herself in the side mirror, pretending to smoke a cigarette.

THELMA'S POV OF A SIGN alongside the road that reads "See you in church on Sunday!"

Thelma pushes in the lighter and waits for it to pop out. Louise gives her a sidelong glance, but does not say anything.

RELATIONSHIP Q&A

Looking through the eyes of Thelma's character, ask yourself questions such as:

- **What's going on for me in relation to the scene?**
  I have just escaped from my horribly oppressive husband to go on an adventure with my best friend, Louise. I'm scared shitless, but exhilarated at the same time.

- **What is my relationship with the other character in the scene (Louise) and how do I feel about her?**
  Louise is my "partner in crime." She pushes me to do things I normally wouldn't have the guts to do. Sometimes she's too tough on me, but deep down, I know she cares.

- **Are there any other characters mentioned in the text? Who are they in relation to my character and how do I feel about them?**
  Well, there's my husband, Darryl. I'm scared of him and sick of him, too. He's a bully. Our relationship is in the toilet on account of he doesn't treat me nice. And, our love life stinks.

Now, step into the environment.

- **Where am I? Where does the scene take place?**
  We are in Louise's vintage convertible on the open road. The wind is blowing through my hair, the truck drivers are honking past us and the radio is blasting!

All too often, when actors get a scene between two characters, they'll read it and say, "Okay, they're friends," and leave it at that. The relationship is tossed into a general bin. Well, that's not good enough! You need specifics to bring your character to life. The more information you have, the better.

Your job is to become a detective and search for clues that reveal what your character is feeling. Owning your character's thoughts and feelings depends on the depth of your investigation. If your investigation is shallow, your portrayal will become a one-dimensional sketch; if your investigation is deep, your character springs to life and the process will feed you, the actor.

From the Studio

Two of my students were given the previous scene to work on from *Thelma & Louise*. When Wendy and Dawn Ann finished the first scene, the critique was opened to the class for discussion.

> **Comment:** Their intention was strong and the use of environment was excellent, but something seemed to be missing in their relationship.

> **Margie:** You're right. Let's see how the five Ego States apply to this scene from *Thelma & Louise*. Thelma begins as the Fearful Child; Louise is the Critical Parent. But this changes: The Playful Child emerges when Thelma realizes she got away with something ("I left him a note. I left him stuff to microwave."). That gets Louise to drop her Critical Parent and step into the Playful Child.

> **Dawn Ann:** In other words, I got stuck in my fearful child.

> **Wendy:** And I got stuck in my critical parent.

> **Margie:** Right! Let's try it again with that adjustment.

In the second read-through, the difference was astonishing! It took only that small adjustment to make the scene come alive. Once Wendy gave up her need to be the Critical Parent, she allowed herself to bring out her Playful Child. And that child said, "Hey, I want to have fun, too! I don't want to be left out."

CHANGING RELATIONSHIPS

When you read a scene and form an initial impression, you assume the scene is going to go in a certain direction. However, you may be overlooking important clues. If you stop, listen and let yourself experience the moment, you may end up taking a detour. All of the sudden, magical things occur that never would have been possible if you weren't available to them in the first place. It's important to understand the dynamics of a relationship and how it grows within the movie.

Actors are usually given two or three scenes in an audition, but they don't always ask themselves, *Where is this character now compared to where she was then? How has she changed? How has the relationship changed from the beginning of the script to the end?*

Thelma & Louise is a good example of a relationship that begins in one place and ends up someplace entirely different. Because, *relationships change*—they evolve in a script, as they do in life. Let's see where *Thelma & Louise*'s journey has taken them.

pg. 111

Louise is rubbing her face. She looks pretty bad. Her hands are shaking.

>   LOUISE
>   (to herself)
>   Shit. I'm gettin' tired.

>   THELMA
>   Are you alright?

Louise does not really seem alright.

>   LOUISE
>   (upset)
>   I think I've really fucked up.
>   I think I've got us in a
>   situation where we could both
>   get killed. I mean, I don't
>   know what's the matter with me.
>   I don't know why we didn't just
>   go straight to the police.

                    THELMA
You know why. You already said.

                    LOUISE
What'd I say again?

                    THELMA
Nobody would believe us. We'd
still get in trouble. We'd
still have our lives ruined.
And you know what else?

                    LOUISE
What?

                    THELMA
That guy was hurtin' me. And if
you hadn't come out when you
did, he'd a hurt me a lot
worse. And probably nothin'
woulda ever happened to him.
'Cause everybody did see me
dancin' with him all night. And
they woulda made out like I
asked for it. And my life
woulda been ruined a whole lot
worse than it is now. At least
now I'm havin' fun. And I'm not
sorry that son of a bitch is
dead. I'm only sorry that it
was you that did it and not me.
And if I haven't, I wanna take
this time to thank you, Louise.
Thank you for savin' my ass.

                    LOUISE
I said all that?

                    THELMA
No, Louise, you said the first
part. I said all the rest.

                    LOUISE
        (tired)
Whatever.

In this later scene, the characters have switched roles: Louise has become the Fearful Child while, affected by her partner's distress, Thelma transforms into the Nurturing Parent and calms Louise's fears. By the end of the film, Thelma and Louise are two strong, united women soaring over the Grand Canyon.

It is always important to take into consideration where your character came from, where she is now and how her relationship changes in the future.

RELATIONSHIP CONTRACT—*HANNAH AND HER SISTERS*

Now let's explore the psychological aspects of relationships. Elaine Harris talked about the "Relationship Contract," a tool to help uncover the different levels of connection in a scene. An excellent example of this is Woody Allen's *Hannah and Her Sisters,* which explores the relationship between Hannah (Mia Farrow) and her two sisters, Lee (Barbara Hershey) and Holly (Dianne Wiest).

In the following excerpt, the sisters meet at a posh New York restaurant for lunch. Unbeknownst to Hannah, her middle sister, Lee, is having an affair with her husband, Elliot (Michael Caine). Meanwhile, her youngest sister, Holly, asks Hannah if she can borrow more money for her latest career venture. Note the underlying tension in the scene and the complex interactions that occur.

> LEE
> (Interrupting, her voice
> slightly higher-pitched as
> she takes off her coat)
> How are you?

> HANNAH
> (Offscreen)
> I'm okay.

> LEE
> (Overlapping)
> You know, how's everything? You
> doing okay? How's Frederick?
> (Laughing) I mean, Elliot.

> HANNAH
> (Offscreen, overlapping)

Hannah walks out of the coat check room without her coat; it's Lee's turn to disappear and check her things. Now only Hannah can be seen onscreen as the

sisters talk. In the background, the waiter once again
walks over to the bar.

>   HANNAH
>   (Continuing)
>   Oh, he's fine. He's-he's, I
>   guess he's fine. I don't know.
>   (Shaking her head, her arms
>   crossed) He's been kinda moody
>   lately, the last few months.

>   LEE
>   (Offscreen, overlapping)
>   Really?

>   HANNAH
>   Yeah. I-I don't know what's
>   wrong with him. He's
>   just...kind of distant and
>   difficult.

>   LEE
>   (Offscreen)
>   Oh...

>   HANNAH
>   (Overlapping, gesturing)
>   I've been trying to talk to him
>   about it. He says everything's
>   fine, but I don't know.
>   Automatically, you know, I leap
>   to the worst conclusions.

>   LEE
>   (Offscreen)
>   Like what?

As Hannah answers her sister, Holly can be seen
entering the restaurant and walking over to the coat
check area, an unlit cigarette in her mouth, her
sunglasses still on her eyes.

>   HANNAH
>   (Gesturing)
>   I mean, I don't know, he's
>   seeing someone else or
>   something, but...

                    LEE
               (Walking back onscreen
               without her coat, reacting)
          Oh, no! I mean, everyone thinks
          things like that.

Hannah mumbles as Holly walks over to her sisters.

                    HANNAH
               (Turning, to Holly)
          Hey, hi!

                    HOLLY
               (Overlapping)
          Well, I just came from an
          audition...

                    LEE
               (Overlapping, leaning
               against the coat check
               wall)
          Hi.

                    HOLLY
               (Continuing)
          ...which I did not get.

                    HANNAH
               (Reacting)
          Awwww...

                    HOLLY
               (Overlapping, sighing)
          So what's new?

She takes off her gloves and scarf, stuffing them in
her bag.

                    HANNAH
               (Helping Holly with her
               coat)
          Boy -

>   HOLLY
>   (Interrupting)
>   They said I was too offbeat
>   looking, whatever the hell that
>   means.

>   HANNAH
>   Oh, what do they know?

Holly gives her coat to the coat check person.

>   HOLLY
>   (To the checker)
>   Thanks. (Turning to her
>   sisters) But guess who was
>   there auditioning?

>   LEE
>   April?

The hostess appears, peeking around the corner of the
coat check area. She signals for the three sisters to
follow her.

>   HANNAH
>   (Reacting to Holly's news)
>   Oh, gosh.

>   HOLLY
>   You got it.

Holly takes off her sunglasses; her cigarette still
dangles from her mouth. Hannah murmurs her sympathy as
the trio follows the hostess into the dining room.

>   HOLLY
>   (Gesturing)
>   I was very polite. I maintained
>   my poise. (Taking out a match
>   for her cigarette) I said
>   hello.

The sisters walk to their seats, at a round table in
the middle of the room; the hostess puts down their
menus.

                   LEE
Hmm. I never trusted April, you
know. She has eyes in the back
of her head.

They sit down. The hostess leaves. Other diners are
seen in the background; a waiter is taking the order
of a couple sitting on a banquette; other waiters
clear off a table. Diners walk in and out. A low
murmur of conversation, as well as the faint clatter
of dishes, is heard. The camera moves closer to the
three sisters, circling the table as Holly speaks.

                  HOLLY
Yeah, well, she and an
architect are now a very
definite item, which I still
cannot believe.

                 LEE
            (Overlapping)
Hmm.

                HANNAH
Oh, God...

                  HOLLY
            (Nodding her head, holding
             her cigarette)
Yeah, although it's put an end
to the Stanislavski Catering
Company. Which is why I have to
speak to you. And... (Gesturing
to Hannah) you're gonna get
impatient, but...I have to
borrow some more money.
(Putting her cigarette in her
mouth and picking up the
matches)

                HANNAH
            (Shaking her head)
Well, that...th-that's fine.

>   HOLLY
>   (Gesturing, her cigarette
>   in one hand, her matches in
>   the other)
> But what I decided to do is
> some writing. Yeah, I think
> I've had it with acting. You
> know, these meaningless
> auditions at cattle calls. And
> I can't handle another
> rejection. (Emotionally) Now
> let's face it here. I gotta,
> you know, latch on to something
> in my life. You know—something
> with a future. I'm not sixteen
> anymore. (Lighting her
> cigarette) It's just... crazy!
> But...(Puffing her cigarette)
> I've got...an idea for a story.
> More than one. And I just need
> a few months, you know, or a
> year even.

As the camera slowly circles the table, Hannah is seen
listening to Holly, her hand on her mouth.

>   HOLLY
> I've picked up a lot about
> dramatic structure from doing
> my scenes in acting class.

Lee, her hand on her mouth, glances briefly at Hannah.
As Hannah replies to Holly, the camera focuses on
Lee's face. She bites her nails; she looks down,
involved in her own thoughts.

>   HANNAH
>   (Offscreen)
> Well, that-that's good. It
> just, uh...it just seems to me
> that-that six months or a year,
> if-if you spent it more
> productively...

                    HOLLY
              (offscreen, the camera
              still focused on Lee)
         Well-well, like what?

Lee looks up, her hand still on her mouth, watching
Hannah, as the camera slowly moves off her to show
Hannah.

                    HANNAH
         Well, I don't know. We'd uh,
         uh, um... Didn't Mom mention
         there was something...
         something at the Museum of
         Broadcasting?

                    HOLLY
              (Offscreen)
         Yeah, that's clerical.

                    HANNAH
         No. She, didn't she say it was,
         um...she said it was in the
         publicity department. That-that
         can lead to other things.

The camera is back on Lee. She looks around tensely,
barely listening to the conversation. She fidgets. An
empty table sits in the background.

                    HOLLY
              (Offscreen)
         Boy, I knew you'd be
         discouraging.

                    HANNAH
              (Offscreen)
         I'm not! I'm not! I'm trying to
         be helpful. A person doesn't
         just say one day, "Okay, now-
         now I'm finished as an actress.
         Now I'm a writer." I mean-

                    HOLLY
              (Offscreen, interrupting)
         Yeah, you mean not at my age.

                    LEE
              (Shaking her head, unable
              to take much more)
          Oh, please! We all came to have
          lunch, didn't we?

                    HOLLY
              (Reacting, now in view)
          Yeah, okay, right. Forget it.
              (Puffing on her cigarette)
          What's to eat?

Holly abruptly picks up her menu.

                    LEE
              (Trying to alleviate the
              tension)
          Boy...Holly...Holly.

                    HOLLY
              (Overlapping)
          I just want a salad. (To
          Hannah) You really think I'm a
          loser, don't you?

                    HANNAH
              (Offscreen)
          What do-? You're being
          ridiculous.

                    LEE
              (Overlapping, reacting)
          You are, Holly. Stop it.

                    HOLLY
              (To Hannah)
          You treat me like a loser.

                    HANNAH
              (Offscreen)
          How?

                    HOLLY
          You never have any faith in my
          plans. You always undercut my
          enthusiasm.

She puffs intensely on her cigarette as the camera
slowly circles to Hannah's face. She is equally
intense, looking at both sisters as she speaks.

>   HANNAH
> Not so! No. I think I've been
> very supportive. I've...I try
> to give you honest,
> constructive advice.

>   HOLLY
>   (Offscreen)
> Hmm!

>   HANNAH
>   (Overlapping)
> I'm-I'm always happy to help
> you financially. I think I've
> gone out of my way to-to
> introduce you to interesting
> single men. There's nothing I
> would-

>   HOLLY
>   (Offscreen, interrupting)
> Uh, losers! All losers!

>   HANNAH
> You're too demanding.

>   HOLLY
>   (Offscreen)
> You know, I could always tell
> what you thought of me by the
> type of men you fixed me up
> with!

The camera, slowly circling the table, is back on
Lee's face. While her sisters argue emotionally on her
right and left, she is looking down, biting her lip.
She is outwardly still, but her face is registering
her seething emotions.

>   HANNAH
>   (Offscreen)
> You're crazy! That's not true.

                    HOLLY
             (Offscreen)
        Hey, Hannah, I know I'm
        mediocre.

                    LEE
             (Interrupting angrily,
             looking as if she's about
             to cry)
        Oh, will you stop attacking
        Hannah?!

                    HANNAH
             (Offscreen, overlapping)
        Oh, now— (Stuttering)

                    LEE
             (Interrupting, shaking her
             head)
        She's going through a really
        rough time now.

                    HOLLY
             (Offscreen)
        Why are you so upset?

                    LEE
             (Sobbing and gesturing)
        You know, you've been picking
        on her ever since she came in
        here. Now just leave her alone
        for a while! I'm just
        suffocating. (Sniffing back her
        tears)

                    HOLLY
             (Leaning over to Lee,
             puzzled, reacting to her
             sister's tears)
        What's the matter with you,
        Lee? Why are you so sensitive
        all of a sudden?

                    HANNAH
               (Offscreen)
          Look. (Onscreen, as the camera
          circles around the table)
          Listen. Listen. (Tapping Holly
          on her shoulder and gesturing)
          You want to write? Write.

APPLYING THE RELATIONSHIP CONTRACT

The "Relationship Contract" isolates three levels of a relationship:

1. **Spoken Data**—In this level, you look at what *your* character says and you fill in the blanks according to what the *other* characters say about your character. Ask the following questions about your character: Who are you; what are you about; how old are you; where did you come from; what do you do for a living.

    What facts do you know about the character (Hannah)?
    I'm Hannah, the oldest sister. I'm the married, responsible one; caretaker of the family, hostess of all seasonal gatherings. I'm also a successful actress and I'm well-off financially.

2. **Unspoken Expectations**—This level is concerned with your unspoken dreams and secret fantasies. You assume that those close to you know them, but they don't always. As your character becomes disappointed, your resentment and anger build, but these emotions never come out verbally. This is where you, the actor, must read between the lines.

    What are Hannah's unspoken hopes and dreams? Are they being fulfilled?
    I expect my sisters to appreciate the selfless sacrifices I make for them. I hope and pray that someday they will take care of themselves.

3. **Unconscious Choices**—These unconscious, sometimes unhealthy choices aren't limited to lovers ("I'm going to choose you because I can't be intimate. You can't be intimate either, so let's get together!"); they can also include friends and family. All those hours of therapy will come in handy when uncovering this level—look into the heart of your character and imagine what it would be like to be him or her.

Why did Hannah choose her mate? What does that say about her? What unconscious role does Hannah play in her family?
I married Elliot because he is strong and stable, unlike my alcoholic mother and philandering father. To compensate for their weaknesses, I have taken on a parental role in my family, refereeing my parents' feuds, unconsciously becoming the mother figure.

SIBLINGS: WHERE IS YOUR CHARACTER IN THE FOOD CHAIN?

Like *Hannah and Her Sisters*, if your scene involves siblings, it can be very helpful to find out where the character falls in the family (first born, middle child, or the youngest). The first child is seen as the hero of the family, blazing all the trails. If it's a boy, then he automatically has certain expectations placed upon him ("This is the one who's going to carry on the family name." "Look at what our son has achieved!"). The middle child needs to live up to the elder sibling—or, he completely rebels against him, never getting the glory. The youngest child will always be the baby—used to being watched over and taken care of.

LOVE RELATIONSHIPS

Love can be many things to many people—beautiful, painful, happy or miserable—depending on what season of love you're in. Is it the beginning of your relationship? Have you been lovers for awhile? Is there jealousy? Do you still have sex? Let's review the tender and bittersweet love story, *The Way We Were,* written by Arthur Laurents and directed by Sydney Pollack, to analyze the stages of love as defined by Elaine Harris.

STAGES OF A LOVE RELATIONSHIP

1. **The Glow of New Love**—Everything is perfect, you can't believe you've met your soul mate. You think alike, feel alike, finish each other's sentences. You are on such a high that you can hardly sleep.

   When WASP-y writer Hubbell Gardiner (Robert Redford) and radical Jewish activist Katie Morosky (Barbra Streisand) fall in love, they look at each other through rose-colored glasses.

2. **You're Not Who I Thought You Were or How Did You Turn Out So Different?** In this stage, the romance begins to fade as the real people emerge and differences appear. The lovers begin to doubt their choices and become critical of each other.

Katie is disillusioned when Hubbell sells out and moves to Hollywood. She now sees him as weak and lacking integrity. Hubbell is tired of Katie's political activism. Her aggressive approach doesn't fit into his laid-back Hollywood lifestyle.

3. **Can I Live With the Differences?** During this stage, you try to change your partner. There's a little bristling, some discomfort and disappointment. And, then you have to make a choice about whether to continue the relationship.

Katie wants Hubbell to leave Hollywood and move back to New York, but when she goes on one last protest, it's the last straw. The relationship is over.

Regardless of the genre, if your character is in love, he will be passing through one of these stages. And realize, you might not get to the first stage until the end of the movie, as in many romantic comedies. (At first, they hate each other, then they start to like each other, and finally, they fall in love.)

As you prepare your audition, ask yourself, *"At this point in the script, what stage of love is my relationship in?"*

Whether you have twenty-five minutes, a full day, or a week to prepare for your audition, a thorough analysis of the relationship will keep you afloat and help you survive.

TIPS

- When you go to an audition and there are more than two characters in a scene, focus on the casting director for the bulk of the dialogue. Then, when a new character enters, create an imaginary person in a different place, *not* the same space as the casting director. Always differentiate between the characters you are talking to if your character's feelings about them are different.

- If the new character has extensive dialogue, take a moment to look away and reestablish the casting director as that new character. It is important to make contact with the reader.

- If you go into an audition and you get only the sides and not a full script, be sure to look at the page numbers to find out where the scene appears in the script. If you get a scene that begins on page 8, you'll know the relationship is in the early stages (as opposed to a scene from page 65). How does it change by the end of the script? How much time has gone by between the scenes? Relationships don't stay the same, they change. What different aspects of your character can you bring out in the two scenes?

- Look for clues in the description section of the script regarding relationships to other characters in the scene.

- If you are limited with time, always be clear on who the other characters are and how your character feels about them.

- Don't just state facts, analyze the relationship on an emotional level

---

QUICK TAKE

RELATIONSHIP—*What do the characters mean to each other?*

READ THROUGH THE SCENE FOR THE FIRST TIME. Become a detective and search for clues that show what your character is feeling about the other characters.

- What is going on for my character in relation to the scene?
- What's my relationship with the main character and how do I feel about him or her?
- Are there any characters *mentioned* in the scene? If so, how do I feel about them?
- Where am I in relation to the environment? Where does the scene take place?
- How does my relationship change during the scene?

—

INTENTION

What do you want from the other character?

EILEEN DAVIDSON / *The Young and the Restless, Days of Our Lives*

When I first started auditioning, I didn't know very much about cold reading. I thought it was best to always recreate the text as much as possible. The character I was reading for was scrubbing a floor in the scene, so I got down on all fours and mimed the same. I pretty much did the whole scene with my butt pointed at the casting director who was moving from side to side, up and down trying to see the rest of me. After I finished, the casting director told me that although he thought I gave a good reading, it would probably be better if I read SEATED in the future. Moral of the story . . . sometimes the K.I.S.S. rule applies: KEEP IT SIMPLE, SWEETHEART!

EILEEN DAVIDSON

How often have you gone into an audition and, in the middle of it, the casting director says, "No, no. Stop right there. There's no energy. It needs more energy!" Of course, you have no idea what they're talking about. Or, the casting director will ask you to speed it up because it's dragging. Even if you feel that something is missing in the scene, how do you translate those vague directions into something you can act? When you hear comments such as, "It's boring" or "Pick up the pace," this usually means your character's need was not strong enough to propel the scene—there was a weak intention.

> *My associate, Annie Grindlay, and I attended an industry showcase in which four of my clients appeared. The audience was filled with casting directors and agents hoping to discover hot new talent. Over a dozen scenes were to be performed, an ambitious task. Twenty minutes into the showcase, a heaviness filled the air. The audience was getting fidgety: a well-known casting director was nodding off, another couple slipped out quietly. Annie and I looked at each other and knew exactly what the problem was. The actors had worked hard on their character choices but they had forgotten the most important ingredient—a strong intention. Their relationships were good, but the scenes weren't going anywhere. They became stagnant, plodding along until the audience soon lost interest.*

Intention is what drives a scene. Without a strong intention, the characters falter (and the audience's attention will drift). Intention is described as goal, objective, need, purpose, etc. Your high school drama teacher may have asked, "What does your character hope to *achieve*?" Or, your director may want to know, "What are you trying *to get* in the scene?" or "What is your character's *goal*?" But, these questions all ask the same thing: *What does your character want in the scene?*

SECOND READ-THROUGH

As you read over the same scene from Thelma & Louise, this time ask yourself, *"What do I want from the other character in the scene?"*

```
Louise is rubbing her face. She looks pretty bad. Her
hands are shaking.

                LOUISE
             (to herself)
        Shit. I'm gettin' tired.
```

                    THELMA
Are you alright?

Louise does not really seem alright.

                    LOUISE
        (upset)
I think I've really fucked up.
I think I've got us in a
situation where we could both
get killed. I mean, I don't
know what's the matter with me.
I don't know why we didn't just
go straight to the police.

                    THELMA
You know why. You already said.

                    LOUISE
What'd I say again?

                    THELMA
Nobody would believe us. We'd
still get in trouble. We'd
still have our lives ruined.
And you know what else?

                    LOUISE
What?

                    THELMA
That guy was hurtin' me. And if
you hadn't come out when you
did, he'd a hurt me a lot
worse. And probably nothin'
woulda ever happened to him.
'Cause everybody did see me
dancin' with him all night. And
they woulda made out like I
asked for it. And my life
woulda been ruined a whole lot
worse than it is now. At least
now I'm havin' fun. And I'm not
sorry that son of a bitch is
dead. I'm only sorry that it
was you that did it and not me.

```
And if I haven't, I wanna take
this time to thank you, Louise.
Thank you for savin' my ass.

        LOUISE
I said all that?

        THELMA
No, Louise, you said the first
part. I said all the rest.

        LOUISE
    (tired)
Whatever.
```

In this scene, what does Louise want from Thelma? Obviously, she is very upset. The situation has gotten out of control and she *wants* reassurance from Thelma that she did the right thing. Thelma, on the other hand, *wants* Louise to be strong. She needs Louise to remain in one piece to get through this awful mess.

"Want" is a powerful word. It inspires us to action. How do you translate character "wants" into tangible terms for your acting? For this, you must ask yourself a second question: *"What am I going to do to accomplish my intention?"*

ACTION VERBS

Now's the time for you to get out of your head and into your body. There's no need for long expositions on the deep psychological needs of your character. At this point, you need to breathe life into your character by physicalizing your intention. Think in terms of simple action verbs that children might use.

Always begin your intention with the words, "I want to . . . "
Then, insert your action verb.

Louise wants *to dump out* her fears in the hope that Thelma will tell her that she did the right thing. Thelma wants *to shake* Louise into realizing that Louise saved her life.

Here are examples of action verbs versus non-action verbs:

action verbs	non-action verbs
push	control
pull	find out
tear apart	discuss
squeeze	examine
force	make
awaken	tell
shake	analyze
tease	delude
stroke	impact
crush	conquer
seduce	beguile
charm	get
kick	operate

Stay away from non-action verbs that are too "heady" and hard to play (i.e., discuss, tell, accomplish, deceive, prepare, blame, describe). Physical, active verbs get you out of your head and into places of passion (your heart, guts, sex).

OPPOSING ADJECTIVES

Everyone has more than one side to his personality. Using opposing adjectives keeps you hooked into the relationship. By including the other character in your intention, you stay connected to that character and the way your character feels about him. It's a simple, but powerful reminder.

Louise's intention is, "I want to dump out my fears to my caring, but naïve friend, Thelma, in hopes that she will say I did the right thing." Thelma's intention becomes, "I want to shake Louise, my frightened, but strong friend, into realizing that she saved my life."

Notice that for Louise's intention, opposing adjectives describe Thelma as "caring, but naïve." Louise is "frightened, but strong."

Following are a few examples of opposing adjectives:

loving, but dangerous
stupid, but happy
sexy, but egotistical
bright, but obnoxious

PHYSICAL BEHAVIOR

Your character's physical behavior should always match your intention. If you are coming from the character's point of view, then your movement should express your character's needs.

Turn on your television but turn off the volume. Can you tell what's going on in the scene? Do you have an idea what the characters are thinking and feeling—without hearing their dialogue? If you do, it's because the actors are physicalizing their life; their bodies are supporting their intentions.

I can't tell you how many times I have seen the following scenario: an actor doing an audition scene is supposed to get angry at the other character; however, just before the scene, the actor takes two steps backwards, shifting his body aimlessly from side to side. The actor feels insecure and withdraws from the scene but his character would not have behaved this way. His character would have gone after what he wants.

Don't get lost in extemporaneous movement. If you have something to express, use your body! Start with a thought; this will create an emotion that is finally expressed in a physical movement.

OBSTACLES

It's not enough to have a strong intention. Once you are clear on what your character wants, ask yourself, *"What is preventing my character from achieving her goal? What are the obstacles in the scene?"* Obstacles are the little bumps in the road that make the character's journey interesting. They may cause the character to take a detour and find a completely different path—a path that may be more rewarding than the one they originally took.

Sometimes a student will come into the scene with a very specific, strong intention. The scene is moving in the right direction, but something is missing. The character is on a one-lane road and we know just where she's going. It becomes predictable; there are no surprises. It shouldn't be that easy to accomplish what you want.

Any given day is beset with obstacles. Let's take a simple example: you have an audition at 10:00 a.m. and your goal is to arrive a few minutes early to prepare. Sounds easy enough, except that your alarm clock is mysteriously set for 7:30 p.m. instead of 7:30 a.m. You wake up an hour late, in a panic. You scramble to find an unwrinkled shirt and you also discover that you're out of coffee. Barely dressed, you stumble into your car, back out of the driveway and smack into the pole that you've been carefully dodging for months. You'll have to assess the damage later. Traffic is horrible! You finally arrive—just in time to hear the last syllable of your name being called. Whew! You just made it!

It wasn't so easy to accomplish your original intention, was it? But, you have to admit—your morning was full of surprises and it certainly wasn't predictable!

TYPES OF OBSTACLES

In life, obstacles always get in our way. Look for them in your work, as well. There are five main types of obstacles that may be found in a scene:

- **Environmental**—any of the elements (air, water, earth and fire), the weather (wind, rain, snow, heat), a specific location (is your character in a crowded restaurant embroiled in a heated discussion? If so, take that into consideration.).

- **Physical**—any type of pain or discomfort your character experiences, including medical ailments and/or physical limitations.

- **Emotional**—including psychological difficulties, your character's inner fears, insecurities and neuroses.

- **Other people**—other characters present or mentioned in the scene that impede your character's actions.

- **Time**—a specific time frame can help create an urgency necessary to drive the scene.

The Fugitive

The Fugitive[1] (written by Jeb Stuart, David Twohy; directed by Andrew Davis), the 1993 feature film version of the 1950s TV series, is an excellent example of different obstacles facing a character. The film opens with Dr. Richard Kimble (Harrison Ford) being convicted of killing his wife, despite his claims to have witnessed a one-armed man commit the crime. Kimble manages to escape and hunt for the real killer, while being tracked by U. S. Marshall Sam Gerard (Tommy Lee Jones). Kimble's overall intention is to evade Gerard long enough to bring his wife's real killer to justice.

---

[1] *The Fugitive* won the Academy Award™ for Best Supporting Actor (Tommy Lee Jones) and was nominated for six others.

- **Environmental Obstacles**
  Dr. Richard Kimble jumps off a huge waterfall; he stumbles through thick woods; faces a gunfight on a moving train; and falls down an elevator shaft.

- **Physical Obstacles**
  During his escape, Kimble is physically injured in a train explosion (shrapnel rips through his side, but he stays on his feet, limping away from the scene); he must keep others from recognizing him (throughout the film, he must take on different identities).

- **Emotional Obstacles**
  Kimble's emotional obstacles take on the form of flashbacks, which occasionally cause him to lose focus at critical times.

- **Other People**
  Gerard's obsessive pursuit is Kimble's main obstacle. Other people present a problem as they begin to suspect Kimble's true identity.

- **Time**
  Time is critical, as Kimble never knows when Gerard will show up, forcing him to constantly stay on the move.

In Kimble's case, he is able to overcome the odds. However, it was not an easy task. In life, you don't always succeed over obstacles; most times, you fail. But that's what makes life challenging.

Julia

The 1977 Academy Award™-winning film, *Julia*[2] (written by Alvin Sargent, based on a story by Lillian Hellman; directed by Fred Zinnemann) is Lillian Hellman's account of her lasting relationship with childhood friend, Julia. The story takes place during the 1930s and '40s, when these two wealthy society women broke away from the traditional female roles. Lillian (Jane Fonda) became a controversial writer, living "in sin" with Dashiell Hammett (Jason Robards, Jr.), while Julia (Vanessa Redgrave) went to Germany, joined the underground forces and helped persecuted Jews escape the death camps. *Julia* offers a strong connection between intention and obstacles.

A crucial scene of the film occurs the last time Lillian sees Julia. Secretly transporting money for the cause, Lillian reunites with her long-lost comrade in a German coffeehouse; they haven't seen each other for years. Their opposing intentions and the many obstacles they face make it a remarkable encounter.

---

[2] *Julia* won Academy Awards™ for Best Adapted Screenplay (Alvin Sargent), Best Supporting Actor (Jason Robards) and Best Supporting Actress (Vanessa Redgrave) and received eight other nominations.

Closer angle - LILLIAN and JULIA - night

LILLIAN closer to her now. For the first time she sees
the crutches. JULIA takes her hand. LILLIAN'S eyes
begin to tear. They do not speak. LILLIAN looks again
at the crutches, then she sits next to JULIA. JULIA
continues to hold her hand. LILLIAN can't speak. Then
finally:

>   JULIA
> Fine, fine.

Lillian studies her, looks at the crutches.

>   JULIA
> I've ordered caviar. We'll
> celebrate. Albert had to send
> for it, it won't be long. Look
> at you. Oh, just look at you!

>   LILLIAN
>   (whispers)
> Tell me what to say to you.

>   JULIA
> It's all right. Nothing will
> happen now, everything's fine
> now.

>   LILLIAN
> I want to say something.

>   JULIA
> I know.

>   LILLIAN
> How long do we have?

>   JULIA
> Not long.

>   LILLIAN
> You still look like nobody
> else. (pause) Why do you have
> the crutches?

Pause.

>   JULIA
>   (quickly)
> I have a false leg!

>   LILLIAN
> What?

>   JULIA
> I have a false leg!

>   LILLIAN
> No! I don't want to hear that.
> Don't tell me that!

>   JULIA
>   (sharp)
> No tears, Lilly.

>   LILLIAN
> I'm sorry.

>   JULIA
> It's done. It's what it is.

>   LILLIAN
> When?

>   JULIA
> You know when. You were there.
> In Vienna.

>   LILLIAN
> I don't want to hear about it,
> please, just let me look at
> you.

>   JULIA
> You have to hear about it, you
> have to hear about everything.
> (taking Lillian's hand) Your
> fingers are cold, here...

She begins to rub Lillian's hands.

>   LILLIAN
> They took the candy box. A man
> and a woman.

>   JULIA
> That's right. Everything's fine
> and what I want you to do now
> is take off your hat, the way
> you would if it - Lilly, listen
> to me, you aren't listening.

>   LILLIAN
> I'm listening, I am.

>   JULIA
> Take off your hat, as if it
> were too hot in here. Comb your
> hair. Put your hat on the seat
> between us. Do as I tell
> you...Make conversation...It
> has to be this way.

Lillian looks around the room. Then she looks at
Julia. She takes off the hat.

>   JULIA
>   (calmly)
> So who were you with in Paris?
> Good friends?

>   LILLIAN
> Yes. Good friends. But they
> don't know anything about this.

She puts the hat on the seat between them.

>   JULIA
> Get your comb.

>   LILLIAN
> Comb...

She reaches for her purse. Opens it. Looks for the
comb. The purse is full.

```
                    LILLIAN
          I still carry too much.

                    JULIA
                (looking in purse)
          There it is, take it out and
          use it.

     Lillian takes out the comb. Starts to comb her hair
     back.

                    JULIA
          Keep talking to me. I read your
          play. Don't look down. Look at
          me. Be natural. You look so
          very well.

     During this Julia has pulled the hat into her open
     coat. Then she'll proceed to pin it deep inside the
     lining.

                    LILLIAN
          Did you like it? My play?

                    JULIA
          I'm very proud of you. It was
          wonderful.
```

Lillian's overall intention is *to be strong for Julia.* But how do you act that? Employing an action verb, *Lillian wants to support her brave, but troubled friend.* She's gotten this far, but when she sees her wounded companion after all this time, the flood of memories is too great. She struggles to hold back her emotions so that she may be of service to Julia. Lillian's obstacle stems from her strong need. She misses Julia terribly. Also, she's scared.

Julia's overall objective is to make sure, without a doubt, that this meeting goes off as planned. *She wants to quiet (or contain) her loving, but frightened friend* so they're not discovered. Due to the urgency of her intention, Julia is acutely aware of the surrounding obstacles:

- **Environmental**—The openness of the public cafe makes it almost impossible to share a private moment.

- **Physical**—Julia's injured leg presents a physical obstacle; the crutches make her more recognizable.

- **Emotional**—Julia must hide her emotions to get the job done.

- **Other People**—The Gestapo surrounds them, watching their every move.

- **Time**—At any moment, Julia could be arrested. Time is ticking away. Julia wrestles with her feelings: her love for Lillian, her memories, joys, fears and the realization that she doesn't have much time make achieving her intention all the more challenging.

ADJUSTMENTS

You've figured out what your character wants and you've pinpointed the obstacles that stand in their way. The next question is: *How do you fulfill your character's intention?* You do this by using adjustments (or tactics), which can best be described as adverbs. For example, if my intention is to shake you into listening to me, how shall I go about that? Lovingly, passionately, angrily. An actor may have a strong intention, but he might hammer away at it until the scene becomes predictable. Adjustments vary the course.

> *Imagine you're playing golf. Your goal is to get the ball into the hole. How are you going to do that? Depending on where your ball is located and after selecting one of your many clubs, you make adjustments. You start out with a driver to hit the ball SOLIDLY and FORCEFULLY down the fairway. Then, along the fairway, you pick either a wood or an iron. Midway, you might select a 5-iron to help you stroke POWERFULLY and give you more loft. Oops! You're lost in a sandtrap. Time to pull out the old sand wedge. You knock the ball DIRECTLY back on course. Finally, you unveil your brand new specialty putter to tap the ball LIGHTLY and EVENLY into the hole. Congratulations! You made it! And, you did it by making choices. Notice how you accomplished your goal by varying your approach for each shot. In other words, you used different tactics—or adjustments—to get what you wanted.*

As you read through a scene, notice the different ways your character tries to achieve his goal. Note the changes by listing as many adverbs as you can. (In Chapter 7, on units and transitions, you will learn how to place specific adjustments.)

The Silence of the Lambs

The Silence of the Lambs[3] (written by Ted Tally and directed by Jonathan Demme) is a phenomenal script, layered with complex characters and their obsessions. FBI trainee, Clarice Starling (Jodie Foster) has been assigned to

---

[3] *The Silence of the Lambs* won Academy Awards™ for Best Picture, Best Actor (Anthony Hopkins), Best Actress (Jodie Foster), Best Director (Jonathan Demme), Best Adapted Screenplay (Ted Tally) and received two other nominations.

profile serial killer, Dr. Hannibal Lecter (Anthony Hopkins), an incarcerated
psychopathic monster who is enlisted to help with unsolved cases.

The first meeting between Hannibal and Clarice is an excellent example
of the characters' strong intentions, obstacles and adjustments. Each exchange is like a chess move: each move requires forethought and invention
to get ahead.

```
DR. LECTER'S CELL
is coming slowly INTO VIEW...Behind its barred front
wall is a second barrier of stout nylon net...Sparse,
bolted-down furniture, many softcover books and
papers. On the walls, extraordinarily detailed,
skillful drawings, mostly European cityscapes, in
charcoal or crayon.

CLARICE
stops, at a polite distance from his bars, clears her
throat.

                    CLARICE
          Dr. Lecter...My name is Clarice
          Starling. May I talk with you.

DR. HANNIBAL LECTER
is lounging on his bunk, in white pajamas, reading an
Italian Vogue. He turns, considers her...A face so
long out of the sun, it seems almost leached - except
for the glittering eyes, and the wet red mouth. He
rises smoothly, crossing to stand before her: the
gracious host. His voice is cultured, soft.

                    DR. LECTER
          Good morning.

CUTTING BETWEEN THEM
as Clarice comes a measured distance closer.

                    CLARICE
          Doctor, we have a hard problem
          in psychological profiling. I
          want to ask for your help with
          a questionnaire.
```

>   DR. LECTER
> "We" being the Behavioral
> Science Unit, at Quantico.
> You're one of Jack Crawford's I
> expect.
>
>   CLARICE
> I am, yes.
>
>   DR. LECTER
> May I see your credentials?

Clarice is surprised, but fishes her ID card from her
bag, holds it up for his inspection. He smiles,
soothingly.

>   DR. LECTER
>   (cont.)
> Closer, please...clo-ser...

She complies each time, trying to hide her fear. Dr.
Lecter's nostrils lift, as he gently, like an animal,
tests the air. Then he smiles, glancing at her card.

>   DR. LECTER
>   (cont.)
> That expires in one week.
> You're not real FBI, are you?
>
>   CLARICE
> I'm - still in training at the
> Academy.
>
>   DR. LECTER
> Jack Crawford sent a *trainee* to
> me?
>
>   CLARICE
> We're talking about psychology,
> Doctor, not the Bureau. Can you
> decide for yourself whether I'm
> not qualified?
>
>   DR. LECTER
> Mmmmmm...That's rather slippery
> of you, Agent Starling. Sit.
> Please.

She sits in the folding metal desk-chair. He waits
politely till she's settled, then sits down himself,
faces her happily.

                    DR. LECTER
               (cont.)
          Now then. What did Miggs say to
          you? (She is puzzled) "Multiple
          Miggs," in the next cell. He
          hissed at you. What did he say?

                    CLARICE
          He said - "I can smell your
          cunt."

                    DR. LECTER
          I see. I myself cannot. You use
          Evian skin cream, and sometimes
          you wear L'Air du Temps, but
          not today. You've brought your
          best bag, though, haven't you?

                    CLARICE
               (Beat)
          Yes.

                    DR. LECTER
          It's much better than your
          shoes.

                    CLARICE
          Maybe they'll catch up.

                    DR. LECTER
          I have no doubt of it.

                    CLARICE
               (Shifting uncomfortably)
          Did you do those drawings,
          Doctor?

                    DR. LECTER
          Yes. That's the Duomo, seen
          from the Belvedere. Do you know
          Florence?

>   CLARICE
> All that detail, just from
> memory...?
>
>   DR. LECTER
> Memory, Agent Starling, is what
> I have instead of a view.

A pause, then Clarice takes the questionnaire from her
case.

>   CLARICE
> Dr. Lecter, if you'd please
> consider -
>
>   DR. LECTER
> No, no, no. You were doing
> fine, you'd been courteous and
> receptive to courtesy, you'd
> established trust with the
> embarrassing truth about Miggs,
> and now this hamhanded segue
> into your questionnaire. It
> won't do. It's stupid and
> boring.
>
>   CLARICE
> I'm only going to ask you to
> look at this, Doctor. Either
> you will or you won't.
>
>   DR. LECTER
> Jack Crawford must be very busy
> indeed if he's recruiting help
> from the student body. Busy
> hanging that new one, Buffalo
> Bill... Such a naughty boy! Did
> Jack send you to plead for my
> advice on him?
>
>   CLARICE
> No, I came because we need -
>
>   DR. LECTER
> How many women has he used, our
> Bill?

                  CLARICE
Five...so far.

                  DR. LECTER
All flayed...?

                  CLARICE
Partially, yes. But Doctor,
that's an active case, I'm not
involved. If -

                  DR. LECTER
Do you know *why* he's called
Buffalo Bill? Tell me. The
newspapers won't say.

                  CLARICE
I'll tell you if you'll look at
this form. (He considers, then
nods) It started as a bad joke
in Kansas City Homicide. They
said... this one likes to skin
his humps.

                  DR. LECTER
Witless and misleading. Why do
you think he removes their
skins, Agent Starling? Thrill
me with your acumen.

                  CLARICE
It excites him. Most serial
killers keep some sort of -
trophies.

                  DR. LECTER
I didn't.

                  CLARICE
No. You ate yours.

A tense beat, then a smile from him, at this small
boldness.

>   DR. LECTER
> Send that through.

She rolls him the questionnaire, in his sliding food
tray. He rises, glances at it, turning a page or two
disdainfully.

>   DR. LECTER
>   (cont.)
> Oh, Agent Starling...do you
> think you can dissect me with
> this blunt little tool?

>   CLARICE
> No. I only hoped that your
> knowledge -

Suddenly he ships the tray back at her, with a
metallic CLANG that makes her start. His voice remains
a pleasant purr.

>   DR. LECTER
>   (cont.)
> You're sooo ambitious, aren't
> you...? You know what you look
> like to me, with your good bag
> and cheap shoes? You look like
> a rube. A well-scrubbed,
> hustling rube with a little
> taste...Good nutrition has
> given you some length of bone,
> but you're not more than one
> generation from poor white
> trash, are you - *Agent*
> Starling...? That accent you've
> tried so desperately to shed -
> pure West Virginia. What is
> your father, dear? Is he a coal
> miner? Does he stink of the
> lamp...?

His every word strikes her like a small, precise dart.

                    DR. LECTER
               (cont.)
          And oh, how quickly the boys
          found *you!* All those tedious,
          sticky fumblings, in the back
          seats of cars, while you could
          only dream of getting out.
          Getting anywhere, yes? Getting
          all the way - to the F...B...I.

                    CLARICE
               (Shaken)
          You see a lot, Dr. Lecter. But
          are you strong enough to point
          that high-powered perception at
          yourself? How about it...? Look
          at yourself and write down the
          truth. (She slams the tray back
          at him) Or maybe you're afraid
          to.

                    DR. LECTER
          You're a tough one, aren't you?

                    CLARICE
          Reasonably so. Yes.

                    DR. LECTER
          And you'd hate to think you
          were common. My, wouldn't that
          sting! Well you're far from
          common, Clarice Starling. All
          you have is a fear of it.
          (Beat) Now please excuse me.
          Good day.

                    CLARICE
          And the questionnaire...?

                    DR. LECTER
          A census taker once tried to
          test me. I ate his liver with
          some fava beans and a nice
          chianti...Fly back to school,
          little Starling.

Let's go to the studio where Steve and Annie have just completed the scene.

From the Studio

Margie: The two of you really hooked into the game-playing aspect of the scene. It's great to see you perform it simply and without pushing your intentions, yet lots of things were going on. I felt you were both observing each other. Steve, what was your intention?

Steve: To chip away at this scared but determined young lady and see if she is a worthy opponent.

Margie: Notice how he grabbed both the relationship and Clarice's opposing qualities: to chip away at this *scared, but determined* young lady . If you can understand her character and what the scene is about, you'll find different ways to test her.
    The fun of the scene is to view it as a chess game. Find out where your next move is and go one up from there. You're thinking about the future and how to achieve your goal. There's an excitement about winning. The game is calculated at times but it can also be impulsive. Some moves are more obvious and others not as apparent.

Annie: Doesn't he have more moves than I do?

Margie: He's the initial game player but you come in with a very strong intention and need.

Annie: I put down "to draw out information from this bizarre, but brilliant monster."

Margie: That's good, but your moves are going to be more difficult than his because you have to make sure you don't give away your hand. He could dismiss you at any minute.

Steve: True, but he hasn't seen a woman in a long time.

Margie: Yes, that changes the game, doesn't it? When Clarice walks in, you smell her womanly scent which brings out your starved sexuality. He's a caged animal. No one's allowed near his cell. He hasn't had a visitor in months. His deprivation intensifies his need to conquer her. To him, she's better than the most delicious sirloin steak. He wants to chew her up and spit her out.

Steve: Isn't his hunger also an obstacle for him?

Margie: Yes. His need for her takes over, to the point where he's not as smooth as he would like to be. He loses control and has to fight his desire throughout the scene. Lecter must contain himself in order to play the game expertly. And Steve, I think you can let yourself have a little more fun with it.

When Clarice scores, there's a part of Lecter that loves the challenge. Then there's the psychotic part of his personality that emerges. So, Steve should consider some adjustments: demeaningly, tauntingly, cruelly, monstrously, insultingly.

Annie: For Clarice, it's hard to stay in the room with him. He's so repulsive.

Margie: True, Clarice's obstacle is to keep from running out of the room, especially when he starts digging into her personal life. He provokes her with demeaning statements suggesting that she's nothing, she's unworthy, her clothes are cheap and she's unqualified for the job. Still, she holds her own. That distaste and fear, that discomfort is something she can't let him see because if he senses it, she's lost the round. Some adjustments for Clarice might be: courageously, professionally, humorously, complimentarily and intelligently.

KEY PHRASE

As you read through a scene, a phrase may pop up that makes you stop and recognize what's going on for your character. That is your key phrase—it's what reveals the truth about your character and why he behaves the way he does.

In the climactic courtroom scene from *A Few Good Men* (written by Aaron Sorkin; directed by Rob Reiner), Lt. Kaffee (Tom Cruise) relentlessly grills Col. Jessep (Jack Nicholson), shouting, "I want the truth!" Nicholson yells back, "You can't handle the truth!" These are memorable lines, not only because they are so brilliantly acted, but because they cut to the undeniable truth of the characters. This exchange defines who they are and explains why they behave the way they do.

The key phrase is not always so obvious. In fact, sometimes it's not written, but implied. If you are given two or three scenes for an audition, you may find that there is only one key phrase for your character. Don't be concerned if you have trouble locating the key phrase. It is just another tool for scene analysis.

TIPS

- Post these three words on your bathroom mirror: PHYSICALIZE! PHYSICALIZE! PHYSICALIZE!

- The more action words you know, the easier it is nail down an actable verb (i.e., your intention). Get a dictionary and make a list of active verbs.

- The same applies for adjustments. The more adverbs you know, the easier it is to recognize them. Your list of colorful adverbs will give you more choices when you have to break the scene down into units.

- Why not raise the stakes? Remember, there's only one first. The first kiss, the first time you say "I love you," the first confrontation. Is there a "first" in your scene? If so, fill it with emotion.

- Make sure that what your character wants is connected to the other character in the scene. It will make your intention stronger.

- Nothing in life is easy so why make it easy to accomplish your character's intention? Find at least one strong obstacle.

QUICK TAKE

INTENTION: *What do you want from the other character?*
Read through the scene a second time to determine:

- What do I WANT from the other character in the scene?
- What am I going TO DO to accomplish that intention? What is my ACTION WORD?
- What OPPOSING ADJECTIVES can I use to describe the other character in the scene?
- What OBSTACLES exist that could get in my way?
- How am I going to get what my character wants? What different ADJUSTMENTS can I use? (Think in terms of "ly" adverbs, such as kindly, gently, forcefully.)
- What is my character's KEY PHRASE?

—

HISTORY

How has the past affected your character's choices?

BIBI BESCH / *Star Trek, Betsy's Wedding*

Bibi was a tremendous actress, a wonderful human being and one of the first people to contribute to this book. I was honored to have her in my class. She told me this story about her worst "nightmare" audition that she wished to share with other actors who may have to go through the same sort of confusing and disorienting experience. Bibi is sorely missed.

. . . .

The worst audition I ever had was for a television show. I had just come to Hollywood from New York and didn't know the ropes here yet. Every audition was a big deal and a bit overwhelming. I walked into a large office and, from behind an imposing desk, a man I'd never met before said to me in front of a dozen people, "NOW I remember why I don't like you." I then had to audition! I was so astonished. I pretended he hadn't said anything and gamely tried to go on. Needless to say, I didn't get the job. And I never did find out what he meant.

BIBI BESCH

You've read through the scene twice and you've answered the basic questions: You know *who* the character is; you know *what* they want; you know *when* and *where* the scene takes place. Now, you are ready to answer the more difficult questions about your character (e.g., Why does the character behave this way? How did he get to this point?). You do this by using your imagination to uncover his history and paint in his background. It's time to peel away the layers of the character, just as you would peel the skin off an onion.

> *Sometimes, actors will complain that they did a lot of work on the history, then when they went into the audition, they forgot everything! When I ask how they prepared, they'll say they wrote a ten-page biography that included all the facts of the character's history. But, that's the problem! You don't have time to do all that. You can't own the history unless you're up on your feet physicalizing it. Basically, the facts are not as significant as coming from the emotional place of the character. This is accomplished by using your physical behavior.*

Too often, actors get stuck inside their heads—they'll intellectualize their character's history instead of experience it. You must get out of your head and into your body! When you're working on your character's history, get out of your chair, get onto your feet and start moving! Talk in an emotional language by using images and sensory work to make it real for you. It's not only the facts of what happened to the character, but how you feel about them and how they affect your character today. Stick to feelings, not facts.

Thelma & Louise

Let's go back to *Thelma & Louise*. Most actresses will look at the opening car scene and interpret it as best friends who are running away from their mates and get into trouble. However, that's a superficial analysis. What they forget to look at are the less obvious questions: Why are they doing this? What makes them capable of this behavior? Where did their actions come from? That's where the history comes in.

In the chapter on Relationships, we learned that Louise was raped. She is angry; she's been violated; her rage was never expressed because the crime was never acknowledged. As a result, no one has heard her inner screams and no one has been punished for the crime. So, now she has an opportunity to scream as loudly as she can—and, she does. We'll get into personalizing those images and talk more about sensory work, but for now, we are coloring in only that part of Louise's history; we are feeding our brain cells with Louise's past.

Although Thelma may not have had a life-changing event in her past, what affects her today is her rocky relationship with her husband. Uncovering this history can be interesting and challenging for the actress. Don't just say, "I have a bad relationship with my husband." Instead, remember the day he hit you and how your face was bleeding. Think about how you sat down in the corner and cried for hours, wishing you had the strength to leave him. Recall how, every time you hear his voice, you cringe. In the first scene, when Louise mentions Thelma's husband, emotional images should automatically pop up for you that connect you to those feelings because you've worked on the history.

Thelma and Louise are a good match because they are both containing enormous rage. Although they come from very different backgrounds, both of them are explosions waiting to happen, each for different reasons. Louise has the rape raging inside; Thelma has suppression caused by an abusive husband. For Thelma, being a wife is what is expected of her, the role she is supposed to play. (Where is she going to go?) For Louise, it's societal too, because a rape victim has few rights. (Where is she going to go with her feelings?) So, if you take these two simmering volcanoes and put them in a situation where they have room to spew—they do.

CREATING THE PAST

Paint in your character's history using your imagination. The information you need won't always be found in the script. In fact, the history doesn't always come from the page, it comes from you. Being able to use your creativity is what makes being an actor exciting. As long as it is appropriate to the character's choices, you have free reign to color in the past.

A word of caution: any history you create must fit the character. Sometimes, an actor may select a history that is not appropriate to the character. (For example, an actor may decide his character was an axe murderer in a previous life, when all that's really happening in the scene is an argument between friends.) So, watch that you don't get carried away. Also, don't try to create a history that is so removed from yourself that you can't relate to it. Start from your own truth. It is the seed of possibility. Grow from there.

From the Studio

In this exchange, two students, Stephanie and Jonathan, read a scene from Neil Simon's film, *The Goodbye Girl* (written by Simon; directed by Herbert Ross)[1], in which a dripping wet Elliott (portrayed by Richard Dreyfuss) fights with Paula (Marsha Mason) over a New York rent-controlled apartment. He's got the keys but she's got possession.

---

[1] Richard Dreyfuss won the Best Actor Oscar® for his starring role as Elliott Garfield; the film received four additional nominations.

INT - APARTMENT

She closes the door. He wipes forehead, still rain-
soaked, with his hankerchief.

                    ELLIOTT
          I'm dripping on your rug.

                    PAULA
          It's been dripped on before.

She walks into the living room and takes a place near
the false fireplace, one arm on the mantle. He follows
her in, looks around.

                    ELLIOTT
          ...Look, I'm sorry about all
          this...I didn't know there was
          going to be any complications.

                    PAULA
          Yeah, well, there's a lot of
          that going around lately.

                    ELLIOTT
          Okay. I don't blame you for
          being hostile. I get the
          picture. Tony rents me the
          apartment, splits with the
          money and you and your daughter
          get dumped on, right?

                    PAULA
          That's your version. My version
          is that Tony and I amicably end
          our relationship, we agreed I
          would keep the apartment and
          you and your six hundred
          dollars got dumped on...get the
          picture?

                    ELLIOTT
              (smiles and nods)
          Very good...very sharp...a
          sharp New York girl, right?

                    PAULA
No. A dull Cincinnati kid. But
you get dumped on enough, you
start to develop an edge.

                    ELLIOTT
Okay, so what's the deal? I
have a lease in my pocket. You
gonna honor that or not?

                    PAULA
I got a daughter in my bed.
That tops the lease in your
pocket.

                    ELLIOTT
Look, I don't want to get
legal. Legal is on my side...I
happen to have a lawyer
acquaintance downtown. Now all
I have to do is call this
downtown lawyer acquaintance of
mine —

                    PAULA
Oh, Jesus! An actor!

                    ELLIOTT
What?

                    PAULA
Another goddamn actor! "I
happen to have a lawyer
acquaintance..." That's right
out of "Streetcar Named
Desire"...Stanley Kowalski in
summer stock, right?

                    ELLIOTT
Wrong! I played it in Chicago
in the dead of winter...Three
and a half months at the Drury
Lane.

```
              PAULA
         (nods)
    Ask an actor a question, he
    gives you his credits.

              ELLIOTT
    You want reviews, too?...
    "Elliott Garfield brings new
    dimensions to Kowalski that
    even Brando hadn't
    investigated"... Okay?
```

The actors looked pleased when asked how they thought the reading went.

Stephanie: Well, I thought it was very honest, but I was surprised that nobody laughed.

Comment: It wasn't funny. It seemed really dark.

Margie: Give us the history of their relationship.

Stephanie: Well, I used my imagination like you told us to. I gave Paula a very strong background. I imagined that my previous boyfriend brutally beat me. I was taken to the hospital with many broken bones and I swore off men.

Margie: No wonder you got yourself into trouble. The scene can work only if Paula finds Elliott attractive and charming. That's where the humor and lightness come in. The history you assigned to Paula set you up with an impossible task because it was inappropriate to the material.

DIFFERENT HISTORIES

Some scenes are more relationship-oriented, some are intention-driven and still others rely heavily on investigating the character's history. And, you may be surprised to learn that there are different types of histories: there is the history of the character, the history of the relationship, the back story of the script, as well as the historical background of the times. Some histories figure more prominently than others.

On the Waterfront

Let's analyze the dynamics between the two brothers in the memorable scene from the classic film, *On the Waterfront*, written by Budd Schulberg and directed by Elia Kazan. Charley Mallory (Rod Steiger) and his younger brother Terry (Marlon Brando) are in a taxi. Charley is conflicted because he has orders to "do away with" his kid brother or make sure he doesn't talk; Terry, on the other hand, looks up to Charley and eagerly wants his advice. Charley has spent his life protecting Terry while Terry trusts Charley and is shocked to find out where this ride is headed. The revelation triggers Terry's memory.

Years ago, Charley had persuaded Terry to throw a career-making fight. Although Terry has a strong character history because of the thrown fight, the main focus of the famous cab scene between the brothers hinges on their thirty-year relationship. Terry and Charlie play out roles they've been perfecting for a lifetime. And siblings know how to push each other's buttons. When Terry realizes that Charlie is about to have him killed, it brings up all the pent-up pain and betrayal that he's been harboring for years. For the first time in his life, Terry is faced with the naked truth of how his older brother sold him out: Charlie never believed in him; he never thought Terry could win the match on his own. That fight was the single, most important moment—the pinnacle—of Terry's life. We're all familiar with Brando's famous lines in this scene, "I coulda been a contender. I coulda had class and been somebody." The lines are memorable because they are steeped in history and pain.

In the next chapter, we'll show you how to personalize the thrown fight so you can own it through Terry's eyes. But, for now, let's simply walk through Terry's history. Take the factual information that you have about him and begin translating it into emotional terms. Do this by letting Terry talk: "I was so good. I was feeling really strong that day, throwin' combinations. How could he do this to me? He shoulda known better. Ever since I was a kid, he never believed in me."

At this point, you (the actor portraying Terry) can fill in an imaginary story that supports Terry's feelings—as long as it is appropriate to the script. For example: "I remember in grade school, getting into a fight. My brother threw his weight around and the other kid went running. I was so embarrassed! He never let me fight my own battles. He overprotected me."

In the Line of Fire

Secret service agent Frank Horrigan (portrayed by Clint Eastwood) has a strong character history in the film, *In the Line of Fire* (written by Jeff Maguire; directed by Wolfgang Petersen)[2]. What is unique about the movie is that we, the audience, get to see Frank's reaction to his grim history, as told to him on the phone by the antagonist Booth (portrayed by John Malkovich).

---

[2] This film was nominated for three Academy Awards®, including Best Original Screenplay.

CLOSE SHOTS: An agent running to Jackie Kennedy...
Frank's eyes... A photo of Frank on the running board
of the follow-up car...

>   BOOTH
>   You were on the opposite side
>   of the follow-up car...Closer
>   to Kennedy than he was...You
>   must have looked up at the
>   Texas Book Depository...But you
>   didn't react...Late at night,
>   when the demons come...I'll bet
>   you see that rifle in the
>   window...Or do you see
>   Kennedy's head coming apart?

FULL SCREEN - FRANK'S EYES brimming with pain

>   BOOTH
>   If you'd reacted to the first
>   shot, could you have gotten
>   there in time to stop the fatal
>   bullet? If you had, it might've
>   been your head coming
>   apart...Do you wish you'd
>   succeeded, Frank? Or is life
>   too precious?

>   FRANK
>   (with great difficulty)
>   What's done is done, Booth.

INT. - BASEMENT ROOM - SAME TIME
The room is dank, furnished with only a cot, table, TV
and armchair where BOOTH sits, watching the tape, with
an old copy of Esquire Magazine in his lap.

>   BOOTH
>   I have the article Esquire did
>   for the tenth anniversary,
>   about you and the other agents
>   there that day... Pretty tragic
>   stuff, how your wife left you
>   and took your little girl. You
>   were so forthright, admitting

```
you hadn't been easy to live
with, your drinking problem...I
was so moved by your honesty.
The world can be cruel to an
honest man, can't it?
```

In this excerpt, the actor has been given an enormous amount of character history, so, if you were preparing for this role, much of your work has already been done for you. It's not hard to picture Frank's tragic past: just as surely as the days of "Camelot" vanished with Kennedy's assassination, Frank's life spiraled downward—his wife left him and took their daughter, he became an alcoholic; and, the enormous guilt he felt almost destroyed him.

As an actor, you must translate Frank's history into an "I" message, which would be something like this: "I screwed up. I was right there and I did nothing. I should've seen the bullet coming. How stupid could I have been? I'll never forgive myself. My wife was right to leave me. I'm unworthy of being a father. I'll just keep drinking to ease the pain."

Julia

Let's revisit *Julia*, which is rich in history (see scene excerpt on page 91). Julia and Lillian were born wealthy. They went to private schools. They were expected to marry in their class, have children and take care of their husbands. Julia left her protected life to fight with the underground while Lillian went to fancy parties given by gossipy, prejudiced women who spoke badly of the Jews. Uncharacteristic of the times, Lillian got angry and spoke out. When Julia and Lillian see each other in the café, their history takes over. The bond they have stems from their childhood and the endless days they spent together as children. They used to lay in bed, arm in arm, talking about their future and the men they were going to marry. The past was filled with joyous moments of tenderness between the two. They grew up with a feeling that they would be together forever.

This story is really about two people—the history of their friendship and how it drove them to actions beyond their capabilities. Julia was always the stronger, more adventurous one; she brought Lillian with her wherever she went. Lillian was always afraid, but her anger was powerful; that's what gave her the courage to smuggle in the money for Julia—her fury made her braver than she otherwise would have been.

If you were to audition for the film, it would also be worthwhile to spend some time investigating the history of the period. Today, for these two women to do what they did would be daring, but, at that time, it was absolutely unheard of. Because, the acts of heroism that both Julia and Lillian display are what make the history in the café scene different for those times. To appreciate their fortitude, one must have an insight into the historical period in which the story takes place.

TIPS

- Always remember to read what the other characters say about your character's history. Don't skim over their lines; they may hold valuable clues.

- As you prepare, get out of your chair, get onto your feet and physicalize!

- Don't simply write down facts; they'll only keep you stuck in your head. Instead, concentrate on emotional history.

- One of your most valuable tools is your imagination. Use it!

- Remember, any made up history must be appropriate to your character's situation.

QUICK TAKE

HISTORY: *How has the past affected your character's choices?*

- What is my character's history?
- What is the history of my relationship with the other character in the scene?
- What is the history of the time in which the scene takes place?
- Try to connect emotionally to the history, rather than intellectualize the information.

—

PERSONALIZATION

How do your feelings and life experiences relate to your character?

TOM ARNOLD / *True Lies, Touch, Nine Months*

I have Attention Deficit Hyperactive Disorder (ADHD) and I was working with Margie on a courtroom scene for the movie, *Touch.* I was having a difficult time staying focused and Margie kept saying, "You have to stop all this moving from side to side. It's very distracting and it's not appropriate for the character." The harder I tried to stop, the worse it got. Then Margie gave me a strong image to work off. She said, "I want you to look at the judge and while you are talking, imagine that she's a woman with huge boobs." (Margie has nice tits!) Suddenly, BOING! All movement came to a halt as her image became clearer and clearer (and her breasts became bigger and bigger!). When it came time to shoot the scene, I seemed to have no problem.

TOM ARNOLD

"I coulda been a contender." When Marlon Brando utters that famous line from *On the Waterfront*, there is no question that he owns the innermost feelings of his distraught character, Terry. In life, those feelings would have been present for Terry, but in an audition, the actor must build the illusion and believe it.

> For example, if you were auditioning for the role of Terry, to make the fight scene real for yourself, you must create the boxing ring vividly: the roar of the crowd, the screams of encouragement from the sidelines, the dull thud of the glove meeting flesh, the sting of sweat falling into your eyes and the emotional pain of having to take a dive knowing all the while that you could have torn your opponent apart.

Smell, see, hear, taste, touch—use your senses! Don't get stuck making factual statements that don't feed you. It's not enough to say, "He hit me and I threw the fight." (When I say those words I feel nothing.) Instead, stimulate your senses by creating your own anger, your own passion. Once you're able to experience on that level, the audience will follow.

PERSONALIZING THOUGHTS AND FEELINGS

Personalization is the process of owning the thoughts and feelings of the character. If you don't own it, you can't play it. Your job is to experience what the character is going through. How many times have you gone into an audition (having had great success in front of the bathroom mirror), only to choke when you've come face-to-face with the casting director? If this has happened to you, your images were not specific enough to sustain you, therefore, you lost touch with your character and blew the audition.

SENSES AND IMAGERY

So how do you stay connected to your character's feelings? By using your senses and imagery to create vivid personalizations. Your senses keep you connected to your emotional life and allow you to stay focused. As you know, there are five senses: sight, hearing, smell, taste and touch. Most people rely heavily on the sense of sight; it may be the easiest to relate to, but it's not necessarily the most lasting. (For me, the sense of smell is very powerful.)

> Growing up on Long Island, my grandmother lived with us and I can faintly recall being in the kitchen while she was preparing dinner. When I try to picture that moment visually, I have a tough time feeling her presence. However, my grandmother always used Ivory soap, so all it takes is one whiff of that soap and I can almost feel her soft, gentle hands holding mine.

> *I remember when my two sisters, Lois and Joan, and I decided it was time for our Uncle Si to cut off his moustache. He loved us so much that he was willing to put his face in the hands of three mischievous youngsters! We sat him in a chair and shaved off his moustache—his pride and joy. Beforehand, he soaked himself in Old Spice and, to this day, I can't walk through the fragrance section of a department store without chuckling as the memory of my uncle pops into my mind.*

Sense memories are like fingerprints: they never go away; they stay in your brain until something triggers them. Think about when you were a child and how heightened your senses were; how you took pleasure in small things; how you noticed minute details of objects. (It never ceases to amaze me how my nine-year-old son can pick out the smallest symbol in the corner of a cereal box and create an entire world around it. It's just Rice Krispies to me!) As an actor, you must go back to that same simplicity—awaken your senses and reactivate your imagination.

Scent of a Woman

In *Scent of a Woman*[1] (written by Bo Goldman; directed by Martin Brest), Al Pacino plays former Lt. Col. Frank Slade, a soldier blinded by a foolish accident during the war. To compensate for his loss of sight, his other senses take over. In fact, the movie gets its name from his extraordinary talent for identifying women's fragrances—not only can he detect a lady's perfume but his senses are so acute that he can even recognize her favorite soap.

In the delightful tango scene, Slade seduces an enticing stranger into dancing with him. His buddy, Charlie (played by Chris O'Donnell), whispers to him the coordinates of the room as he whisks his partner to the dance floor. Slade's imagination is so sharp that he dances freely. He feels the room, he hears the nearby murmurs and he holds his partner tightly as her sweet aroma guides his steps. The irony of the scene is that, without ever seeing her, Slade appreciates the woman's beauty and charm more fully than her preoccupied boyfriend, who arrives late and abruptly removes her from the restaurant, oblivious to her magnetic appeal. This is because Slade successfully painted her portrait in his imagination. As an actor, learn to develop your other senses strongly, like Pacino's Slade. Don't rely only on your sense of sight.

BLOOD AND GUTS

The current slew of medical shows and police dramas are full of blood, screams, action and the frantic dance between life and death. Unfortunately, the chaotic emergency room and the noisy police station do not exist in the

---

[1] Al Pacino won the Best Actor Oscar® for his performance in *Scent of a Woman*, which received three other nominations.

audition room! So, you must depend on your senses to make the scene believable for both you and the auditioners. (Hospitals, especially, have very distinct characteristics—the bright lights, the antiseptic smell and the sterile surroundings are unmistakable features of that environment.) In the artificial setting of the casting office, you have to "see" the commotion, "hear" the beeps of the monitors and the crash of the paddles; you have to "feel" the cold glass doors on your palms as the attendants push you out of the way. It's not always easy to call up those images. You must spend time exploring the hospital world so that, during the excitement of the audition, it's there for you. The work is very detailed—that's why preparation is critical.

> *A client, Chase, guest-starred in an episode of* ER, *playing a mother whose young bicycle-riding daughter has been hit by a truck. Chase's first scene, when she arrives at the ER to find her child hooked to machines, is filled with emotion. During her audition, Chase had to experience those images before saying her first line. It's a stimulus-response: first you see it, then you react to it. In her final scene, Chase's character runs into the trauma room as the doctors and nurses desperately try to revive her child. In the audition, Chase used her senses to help stay connected to her emotional life.*

In the Line of Fire

Now, let's take Agent Frank Horrigan's (Clint Eastwood) dark history and paint it with images in order to give it life (see scene excerpt on page 116). When Booth (John Malkovich) recalls to Horrigan the fateful day of Kennedy's assassination, it triggers a flood of sense memories. The actor auditioning for the role of Horrigan might imagine *the hysterical screams of Jacqueline Kennedy, the stench of blood permeating the air; the splattering of brains and blood everywhere; accusatory eyes staring back at him from the crowd.*

When Booth talks about Frank's life after the assassination, it touches a different nerve. Here the actor might imagine feeling *the moist tears on his little girl's cheek as he kisses her goodbye for the last time; the slow burn of alcohol as it flows down his throat.* Only through these textured images can Horrigan's history truly come alive.

STANISLAVSKI'S MAGICAL "AS IF"

Stanislavski uses a magical phrase—"as if"—to make it easier for actors to understand personalization. You start by using your own feelings in an imaginary situation. For example, if you were auditioning for the scene from *ER*, you would say to yourself, "I am going to play the role of the mother *as if* this happened to me." As you create the scenario, you would ask yourself, "If I had to go to the hospital and see my little girl laying on a stretcher, hooked up to machines, how would I feel?" If you have a child of your own, you would incorporate those feelings and expand on them; if not, you would rely on your imagination. So, explore the situation in detail, being aware of your feelings: pain, fear, panic, helplessness, guilt. (Now, all that sensory preparation comes in handy.)

Images should begin popping up for you as you explore your "as ifs." If you were pressed against the ICU door, what thoughts would enter your mind? Would you feel guilty? Have you, as a parent, ever felt as if you didn't do the right thing or that you somehow caused your child pain? It is important not to stop there—the next question is, if this happened to my character, how would she feel? Personalizing from your own experiences is the spark that keeps you truthful and merges you with the character's feelings.

SUBSTITUTION

When an actor has difficulty connecting to his character's circumstances, he may use a technique called "Substitution," in which he substitutes a similar experience from his own life. Use substitution as a way to emotionally understand where the character is coming from. It also will help to jump-start your emotions.

An example of a good use of substitution would be if you were auditioning for the role of Indiana Jones (portrayed by Harrison Ford) in the first film of the series, *Raiders of the Lost Ark* (written by Lawrence Kasdan; directed by Steven Spielberg). Remember the scene in which Indiana (who has a snake phobia) is stuck in the snake pit with hundreds of slithering vipers? In this case, you would think about what you, the actor, are deathly afraid of. I'm allergic to bees and therefore petrified of them, so if I were auditioning, I would substitute bees for snakes. I would surround myself with imaginary bees buzzing around my ankles. It would scare the hell out of me!

Or, if I'm playing an alcoholic but I'm not a drinker, then during preparation, I could substitute my insatiable need for chocolate. Chocolate, then, becomes the seed of my addiction.

It is my feeling that substitution should be used as a tool during preparation only and not during the actual audition. It can be dangerous to rely completely on your substitution because it may not be appropriate to what the character is experiencing.

For example, an actor may tell me that he doesn't have a child, but he does have a dog that he loves very much. A child is an extension of yourself with access to language and a whole range of complex emotions. In this instance, substitution alone might weaken the actor's audition. Too often, actors stop the process of personalization too soon by relying on substitution.

From the Studio

An interesting problem arose in class regarding substitution. Two actors had just completed a scene from *I Never Sang for my Father*, in which a brother and sister, who love each other, have their own agendas and end up confronting each other. Though the conflict was present in the reading, the love between the siblings was missing (see scene except on page 231).

Margie: Where is the love in the scene?

Peter: I couldn't relate to this character so I used my own sister as a substitution.

Margie: Well, how do you feel about your sister? Are you close to her?

Peter: I can't stand my sister. We don't get along and I'm in therapy now dealing with my anger towards her.

Margie: In this scene your character is angry with his sister, but he still loves her very much. It sounds like your negative feelings for your own sister got in the way.

Although he used a strong image, Peter's substitution was inappropriate. It would have been better for him to use the "as if" method and invoke his imagination instead of substituting such a powerful negative image.

Thelma & Louise

In this scene from *Thelma & Louise*, Louise struggles with her rage brought on by Thelma's mention of Louise's rape. Notice Louise's intense need to block out the nightmarish images that come up for her as Thelma continues. Sarandon's personalization of the rape needs to be both specific and graphic in order to feed her character's volatile reaction.

```
EXT. CLOSED GAS STATION - DAWN

Louise is walking back over to the car, a bare smile
left on her face. Thelma watches. All of a sudden, a
look of shocked realization comes over Thelma's face.
It startles Louise.
```

                    LOUISE
What?

                    THELMA
                (carefully)
It happened to you... didn't
it?

Louise knows what she is talking about. She becomes
immediately agitated.

                    LOUISE
I don't want to talk about it!
Thelma, I'm not kidding! Don't
you even...

                    THELMA
... in Texas... didn't it?
That's what happened... Oh my
God.

                    LOUISE
                (vehemently)
Shut up! Shut up, Goddamnit,
Thelma! You just shut the fuck
up.

Louise looks as if she is looking for a way to flee.
She opens the car door and then slams it closed. She
paces around the car.

                    THELMA
                (quietly, almost to
                herself)
Now I see... that's what
happened.

                    LOUISE
                (fighting hysteria, through
                clenched teeth)
I'm warning you, Thelma. You
better drop it right now! I
don't want to talk about it!

                    THELMA
                (gently)
Okay, Louise... It's okay.

Louise's reaction is as immediate as an oncoming freight train. Snapshots of horror flash into her mind, one after the other, as she fights to push them aside. When you work, you've got to feed yourself with images that will cause the same reactions. For example, his filthy smell, his wetness touching your body, the knifelike pain of his penetration. That's what will bring it all back to you.

Now that you're in touch with your senses and the images are meaningful to you, you're ready to look at the scene from the character's point of view. It's time to begin sifting through your emotions to uncover those which are true to the part.

TIPS

- Even if you only have a few short lines in a scene, you still have to do the work to uncover the character's emotions. Many actors figure the part is so small, why bother? If you are a supporting character, often your purpose in the scene is to react to what's going on. Your senses have to be sharp and alive.

- If you start to feel distant from your image and it begins to fade in and out, go back to the five senses to enhance your work.

- Substitution is a good technique to use during preparation, but don't rely on it while you're actually auditioning.

- It's not enough to ask, "If this happened to me, how would I feel?" Your job is to go further by then asking, "If this happened to my character, how would they feel?" Then, compare the two.

- If you don't own it, you can't play it.

QUICK TAKE

PERSONALIZATION: *How do your feelings and life experiences relate to your character's?*

- If this happened to ME, how would I feel?"
- If this happened to my CHARACTER, how would they feel?"
- SUBSTITUTION—During preparation, you may substitute your own feelings or situation if an event has happened to you.
- What images and sensory work can I use to connect me to the character's feelings?

—

V.I.P.S.
(Values, Intellect, Physical traits, Social status)
*What are the similarities and differences
between you and the character?*

STEVE GUTTENBERG / *Three Men and a Baby, Cocoon, Diner*

When I first began my career, I auditioned for a pilot at NBC for a casting director whom I'll refer to as "Joyce Doe." I came into the interview to play an Italian grease monkey mechanic type; she looked at me and said, "There's no way you're going to get the part." So I went home. I was staying with my godfather, a fellow actor named Michael Bell, who said to me, "You don't have to take that. Put some Vaseline in your hair, put on a motorcycle jacket and go back there unannounced."

So that day, I went back to the audition. I greased my hair up with Vaseline—which I couldn't get out for the next three or four weeks—I put on a leather jacket and my best tough attitude and went back to the audition, thinking that I would be welcomed with open arms. But when I went in, the secretary said, "You've already been here." And I said, "Yeah, I know, but this is a different look. I want them to see me." And she called Joyce Doe, who was furious that I was wasting her time. She yelled at me in front of everybody in the waiting room and tossed me out.

I felt pretty dejected after that but I went back to auditioning for other pieces. A few years later, I was actually doing my own show and the casting director assigned to that show was none other than Joyce Doe, who was, in essence, working *with* me. I don't know if she remembered the incident, but it sure was sweet for me to be working in a piece that she was casting—for which she had nothing to do with me being cast (I was cast by the producer). So it was sort of a sweet story for me.

STEVE GUTTENBERG

Recently, I held interviews at my studio for new students. Sitting in the back row, a bright, cocky, stand-up comic named Davis looked at me enthusiastically and said, "I've never acted before, but how hard can it be? All I have to do is be myself—and I'm damn good at that!"

W-R-O-N-G! You cannot simply BE yourself. You must USE yourself and then begin to wear the costume of the character. There's no doubt that charm and personality are important, but characterization is what sets apart actors from mere performers.

If you are in a play or a television series, you'll have plenty of time to try on different aspects of your character. You'll develop your character, change him, grow with him—eventually owning the role.

I attended an initial performance of *Phantom of the Opera* to watch the performance of Amick Byram, who had one of the lead roles. Months later, I returned to see his astonishing transformation, as he had truly begun to eat, drink and breathe his role. How wonderful to have the luxury of living with a character, keeping what works and throwing out what doesn't.

The audition is a different animal. With little time to spare, you must learn to delve into the part quickly but thoroughly. So how do you get into character in such a short period of time? You can do this by using a checklist that I have developed called "V.I.P.S.," an acronym which stands for Values, Intellect, Physical traits, and Social status. During auditions, you usually don't have time to flesh out the character. Using the V.I.P.S. checklist is an easy and quick way to determine the similarities and differences between you and your character. Actors using the V.I.P.S. feel secure in the knowledge that they will not overlook any important traits.

Murphy Brown was a funny and popular CBS sitcom, which owed much of it's success to it's sharply defined characters. Who can forget Miles, the paranoid producer; Jim, the stuffed-shirt newscaster; Corky, the Southern fruitcake; Frank, the eternally depressed bachelor; or Eldon, the sensitive artist? Candice Bergen won numerous Emmy Awards for her portrayal of the tough, wise-cracking Murphy. Let's analyze her character, with respect to her V.I.P.S.:

V   =   **Values/Morals**
Murphy is ruthless with regard to her career. She would do anything to get a story and is fiercely competitive. In her personal life however, she has a baby boy to whom she is devoted.

I = **Intellect**

Murphy's intellect is bright and quick; her humor is sharp and sarcastic. She rarely loses a battle of wits. In fact, her mind is a very important part of her arsenal. Emotionally, it is easier for Murphy to tap into her anger than into her vulnerability.

P = **Physical Traits**

Murphy moves with confidence and purpose. When she walks into a room, she commands your attention. She dresses in smart, stylish, no-nonsense suits.

S = **Social Status**

Murphy is extremely ambitious. She likes to be the center of attention and hates to be excluded. She dines with ambassadors and heads of state and is at ease in the company of presidents and congressmen. She enjoys her success and is at the top of her profession.

If you were asked to audition for the role of Murphy Brown, you would begin by asking yourself the following questions:

- What are the similarities between Murphy and me?
- What kind of *values* do I uphold? Am I a bitter rival or a friendly competitor?
- What about my *intellect*—am I street smart or book smart? Funny or boring?
- Am I emotionally available or closed off?
- What are my *physical* traits? Do I stand confidently or do I cower? Do I dress to kill or live in sweats?
- What are my *social* ambitions? Do I love to party or enjoy staying at home? Would I like to be more successful or am I content with where I am?

As you answer these questions, you'll begin to identify the similarities and draw out the differences between you and your character. Let's go to the studio.

From the Studio

Karen and Sarah were asked to prepare as a "callback" a scene from the film *Beaches* (written by Mary Agnes Donoghue from the novel by Iris Rainer Dart; directed by Garry Marshall). In the scene, Sarah read the role of Hillary (played by Barbara Hershey in the film), who has been diagnosed with terminal cancer. C.C. (the Bette Midler role) was played by Karen; she is Hillary's

best friend and is taking care of her at the beach house. The following scene
is a tough one, with built-in emotional traps, but the screenwriter has given
us some clues to avoid sentimentality. See if you can you find them.

```
INT. SUMMER HOUSE - LIVING ROOM - AUG. 1988 - MORNING

Hillary, wearing a nightgown, is stretched out on the
couch, under a blanket in the semi-darkened room
reading a book. Pills litter a nearby table. The phone
is ringing O.S., it is answered, then we hear:

                    C.C. (O.S.)
                (shouting)
            Hillary! It's for you!

                    HILLARY
                (reading, grim)
            Tell whoever it is I'm not
            here.

A moment passes, then C.C. walks in from the hallway
wearing a bathing suit and carrying a towel, suntan
lotion and magazines.

                    C.C.
                (tense smile)
            You make me say that to
            everyone. Your friends will
            think I'm holding you prisoner.

                    HILLARY
                (reading)
            I don't care what they think.

We can HEAR children playing outside. C.C. stares at
her for a moment, then heads for the door. Just as she
reaches it, she turns back.

                    C.C.
            We're going down to the dock to
            buy steamers later. Want to
            come?

                    HILLARY
                (reading, sharp)
            You know I can't walk that far.
```

                    C.C.
          I'll drive.

                    HILLARY
                    (reading)
          I'd rather not.

                    C.C.
                    (belligerent)
          Okay, then why don't you get
          dressed and sit outside on the
          beach with us.

                    HILLARY
                    (cold)
          I'm happy here.

                    C.C.
                    (grim)
          It's a beautiful day.

                    HILLARY
          I don't care.

                    C.C.
                    (exploding)
          Okay, stay in! But will you at
          least get dressed?! You haven't
          been out of that nightgown for
          over a week!

                    HILLARY
                    (throwing down book,
                    furious)
          So what?! Who the hell are
          you?! The clothes police?!
                    (getting up)
          Just leave me alone, okay?
          That's all I want! To be left
          fucking alone!

Breathing harshly, she walks out of the room. A moment
later, we HEAR the bedroom door slam shut. C.C.
hesitates, then goes after her.

INT. SUMMER HOUSE - HILLARY'S BEDROOM - AUG. 1988 -
MORNING

Hillary sits in a chair by the window staring out at
the sea, her face expressionless. There is a KNOCK on
the door, but she doesn't respond. A second later,
C.C. walks into the room.

>   C.C.
>   Listen, Hill, I'm sorry I blew
>   up like that. I know how hard
>   this is for...

>   HILLARY
>   (shrieking)
>   No, you don't!
>   (spinning around, hard)
>   You don't know what this is
>   like at all! My chances of
>   seeing my child grow are next
>   to nothing! My chances of
>   living a normal life have
>   vanished! My chances of even
>   living a few more years aren't
>   worth more than a two dollar
>   bet! Don't say you know what
>   that's like because you don't!
>   You're still in the land of the
>   living!

>   C.C.
>   (shouting)
>   So are you!

They stare at each other.

>   C.C.
>   (continuing, fierce)
>   You're not dead yet, Hillary so
>   stop living as if you are!

C.C. slams out of the room. Hillary stares at the
door, showing no traces of emotion, then turns and
looks back out the window.

Margie: Let's open the critique to the class. What was your response to their relationship, intention, V.I.P.S., etc.?

Comment: Their relationship was there and the intentions were clear, but something was missing.

Karen: I felt connected to the part. I really experienced the loss of my friend.

Margie: Yes, you were very emotionally connected. But the question is, did you react the same way that the character C.C. would have?

Karen: I thought I might have been too loving, but when Sarah started to cry, I just went with the moment and cried with her. It felt so right.

Margie: Right for you, maybe. But not for C.C. It is important to respond to the moment, but from the character's point of view, not your own. The screenwriter gave you clues in the screen directions to avoid focusing on the sentimentality: belligerent, grim, exploding, fierce. You are similar to C.C. in certain ways and different in others. Let's review your checklist (see next page).

C.C.'S V.I.P.S.
(Values, Intellect, Physical Traits, Social Status)

| | – SIMILARITIES – | – DIFFERENCES – | |
		C.C.	KAREN
VALUES/ MORALS	when push comes to shove, will be there for friend honest	tough not always considerate of others	gentle very considerate
INTELLECT	bright quick thinker	street smart less sophisticated	book smart more wordly
EMOTIONAL	humorous	afraid of being hurt shuts down feelings of love expresses anger	more vulnerable more open afraid of anger
PHYSICAL TRAITS	casual style	aggressive walk flamboyant dresser touchy-feely	laid back more conservative not as demonstrative
SOCIAL STATUS	ambitious go-getter	not from money seeks fame	family has money values love more than fame or money

Margie: Now that we've compared your V.I.P.S. with the character's, what do you think was missing in your analysis?

Karen: I didn't take into consideration that C.C. is afraid to show her vulnerability.

Margie: Right! So the scene would have played very differently. C.C. would never show her pain and sadness in front of Hillary. She wouldn't support Hillary's victim role. C.C. always brings out Hillary's strength. She gets very angry with Hillary in the scene when she says, "You're not dead yet, Hillary, so stop living as if you are!" C.C.'s reaction to Hillary's self-pity is very different from your own. Because of your compassion and vulnerability, you took the scene in a completely different direction. If it were to continue on your path, C.C. and Hillary would be wallowing in tears instead of laughing and playing cards together two pages later. (That scene appears below.)

```
          HILLARY
Why are you smiling...?

          C.C.
Do you remember that Christmas
we spent in the loft?

          HILLARY
     (frowning, vague)
Sure... we had a tree, didn't
we...?

          C.C.
A stick.
     (shaking head)
I was just remembering those
stinking Christmas carols.

          HILLARY
What Christmas carols?

          C.C.
What Christmas carols? The ones
you forced me to sing every
night.
```

```
        HILLARY
I didn't force you! You loved
it!

        C.C.
By the time we hit Good King
Wenceslaus for the fifth time I
was ready for a Drano cocktail!

        HILLARY
Gin and game, as usual.
    (smug)
You will never beat me at
cards.
```

Margie: You'd never get to the card scene if you encouraged Hillary's victim role. C.C. helps her friend the most by forcing her to wake up and enjoy her last days. C.C. covers up her own pain with brashness and personality. That's who she is. It is an important adjustment to her V.I.P.S. and changes the scene dramatically. The clues are there in the non-dialogue descriptions. Don't forget to read them.

It might have helped Karen dissect her character if she reviewed the Five Ego States. Karen, which ego state is most prominent in your life?

Karen: I'm definitely a caretaker. My Nurturing Parent, as you can tell from my choices, is very powerful. I always stroke myself as well as my friends.

Margie: Let's look at C.C. She has a huge Critical Parent. C.C. never thinks that she's enough. Being a singer, she's always striving for that perfect note and is very hard on herself as well as others.

Karen: I never thought to use the Ego States to analyze the character's V.I.P.S. If I had recognized C.C.'s Critical Parent, it would have been impossible to react so compassionately. I also wish I'd paid more attention to the writer's comments in parenthesis.

Margie: That's what they're there for—to keep you on course. It's so easy for a scene to get sidetracked if your V.I.P.S. aren't all there. Most scenes can be read any number of ways. Finding the essence of your character will lead you in the right direction.

Forrest Gump

Forrest Gump[1] (written by Eric Roth; directed by Robert Zemeckis) opens with a memorable line, uttered by the main character, portrayed by Tom Hanks: "Mama said, 'Life was just a box of chocolates...'" We remember the line not just because of its wisdom, but because of the refreshing innocence of the character who spoke them. We fell in love with Forrest Gump, a man with an I.Q. of 75 and the heart of a giant because we saw a little piece of Forrest in ourselves; we recognized in Forrest our own humanity.

How could a character so different from ourselves touch us so deeply? I believe that part of the answer lies with Hanks, who won an Academy Award™ for his portrayal of Forrest. Instead of getting stuck in the trap of playing the character's stupidity or mental incapacity, Hanks acknowledged the differences but embraced the similarities between himself and the character. Though some roles may seem to be more of a stretch, if you start out with the similarities, you will avoid creating a caricature.

> *An actor asked me to help him prepare for the role of a man with the mental capacity of a twelve-year-old year old. The actor was stuck in the character's slowness and overemphasized his speech impediment and crooked gait. It was hard to feel compassion for the character, because he left out an important ingredient—the character's relationship. That's one reason why we concentrate on the development of the V.I.P.S. AFTER we establish the relationships and intention. You need to be aware of the character traits from the beginning of your analysis, but slowly bring them into the work so that by the time you get to the V.I.P.S., the other elements are cemented.*

The key to analyzing a character is to start with yourself. Begin by asking, "What are the similarities between me and the character?" Then move on to the differences. The fusion of the two leads to the success of the part. Focusing on the similarities and differences helps to bring the illusion into reality, thus allowing you to own the role.

> *A client, Michael Easton, was going to read for the starring role in a television series called Two. He came to me perplexed: it wasn't a typical audition because he was up for the part of twins, which involved playing two brothers (one good, one evil) opposite each other in the same scene. In the series, the parents had given away one of the twins (Booth) at birth. One day at a park, when Booth is seven, he sees a boy*

---

[1] *Forrest Gump* received 13 Academy Award™ nominations and won Oscars® for Best Picture, Best Director (Zemeckis), Best Actor (Hanks), Best Adapted Screenplay (Roth), Best Editing, Best Visual Effects.

who looks exactly like him being pushed on a swing by loving parents. For the next twenty years, Booth is obsessed with finding his twin. Having spent most of his life with foster families and later in jail, Booth grows up differently from his twin, Gus, who was blessed with a perfect life. Eventually, Booth murders Gus' wife and frames him, forcing Gus to take on Booth's life-style and become a fugitive from the law.

The role presented Michael with three challenges: First, he had to analyze the similarities and differences between himself and Booth; secondly, between himself and Gus; and finally, between the twins themselves. Before we worked together, Michael struggled to own both characters, mainly because he had not spent enough time finding the similarities between himself and the characters. For example, it was very easy for Michael to connect with Gus' kindness and intelligence, but what dark secrets were hidden in Michael's own psyche that he could call upon? Michael fell into the trap of seeing only Gus' kindness, but what about Gus' fears? Would Michael have reacted the same way as Gus in a life-threatening situation? Michael and I worked very hard on the dual characters' V.I.P.S. and I'm happy to say that he booked the series.

Thelma & Louise

In any good story, the hero undergoes a character transformation. Now that you have a clear understanding of V.I.P.S., it is important to realize that some parts of the V.I.P.S. may change throughout the course of the script. When you are given two or three audition scenes from different pages in the script, always look for parts of the character that might have changed.

Thelma is an excellent example of a character's metamorphosis. She starts out as a law-abiding (VALUES), dizzy (INTELLECT), impeccably made-up, fully accessorized, perky (PHYSICAL traits), obedient, subservient wife (SOCIAL status). By the end of the film, a whole new character emerges: Thelma becomes a fugitive of the law; she has used her clever, cunning ways to impersonate a convenience store robber. Gone is the matching scarf and perky walk. Her long tresses blow wildly in the wind, her jeans are torn and her manicured nails are chipped and dirty. No longer does she need to be taken care of. In fact, the final scenes show Thelma calling the shots and pulling Louise together.

As you audition with scenes from different parts of the script, don't ignore the character's growth. Look for lines or action revealing another side of your character that the audience may not have seen before. Don't invent them, but do highlight the areas of transformation. As you breathe life into the character, don't forget that we are all beings capable of change.

TIPS

- Start giving your character life as soon as you get the sides. Spend time thinking and behaving as your character would.

- Even if your audition scene is heavy in V.I.P.S., always focus on the relationship first, slowly introducing the character analysis, before concentrating on the V.I.P.S.

- Always start out with the similarities between you and the character to avoid caricatures.

- Look for how the character changes during the script.

QUICK TAKE

V.I.P.S.: *Values/Morals, Intellect/Emotions, Physical traits, Social status*

- What are the similarities and differences between me and the character?

- Describe your character using V.I.P.S.:
  - V   = Values/Morals
  - I   = Intellect/Emotions
  - P   = Physical traits
  - S   = Social status

—

OPENING BEAT

*What has occurred the moment before
the scene begins?*

JOSIE BISSETT / *Melrose Place, Book of Love*

My most memorable audition was the time I was interviewing for a movie of the week. I was feeling pretty confident with the material, so I decided to bring in some props: In the scene, I was going to eat cookie dough, so I brought some with me, along with a spoon. So, I have my sides and I'm eating my cookie dough and the scene is going really well . . . and I had a blast! I usually don't bring props unless I'm feeling comfortable. Well, I got the part and the funny thing is, the producer loved it so much that I was eating cookie dough, because he does the same thing! Eats it right out of the tube! That was honestly one of my favorites!

JOSIE BISSETT

Years ago, I traveled to Vancouver, B.C. to visit friends, Steve and Adrienne Downing; he was in his fifth year as executive producer of the hit TV series, MacGyver. One afternoon, I sat down with Steve in his office to look at some casting tapes and saw the process from the producer's point of view. Since MacGyver was filmed in Canada, most of the guest-starring roles were cast via videotape. It didn't take me long to figure out how the system worked. Steve sat in front of the monitor with one finger on the fast-forward button and, usually, it was only a matter of seconds before his finger pressed it.

In life, as well as acting, we are quick to form first impressions. The first few moments in an audition are critical because it's the casting director's first impression of your work. As an actor, one of the ways to hook your audience is through a strong opening beat, which is the moment before the scene begins.

The opening beat is the life that your character brings into the scene before he utters a line. The opening beat feeds you, the actor, and enables your character to come from someplace truthful.

Think of each scene as a slice of life. Something has occurred in the life of your character before the scene begins. For example, if your character has just had a huge fight with her husband, she must enter the scene feeling that angst.

I can always tell when an actor doesn't know where they're coming from, especially if they simply walk in and sit down. What is your character feeling? You must bring those feelings into your physical life. When I say, "Action!" and an actor quickly spits out his first line, it's wrong! The character wouldn't blurt out his lines that way. First, he would experience his thoughts and feelings.

Instead of just practicing the line, find out what makes your character *say* that line. Don't just stumble onto the dance floor. Feel the music, then move to it.

Like a race car on the starting line, the opening beat revs up your motor for the countdown so that, by the time the gun is fired, you're already at full speed. Can you imagine going into a race with a cold engine?

> *I like to assign a scene from the film, Marathon Man (written by William Goldman; directed by John Schlesinger) in which Babe Levy (portrayed by Dustin Hoffman) has been out running, hoping to meet an attractive woman he has seen before. When she asks him his name, he replies, "I'm Tom Levy, the marathon man." I usually have to stop the video before the first lines are even spoken. Most actors don't take into consideration the fact that the character has been running for several miles before the scene begins. The actor should be panting, trying to catch his breath—physical manifestations of the sport. Usually, I have the actor do twenty-five pushups to create the same sense of being out of breath. Then, when he begins his dialogue, I know that he has come from some place truthful.*

THE FIVE "W'S"

Here are five questions that are designed to help you develop your opening beat. Ask yourself:

- Where am I?
- When does the opening beat take place?
- Who else is in the environment?
- What am I feeling?
- What is my physical action?

WHERE AM I?

One of the actor's main obstacles when auditioning is the lack of environment. For example, how do you turn the cold, cramped casting office into a hot steamy desert? You must use your senses and imagination to create the "where" of the scene: you create the scenery; you build the sets and hang the backdrop in your mind. Some opening beats require a stronger use of your senses. If you start off with a strong environment, it's less likely that you'll pull out of the scene.

> *There's a scene I do in class, in which two lonely soldiers are sitting at a bar. The first line is, "A beer, please." This seems like a simple line, but so much needs to be set up before the words are spoken. First, you have to set up the bar—the stale smell of smoke, music blaring from the jukebox, the bartender (is she fat with a mole growing out of her face? Or does he have stained teeth and bad breath?) You must imagine how the cold beer will taste. Imagine looking at the stranger next to you without invading his territory. Creating these thoughts and moments takes time. Actors worry that they take too long to prepare, but if you fill up your moments with real thoughts and images, the time will be well-spent.*

The "Fourth Wall"

Included in your environment is a concept called the "fourth wall," which is the imaginary wall between you and the people watching (or you and the camera). Using the fourth wall as a part of your environment can be very effective during your audition. Painting in the fourth wall with your imagination protects you from the fear of being judged and helps you stay connected to the scene. However, in terms of camera technique, you never want to break the fourth wall by looking directly into the camera.

> *Let's set up a scene from the daytime serial,* The Young and the Restless. *The characters, John and Jill, are stuck in an elevator. If you were to audition for this scene, how would you create the environment? Through your imagination, you would place the elevator door as your fourth wall, giving the character the effect of claustrophobia. You would listen through the imaginary crack in the door to see if anyone is outside. Feel the cold metal of the door on your palms. When Jill says her line, "How long have we been here? It seems like hours!" she has to believe it. If she believes it, then everyone else will. Don't be afraid to create the fourth wall.*

WHEN DOES THE OPENING BEAT TAKE PLACE?

For most people, waking up in the morning offers two, distinct possibilities. First, it can offer freshness, new possibilities and a sense of adventure. On the other hand, waking up can find you in a foul and pessimistic mood. In the same manner, a morning scene usually has a different tone than a business luncheon or a romantic evening by the fire. So, when preparing for your scene, notice the time of day—some scenes have a more specific time of day than others; some aren't even noted. When does your opening beat take place?

My associate, Annie, uses a scene from *Kramer vs. Kramer*[1] (written and directed by Robert Benton from a novel by Avery Corman) as a good illustration of an opening beat. It's a scene between Ted, the father (Dustin Hoffman) and Billy, the son (Justin Henry) that takes place hours after they've had an ugly fight.

When the scene opens, Ted walks into Billy's room and Billy wakes up.

```
INT. BILLY'S ROOM - NIGHT

TED'S P.O.V.: Billy lies sprawled across the bed, all
tangled up in the covers.
```

---

[1] *Kramer Vs. Kramer* was nominated for nine Academy Awards® and won for Best Picture, Best Director (Benton), Best Adapted Screenplay (Benton), Best Actor (Hoffman) and Best Supporting Actress (Meryl Streep) .

```
ON TED—as he crosses to the sleeping child and starts
to straighten the covers.

                    BILLY
                (tentatively)
          Daddy?

                    TED
                (all anger gone)
          Yeah?

                    BILLY
          I'm sorry...

                    TED
                (kisses him)
          That's okay, pal. Go back to
          sleep. It's very late.

He starts to get up...
```

The lines seem so easy, but let's examine *when* the opening beat takes place. It's late—hours after a nasty fight. You tiptoe into your child's room; he's fast asleep with the nightlight on. The dim light spills onto the flannel cowboy-and-Indian sheets that bring a smile to you. You feel a quiet regret that comes with the calm of the night. It only takes a few seconds to bring this emotional, heartfelt scene to life.

WHO ELSE IS IN THE ENVIRONMENT?

Rarely does a scene involve only one person. Certain types of scenes require you to invent imaginary people for the audition. For instance, in courtroom or medical scenes, there are usually more than two eyes observing. If you audition for a project that features many speaking roles, it can get very confusing. Therefore, it is imperative that you keep track of where the different voices are coming from, even though they may all be read by the casting director. If you don't differentiate between the characters, you'll lose an important part of the reality of the scene. Let's see how you would handle a roomful of characters during one of these types of scenes.

Courtroom Scenes

In an episode of *The Practice,* during the attorneys' summation, the defense attorney, Lindsay, uses her final speech to address the prosecution's case against her old law school professor. Imagine you are auditioning for the role of the defense attorney. Who else is in the courtroom? You've just heard from opposing counsel, on your right, and you watch him as he returns to his seat; you smile reassuringly to your own client on your left; then you nod to the judge whom you've placed in the center of the fourth wall (where the casting director now sits). You slowly rise, taking the time to acknowledge each member of the jury. Now, you're ready to begin.

Here's a hint: don't try to make eye contact with every member of the jury. It's best to establish just three jurors, each of whom will have a separate and distinct reaction to you (the first juror waits in anticipation of your brilliance, the second won't look at you and the third is skeptical).

Operating Room Scenes

Imagine working in the trauma room with six doctors and nurses yelling at you at the same time:

> "BP's dropping."
> "Where's the blood gas?"
> "He's arresting! Get me the paddles!"
> "Here."
> "Step back. Okay . . . Now."
> "Nothing."
> "Again."
> "I'm getting something."
> "Good. You take it from here."

As complicated as this may seem, you don't have to create all six doctors and nurses to get a sense of commotion. Once again, focus on three distinct characters (that you have different feelings for) and place them in three separate locations (one of them between the casting director).

WHAT AM I FEELING?

Oftentimes, actors feel frustrated after finishing a scene. I've heard such comments as, "I shut down during the first half of the scene. I wasn't there emotionally." "My emotions didn't kick in until the scene was almost over." If this happens, it's because the actors didn't give themselves strong enough emotional images to begin the scene on the right footing. Therefore, they find themselves playing catch-up for most of the scene. Commonly, the scenes that are used to audition actors are the emotional climaxes for the character and may involve such complex emotions as fear, anger, pain, sadness, exhilaration or rage. The climax may not occur until the middle of the scene, but the character is feeling those powerful emotions from the top.

Let's analyze a scene from Clifford Odets' classic, *The Country Girl*[2] (written by George Seaton from Odets' play; directed Seaton). Georgie (portrayed by Grace Kelly) is married to an alcoholic actor, Frank (portrayed by Bing Crosby), and spends her life mothering him, trying to keep him away from the bottle. Bernie (played by William Holden), Frank's passionate stage director, has been lied to and blames Georgie for Frank's drinking problems. The scene opens with Georgie in Frank's dressing room. Bernie knocks at the door. Georgie calls out, "Come in." Georgie's first line to Bernie is, "Frank's on stage."

What choice can you give the character of Georgie that would feed her first line? We know her husband is an alcoholic; we know that he is also a pathological liar; from the history that we have about Georgie, we know that she is constantly struggling with Frank's addiction and is always disappointed by the outcome. So, let's give her something that is sensory-oriented to feed her emotional life. At the top of the scene, let's say Georgie finds a bottle of cough syrup under the makeup table. She picks it up and takes a whiff of the bottle and smells alcohol instead. Now, the character is ready to begin the scene as her sadness and hopelessness permeate her being.

Bernie, on the other hand, comes from a different emotional place. Through your imagination, you must create a specific incident that happens just before the scene. Since you get to paint the picture, why not paint it with a full sensory palette: Frank is on stage; Bernie and the producer, Mr. Dodd, have been sitting in the theater during rehearsal and observe Frank beginning to sway and slur his words. Suddenly, Frank vomits and falls. As you are reading this, are you experiencing clear images? Does your face distort as you smell the vomit? Does it repulse you? Now you are in the moment. The producer turns to you, yelling, "Get rid of him!" As Bernie, you might think, "That's not the problem. It's that bitch wife of his." Now your character is filled with purpose as he enters the dressing room—his production is at stake.

WHAT IS MY PHYSICAL ACTION?

Novice actors will always ask if they should stand or sit for an audition. Acting is not about sitting or standing. Acting isn't only with your head. Yes, I know you feel stuck with this piece of paper, the script, but guess what? It doesn't stop you from connecting with the rest of your body. As an actor, you must use your body to express your feelings and thoughts. When you feel something, you should respond physically. Your physical life doesn't just begin when you read the lines. And many times, your lines won't make sense if you haven't had a physical action first.

Here are a few examples of lines that could occur in the opening of a scene. "Ouch, that hurts." "Ooh, that feels good." "That was delicious." "Watch

[2] *The Country Girl* received seven Academy Award™ nominations and won Oscars® for Best Original Screenplay (Seaton) and Best Actress (Kelly).

out!" "Isn't it a beautiful day?" Before any of these lines are spoken, something physical should have occurred, otherwise the lines don't make sense. You might be holding your hand in pain before shrieking, "Ouch, that hurts." Or, you may receive a tender kiss before moaning, "Ooh, that feels good." You could be chewing a juicy steak as you exclaim, "That was delicious." Or, you might stop your child as he crosses the street while you shout, "Watch out!" You could be watching the sunrise before remarking, "Isn't it a beautiful day?" Not only are the physical actions necessary, but they also enhance the lines and allow the audience to further experience your feelings.

Your physical life should be indigenous to what is happening in the scene and, no pantomimes, please! For example: If your character is pushing a gurney, use your chair and apply pressure to it so you can feel the weight. This will help make the opening beat truthful and then it will feed you.

Love Scenes

I worked with a client who had an audition for a network series. In the scene, she is supposed to be making love; while the characters are engaged, the woman notices a shuttle taking off in the sky. She utters her first line, "Look, there it is!" Now, the actress has all the time in the world to set up her opening beat because she has the first line. Take advantage of that time, as long as you don't do a three-act play in fifteen seconds!

The challenge of a love scene is to receive the stimuli rather than to cause it. Receiving is a more truthful experience for the character as well as for the viewing audience. But, how do you go from making love and feeling passion to uttering a line that breaks the mood? Please don't do what I've seen many actors do: don't start with your eyes closed, open them and then say your line.

Let me describe how this opening beat would work for both characters. For the woman, she would relax in the chair, experiencing the kisses on her neck, letting herself enjoy the feeling. She opens her eyes and all of a sudden there's a most amazing sight piercing the sky—the shuttle. Now, she is able to say her line, "Look, there it is." For the male character, he is also receiving that marvelous, sensual touch. He's in his own world when he is jarred into his reality by her observation. His first line, "Annie," is uttered differently when his libido is interrupted!

Thelma & Louise

As we continue our breakdown of *Thelma & Louise*, let's examine Louise's opening beat from the scene in which Thelma realizes that Louise had been raped. Here's how the scene begins:

```
EXT. CLOSED GAS STATION - DAWN

Louise is walking back over to the car, a bare smile
left on her face. Thelma watches. All of a sudden, a
look of shocked realization comes over Thelma's face.
It startles Louise.

                    LOUISE
          What?

                    THELMA
               (carefully)
          It happened to you... didn't
          it?
```

Now, let's go through the five questions:

- **Where am I?**
  Outside a gas station in the middle of nowhere.

- **When does the opening beat take place?**
  It's dawn. I'm beyond exhaustion. I've just gotten off the pay phone with my boyfriend who might as well be a million miles away.

- **Who else is in the environment?**
  Thelma is waiting by the car. The gas station attendant is walking towards the station. It's pretty deserted.

- **What am I feeling?**
  The phone call has left me sad and nostalgic. Maybe I should have just married him. We did have some raucous good times together. Damn!

- **What is my physical action?**
  I'm wandering back slowly to the car, still caught up in my recollections. I look up at Thelma and jerk my head back, surprised to see her staring at me with a strange expression.

Now, when Louise says her first line, which is only one word, the stage is set—her emotional life is complete.

From the Studio

In my classes, I find that most actors tend to race toward their lines and treat their lines like a security blanket. However, in reality, some of the most interesting moments are those which take place before the dialogue begins.

Barbara read a scene from a show set in a hospital, as a woman who recently had a heart transplant. In the scene, she is attached to an EKG, which limits her physical movement. As she wakes up, she notices a stranger sitting across from her. Her first line is, "Is it nice out?"

Margie: The scene was slow to start. I didn't know where your line came from.

Barbara: I know you're a stickler for opening beats, but I just didn't know how to get there, so I guess I was too general.

Margie: Before you get to the line, there has to be a thought which causes a physical action and prompts the line. You're really taking three steps: thought, physical action, line. What was your character thinking?

Barbara: She was wondering what this guy was doing in her room.

Margie: That's too late! What is her first thought before she even sees him?

Barbara: I guess she's happy to be alive.

Margie: Exactly! The character opens her eyes and thinks, "How lucky I am to be alive." Her physical action is to look out the window. She breathes a sigh of contentment then feels the presence of someone in the room.

Barbara: And then I say my line. Now it makes sense.

Margie: Thought, physical action, line. It happens with each new unit, especially an opening beat.

"HELP, I'M NEXT!"

A strong opening beat keeps you from getting nervous. Your brain cells are filled with all the thoughts and emotions that occur within your character before the scene begins, so there is no room for doubt or hesitation. Your fear is replaced by the work that is required to answer those five questions about your character. When your character thoughts are strong, they erase the nervous thoughts that you may have (e.g., "Will they like me?" "Am I prepared?").

TIPS

- Keep your opening beat simple. Don't rush into the lines. Sometimes just a simple thought can help you connect to your first unit.

- Don't use pantomime or props for your opening because it takes the focus away from your reading.

- A reaction to another character can be as powerful as starting the scene with dialogue. Be specific about your choice!

- Remember, the opening beat is to feed you, not to impress the casting director.

QUICK TAKE

OPENING BEAT: *What has occurred the moment before this scene begins?*

- Where am I?
- When does the opening beat take place?
- Who else is in the environment?
- What am I feeling?
- What is my physical action?

—

UNITS AND TRANSITIONS

In the scene, where do the changes occur that cause the focus to shift?

VONDIE CURTIS-HALL / *Chicago Hope, Passion Fish*

I don't really audition anymore, but one of the last auditions I had was a screen test for *Vampire in Brooklyn* starring Angela Bassett and Eddie Murphy. I was one of the final two guys. Angie and I had talked about the scene and then we were getting ready to do it. I was supposed to knock on the door, burst in, lean against the wall, catch my breath and discover her already there.

So, I come in. I lean against the wall. Now the camera's rolling and this is the first scene of two or three we're supposed to do. I look around, I see her, I start talking and the lights slowly begin to go down. I'm trying to stay focused, but I notice that, incrementally, it's getting darker and darker and darker in the room. I just keep going until all of a sudden I'm in the dark and the director yells, "Cut." I was leaning on the dimmer! Obviously, I was extremely nervous . . . kind of acting in the dark. Then everybody burst out laughing. Of course, we did it again and the next time I didn't lean against the door.

That was one of the weirdest things I can recall happening to me during an audition. And, of course, the next day, I didn't get the job, but I did the best audition. It turned out that Eddie Murphy wanted another guy for the role.

And instead of doing that job, I took *Chicago Hope*. In fact, *Chicago Hope* was waiting on me, so it all worked out in the end.

VONDIE CURTIS-HALL

You've reached the point in your preparation when you're ready to start marking up your sides. I know you're excited but don't get ahead of me! For the third read-through, follow along as we learn to break down the scene into units and transitions.

A unit is a section of a scene defined by a common focus or topic. Some actors use the word "beat" (to me, the words are interchangable). Some units are more obvious than others. See if you can determine the unit breaks in the following example:

M: I just love your shirt. Where did you get it?
B: I bought it at Neiman's.
M: I love the colors. They look fabulous on you.
B: Really? I wasn't sure about the chartreuse.
M: (looks at her watch) Oh my God! Look at the time.
   Darling, I have to run!
B: Me, too! Call me later.

The above lines can be clearly broken into two units. The end of the first unit comes after:

B: Really? I wasn't sure about the chartreuse.

Now, draw a box around the first unit with your pencil. A new unit begins with:

M: (looks at her watch) Oh my God! Look at the time.

The second units ends with:

B: Me, too! Call me later.

Draw a box around the second unit.

It's important to mark the units in boxes so that when you audition, you won't get lost. If you concentrate on one unit at a time, you won't get overwhelmed by the material. Here's how the scene should look once you've penciled it in.

M: I just love your shirt. Where did you get it?
B: I bought it at Neiman's.   *unit 1*
M: Ooh. I love the colors. They look fabulous on you.
B: Really? I wasn't sure about the chartreuse.

M: (looks at her watch) Oh my God! Look at the time.
   Darling, I have to run!   *unit 2*
B: Me, too! Call me later.

Each unit is connected by a character thought or an image called a "transition." The transition acts as a springboard to the next unit. In the above example, the following takes place:

- A *thought* prompts "M" to look at her watch.

- This thought then leads "M" into the next unit.

Think of the scene as a quilt, with each unit comprising one square. In a quilt, different squares are pieced together by a common thread. Similarly, every scene is composed of units linked by thoughts and images.

Sometimes an actor will pause, thinking she's completed a transition. But, a pause is merely a vacant silence; it doesn't allow you to experience your imagery.

I tell my clients, "A truth follows a truth. A lie follows a lie." If you have nothing churning inside to stimulate you during the empty space, there's nothing to build on.

Like dominoes, a strong transition carries you into the next unit. It is a charged moment that the audience can also experience.

Some units are easier to detect than others and the amount of units in a scene will vary. An entire scene may have only one or two units. When breaking down a scene, some actors feel the need to insert more units than necessary but inserting transitions where they don't belong can cause a scene to drag. (In comedy, it's death.)

In the following scene from *Thelma & Louise*, there are only three units. It's tempting to split Thelma's monologue into unnecessary beats, but if you break up the paragraph, you sacrifice the natural arc of the scene and ruin Louise's punch line, "I said all that?" In this case, less is more.

Louise is rubbing her face. She looks pretty bad. Her
hands are shaking.

>   LOUISE
>   (to herself)
>   Shit. I'm gettin' tired.

>   THELMA
>   Are you alright?

Louise does not really seem alright.

>   LOUISE
>   (upset)
>   I think I've really fucked up.
>   I think I've got us in a
>   situation where we could both
>   get killed. I mean, I don't
>   know what's the matter with me.
>   I don't know why we didn't just
>   go straight to the police.

>   THELMA
>   You know why. You already said.

>   LOUISE
>   What'd I say again?

>   THELMA
>   Nobody would believe us. We'd
>   still get in trouble. We'd
>   still have our lives ruined.
>   And you know what else?

>   LOUISE
>   What?

>   THELMA
>   That guy was hurtin' me. And if
>   you hadn't come out when you
>   did, he'd a hurt me a lot
>   worse. And probably nothin'
>   woulda ever happened to him.
>   'Cause everybody did see me
>   dancin' with him all night. And

```
                    they woulda made out like I
                    asked for it. And my life
                    woulda been ruined a whole lot
                    worse than it is now. At least
                    now I'm havin' fun. And I'm not
                    sorry that son of a bitch is
                    dead. I'm only sorry that it
                    was you that did it and not me.
                    And if I haven't, I wanna take
                    this time to thank you, Louise.
                    Thank you for savin' my ass.

                         LOUISE
                    I said all that?

                         THELMA
                    No, Louise, you said the first
                    part. I said all the rest.
```

```
                         LOUISE
                       (tired)
                    Whatever.
```

You should break down the entire scene, including all of the other characters' beats. You may even discover clues from the other characters' transitions. If you don't acknowledge these changes, you could miss vital information that affects your character's choices. So, pay attention to the whole scene, not just your own lines.

Let's explore a scene from one of the most successful comedy writers of all time, Neil Simon. His writing is a road map of clear, precise unit breaks and changes. I use his work to demonstrate what a clearly-defined unit looks like. *The Prisoner of Second Avenue* is the story of married couple Mel and Edna who live in New York City. In the scene that follows, Mel comes home to find that their apartment has been robbed. Notice the clearly boxed units.

```
                         MEL
                    What happened here?...Why is
                    this place such a mess?

                         EDNA
                    We've been robbed.

                         MEL
                    What do you mean robbed?
```

                    EDNA
Robbed! Robbed! What does
robbed mean? They come in, they
take things out. They robbed
us!!!

                    MEL
I don't understand...What do
you mean, someone just walked
in and robbed us?

                    EDNA
What do you think?...They
called us up and made an
appointment? We've been robbed!

                    MEL
Alright, calm down. Take it
easy, Edna. I'm just asking a
simple question. What happened?
What did they get?

                    EDNA
I don't know. I left. I was
only gone five minutes.

                    MEL
You couldn't have been gone
five minutes.

                    EDNA
Five minutes. That's all I was
gone.

                    MEL
Five minutes, huh? They must
have been gorillas to lift all
that in five minutes.

                    EDNA
Well, that's what they were
because I was only gone five
minutes.

                    MEL
When you left the building, did
you notice anyone suspicious
looking?

                    EDNA
Everyone in this building is
suspicious looking.

                    MEL
Did you notice anyone leaving
with packages or bundles?

                    EDNA
I didn't notice.

                    MEL
What do you mean, you didn't
notice?

                    EDNA
I didn't notice. You think I
look for people leaving the
building with my television
set?

                    MEL
They took the television? A
brand new color television?

                    EDNA
They're not looking for the
1948 Philco's. It was here.
They took it. I can't get a
breath out.

                    MEL
Alright, sit there. I'll get a
drink.

                    EDNA
I don't want a drink.

                    MEL
A little scotch. It'll calm you
down.

                    EDNA
It won't calm me down because
there's no scotch. They took
the scotch too.

                    MEL
All the scotch?

                    EDNA
All the scotch.

                    MEL
The Chivas Regal too?

                    EDNA
No, they're going to take the
cheap scotch and leave the
Chivas Regal. They took it all,
they cleaned us out.

                    MEL
Sons of bitches. Sons of
bitches! All in five minutes,
heh? They must have been
gorillas to lift all that in
five minutes.

                    EDNA
Leave me alone.

                    MEL
Sons of bitches.

                    EDNA
Stop swearing, the police will
be here any minute. I just
called them.

                    MEL
You called the police?

                    EDNA
Didn't I just say that?

                    MEL
     Did you tell them we were
     robbed?

                    EDNA
     Why else would I call them? I'm
     not friendly with the police.
     What kind of questions are you
     asking me? What's wrong with
     you?

                    MEL
     Alright, calm down because
     you're hysterical.

                    EDNA
     I am not hysterical.

                    MEL
     You're hysterical.

                    EDNA
     You're making me hysterical.
     Don't you understand, my house
     has just been robbed.

                    MEL
     What am I, a boarder? My house
     has been robbed too. My color
     television and my Chivas Regal
     is missing the same as yours.

                    EDNA
     You didn't walk in and find it.
     I did.

                    MEL
     What's the difference who found
     it? There's still nothing to
     drink and nothing to watch.

                    EDNA
     Don't yell at me. I'm just as
     upset as you are.

```
                    MEL
      I'm sorry. I'm excited, too. I
      don't mean to yell at you. Let
      me get you a Valium, it'll calm
      you down.

                    EDNA
      I don't want a Valium.

                    MEL
      Take one. You'll feel better.

                    EDNA
      I'm not taking a Valium.

                    MEL
      Why are you so stubborn?

                    EDNA
      I'm not stubborn. We don't have
      any. They took the Valiums.

                    MEL
      They took the Valiums?

                    EDNA
      The whole medicine chest.
      Valiums, Seconals, aspirin,
      shaving cream, tooth paste,
      razor blades. They left your
      tooth brush. You want to go in
      and brush your teeth, you can
      still do it.

                    MEL
      I don't believe you. I don't
      believe you!
```

As you can see from this excerpt, Simon writes definite, obvious changes from one topic to another. His writing flows confidently from the "robbed" unit to the "five minute" unit to the "suspicious" unit to the "Scotch" unit to the "police" unit to the "hysterical" unit and finally to the "Valium" unit. As you learn to break down a scene, you'll have an opportunity to experience the difference between specific beats and nebulous ones.

BABY BEATS

Sometimes you'll find a brief transition that is not really a complete change. I call this a "baby beat," a slight, temporary shift that is mercurial in nature. A baby beat gives the character an opportunity to take that extra second to absorb the new information that has been given to him. Baby beats may be present or absent with each different read. Mark them in your script as ("b.b.") and let your feelings in that moment dictate whether or not the shift occurs. Here's an example:

```
                    EDNA
       ...You think I look for people
       leaving the building with my
       television set?

       (b.b.)

                    MEL
       They took the television? A
       brand new color television?
```

Another example would be:

```
                    MEL
       Take one. You'll feel better.

                    EDNA
       I'm not taking a Valium.

                    MEL
       Why are you so stubborn?

                    EDNA
       I'm not stubborn. We don't have
       any. They took the Valiums.

       (b.b.)

                    MEL
       They took the Valiums?
```

Sometimes you might break down a section into a full transition only to discover that, in your next read, it is instead a baby beat.

```
                    EDNA
        Stop swearing, the police will
        be here any minute. I just
        called them.

                    MEL
        You called the police?
```

or

```
                    EDNA
        Stop swearing, the police will
        be here any minute. I just
        called them.

        (b.b.)

                    MEL
        You called the police?
```

Most transitions are not set in stone. During a reading, your character could be suddenly influenced by a stimulus brought on by another character or by an element in the environment that would require a longer, more intense transition.

Because transitions may change, use pencil instead of ink when marking off units.

ADJUSTMENTS

Now that you've broken down the scene into boxed units, it's time to lay in the adjustments, or tactics, which are the different ways to meet your intention. Every unit has one or more adjustments. As you examine the first boxed unit of your scene, decide on an appropriate tactic, which may take you all the way through the unit—and even into further units. Or, you may need to change your approach along the way.

From the Studio

Let's return to the studio where my clients, Stephanie and Jonathan, have continued their work from *The Goodbye Girl*. We met Stephanie in an earlier chapter, when she realized she had gone overboard with Paula's history. Now let's see how Jonathan deals with Elliott's adjustments.

When Stephanie and Jonathan performed the scene, there was unanimous agreement that it didn't go anywhere. In comedy, the characters try to win out; they try to beat each other at the same game. Therefore, adjustments are very important, because that's how the character prevails.

Comment: I never felt that Elliott stood a chance of getting the apartment.

Margie: Well, his intention seemed clear enough. "I want to force this attractive, but stubborn woman into giving me the apartment." But Jonathan got stuck being charming. He limited himself by choosing only one way to get his intention met—charmingly. Let's go back to the beginning of the scene and see if we can find other adverbs to help him achieve his goal.

```
INT - APARTMENT

She closes the door. He wipes forehead, still rain-
soaked, with his hankerchief.

          ELLIOTT                    (apologetically)
     I'm dripping on your rug.

          PAULA
     It's been dripped on before.

She walks into the living room and takes a place
near the false fireplace, one arm on the mantle. He
follows her in, looks around.
```

                    ELLIOTT   **(sincerely)**
...Look, I'm sorry about all
this...I didn't know there was
going to be any complications.

                    PAULA
Yeah, well, there's a lot of
that going around lately.

                    ELLIOTT   **(charmingly)**
Okay. I don't blame you for
being hostile. I get the
picture. Tony rents me the
apartment, splits with the
money and you and your daughter
get dumped on, right?

                    PAULA
That's your version. My version
is that Tony and I amicably end
our relationship, we agreed I
would keep the apartment and
you and your six hundred
dollars got dumped on...get the
picture?

                    ELLIOTT
     (smiles and nods)
Very good...very sharp...a
sharp New York girl, right?

                    PAULA
No. A dull Cincinnati kid. But
you get dumped on enough, you
start to develop an edge.

                    ELLIOTT   **(threateningly)**
Okay, so what's the deal? I
have a lease in my pocket. You
gonna honor that or not?

                    PAULA
I got a daughter in my bed.
That tops the lease in your
pocket.

                    ELLIOTT
Look, I don't want to get
legal. Legal is on my side...I
happen to have a lawyer
acquaintance downtown. Now all
I have to do is call this
downtown lawyer acquaintance of
mine —

                    PAULA
Oh, Jesus! An actor!

                    ELLIOTT
What?

                    PAULA
    Another goddamn actor! "I
    happen to have a lawyer
    acquaintance..." That's
    right out of "Streetcar
    Named Desire"...Stanley
    Kowalski in summer stock,
    right?

                    ELLIOTT   *(boastfully)*
Wrong! I played it in Chicago
in the dead of winter...Three
and a half months at the Drury
Lane.

                    PAULA
    (nods)
Ask an actor a question, he
gives you his credits.

                    ELLIOTT
You want reviews, too?...
"Elliott Garfield brings new
dimensions to Kowalski that
even Brando hadn't
investigated"... Okay?

By the fourth unit, Elliott obviously has shifted gears, "Okay, so what's the deal?" Jonathan, consequently, needs to change tactics, too. He might attempt to persuade Paula *threateningly.* He doesn't stay that way for long, though. In response to Paula's accusation, he defends his craft *boastfully,* "Wrong! I played it in Chicago in the dead of winter . . . " As you can see, it's possible to have more than one adjustment within a given unit. It's also not uncommon to ride a few units with the same tactic.

Making adjustments is like surfing. You're riding a wave and it's going strong. Then before it slows down, you catch another wave and ride it for a while until it's time to change again. The excitement of surfing is riding each new wave as it comes. How boring it would be to ride the same wave all the way in. You want to stay where the action is. It's the same thing when you're doing a scene. Many actors get stuck in the same approach, which soon becomes predictable.

Always remember to look for those opportunities in the script when you can engage a new strategy to help fulfill your goal.

CLOSING BEATS

Acting is storytelling. And every story has a beginning, a middle and an end. The closing beat is the button at the end of the scene that completes the moment. Actors tend to give up their characters too quickly, jarring the audience out of the imaginary world they've created. A closing beat should be acknowledged with the same importance as an opening beat.

To illustrate the Closing Beat, I like to use a scene from the series *C-16,* featuring the character Amanda. It's her first day on the job as an FBI agent and she's paired with a no-nonsense, seasoned pro. In all her eagerness to involve her partner and get him to talk to her, she mistakenly says the wrong thing by inquiring about his recent leave of absence. His curt answer is, "It wasn't self-imposed"—this response puts her in her place. Although he has the last line, her closing moment provides the comedic element of the scene. Her thought could be, "Oops! I really screwed that one up! What an idiot! Good job, Amanda." As my associate, Annie Grindlay tells her students, "You have a line at the end . . . it's just not written!"

TIPS

- If a new unit occurs in the middle of a dialogue paragraph, try using a backwards "L" to mark the break instead of boxing the unit. In this case, it is less cumbersome.

- Remember, transitions don't occur only during *your character's* dialogue. Be aware of all the transitions in the scene.

- Some units are subjective. Don't be surprised at how easily they change from one read to the next, depending on what is happening at the moment.

- Using a pencil rather than a pen is a reminder that a transition may not be permanent.

- When you box your units, you have less chance of getting lost.

QUICK TAKE

UNITS AND TRANSITIONS: *In the scene, where do the changes occur that cause the focus to shift?*

NOW READ THROUGH THE SCENE FOR THE THIRD AND FINAL TIME to break it down into units or beats.

- Use a pencil to draw a box around each UNIT.
- Write down your ADJUSTMENTS as they occur in the scene.
- Are there any BABY BEATS in the scene?
- What is your CLOSING BEAT?

—

CORE AND MASKING

What are the character's true feelings?
Which are exposed vs. concealed?

MICHAEL EASTON / *Total Recall, Ally McBeal*

I remember going in to audition for the film, *Thelma & Louise*, believing that I had no real shot at it. I walked into a room filled with name actors; at the time, I had only done a lot of theater in New York. I did four consecutive privates with Margie and ended up screen testing for the role. Each time I worked with Margie, she added a layer to my audition. Each time, I went past the process until I finally got to test for the role.

I didn't get the role because Margie was also working with the guy who did get it—Brad Pitt.

MICHAEL EASTON

As children, one of the first images we recognize is the clown, smiling and joking as he gets us to laugh. As adults, we see behind the clown's mask—he may be laughing on the outside, but he's crying on the inside. As we prepare to go out and greet the day, each of us puts on our own mask that may cover our insecurities, doubts, fears, pain, disappointment and helplessness. When an acquaintance stops us with the requisite, "Hi, how are you?" we don't dig into the core of our being for an honest answer. We go for cover with an easy line like, "Fine, thanks. How are you?"

The core is the center of our true feelings. The mask is our coverup. That's how we survive our humanity, frailties, everyday existence.

Some people live closer to the core than others; some mask with thin gauze, allowing you to see through; others mask with lead and hide behind it completely. For example, mentally unstable patients completely expose their cores, saying and doing whatever pops into their heads without regard to what others may think. Politicians, on the other hand, wear heavy masks, working hard to present a singular, positive image to voters.

Each of us masks our core in different ways—through humor, indifference, even anger. Many people believe that anger is a core feeling, but it usually hides a deeper emotion—like pain or hurt—that we find more difficult to express. For example, if Judy finds out that her boyfriend has been cheating on her, she might start by yelling at him, "I hate you! How could you do this to me? I never want to see you again!" But if you stripped away this layer of anger, her dialogue would sound different. Judy might instead say something more revealing, such as, "I'm so hurt. I'm in such pain over your betrayal. I'm scared I'm going to lose you forever."

LAYERS OF CORE AND MASKING

Think back to your third grade science class—when you studied geology. Do you remember the different layers of the Earth's core? (The crust is made up of igneous, sedimentary and metamorphic rock, cutting through to the mantle, outer core and inner core.)

Compare this sparse recollection to your own personal makeup—can you identify your own layers of core and masking? It seems that we are most fragile when we experience our deepest emotions created by fear: fear of abandonment, fear of rejection, fear of pain, fear of being hurt. Like the layers of the Earth, our fears may be layered. To protect ourselves from experiencing these core feelings, we wear a series of changing masks.

In Judy's case, the cross-section of her emotions might look like this:

ANGER—outer layer
HURT—middle layer/core
FEAR OF ABANDONMENT—deepest core

Let's say, though, that Judy is not the type of woman who screams; she's not comfortable dealing with her anger. Instead, she chooses to cover her feeling with yet another mask. So, when her boyfriend comes home and asks, "Can you ever forgive me?" Judy might respond with, "Hey, you want to have an affair, have an affair. I really don't care one way or the other." Now, we've added an extra layer:

> INDIFFERENCE—cover-up
> ANGER—outer layer
> HURT—middle layer/core
> FEAR OF ABANDONMENT —deepest core

Layering of core and masking adds dimension to your character. Look at Heather Locklear's character, Amanda, in *Melrose Place*. She began as the cold, calculating head of D&D Advertising and she moved on to be president of her own company. In the show, she wore her mask proudly, defiantly shielding her real emotions with tough talk and swift action. In fact, her exterior was almost impenetrable. We watched her every week to see how ruthless she could be. Those moments when she did let down her guard and expose her core were what made her character likable. Without her vulnerability, Amanda would have been a cardboard character and the audience would have had no way of relating to her. Those flashes of core allowed us to feel empathy and compassion for Amanda: we reveled in her ruthlessness, but we stayed hooked to her character because of her vulnerability.

As you search through your scene to find your character's core, ask yourself the following questions:

- What are my character's inner feelings throughout the scene?
- Do these feelings change?
- How does the character cover up these feelings?
- What masks does my character wear?
- Do the masks change during the scene?
- How easily penetrable is the mask?
- How dense or how porous is it?

PERIOD PIECES
Period pieces are known for their heavy masking. For example, the story of *Sense and Sensibility* (written by Emma Thompson; directed by Ang Lee), the Oscar®-winning adaptation of Jane Austen's novel,[1] entirely revolves around

---

[1] *Sense and Sensibility* received seven Academy Awards™; Emma Thompson won the Oscar® for Best Adapted Screenplay.

the dilemma between core and masking and whether a woman should show her true feelings or be "sensible" enough not to wear her heart on her sleeve. Marianne (played by Kate Winslet) is nearly ruined for revealing her love for the scoundrel Willoughby (Greg Wise). She is dishonored and almost dies because of her unabashed show of affection. Contrary to Marianne's weakness for exposing her passionate core, her sister Elinor (played by Emma Thompson) almost loses her chance at love by concealing her innermost desires—she wears her mask so well that Edward (Hugh Grant) has no idea that he is the object of her affection. The film's climactic moment occurs when Elinor can no longer hide her true feelings. Upon learning that Edward is not married, as she had thought, she lets out a huge sigh of relief. Her all-too-proper mask dissolves into a flood of tears and joy.

The magnificent period films from Merchant-Ivory usually deal with themes of masking. In fact, *The Remains of the Day* (written by Ruth Prawer Jhabvala from the novel by Kazuo Ishiguro; directed by James Ivory) is a bittersweet lesson in masking. In it, Stevens' (Anthony Hopkins) station in life as the butler prevents him from expressing his real feelings. When Miss Kenton (Emma Thompson) is hired as one of the maids, Stevens' convictions are put to the test as he becomes desperately conflicted between his desire for her and his duty to his master. It is a love story of the most tender kind—yet, the two principals never share a kiss! They each mask brilliantly, with Stevens winning out over his feelings but losing his love in the end because he cannot overcome the constraints of his occupation to let down his staid mask.

MASKING WITH ANGER

Don't fall into the trap of believing that anger is a core feeling. Usually, anger serves to protect us from our raw, sometimes unbearable emotions. Recall *Scent of a Woman*: Lt. Col. Frank Slade (Al Pacino) starts out with a thick, impenetrable shield of anger, barking out commands and stripping Charlie (Chris O'Donnell) and anyone else of their dignity. Slade's motto is "Destroy them before they destroy you." His cruel and uncouth behavior effectively keeps the world at a distance and yet his underlying core is his fear of being alone. If he were to let anyone come close to his being, he would risk losing that person and would again be faced with loneliness. So, instead, he spends his days in the dark by himself, afraid to show his vulnerability.

As the story unfolds, Slade peels away his anger and begins to connect with Charlie. We see this shell of a man emerge into a caring human being. By the end of the film, Slade has gone from planning his suicide to standing up and fighting for Charlie against the school. His love for the boy replaces his core of despair. Through it all, the two develop a bond more powerful than all of Slade's pain.

MASKING WITH INDIFFERENCE

The successful cop series, *NYPD Blue*, owes much of its appeal to the tough, streetwise character, Andy Sipowicz, portrayed beautifully by Dennis Franz[2]. His rough exterior is meant to keep us from getting too close to him; it's not unusual to find him bellowing at hapless criminals who stumble into his path. His mask of anger is an easy fit but Andy is equally comfortable wearing a mask of casual indifference. Both his physical behavior as well as his words are an attempt to make us believe that he doesn't care. He would rather appear apathetic than show us how he really feels. However, nothing could be further from the truth! Andy's fear of being hurt and rejected is his core. Underneath it all, he is a gentle soul with the passions and emotions of a giant.

In one extremely touching episode, Andy's older son stops by the station to talk with him, but Andy is in the middle of a case and can't talk. The rest of that day, Andy's imagination runs wild because he doesn't know why his son wanted to talk to him—Andy angrily yells at make-believe Army sergeants or threatens to put his son in rehab if he finds out the boy is hooked on drugs. Not knowing the problem, Andy fears the worst and masks his fear with anger.

But the mask changes when Andy gets home. Face-to-face with his son, Andy feigns indifference and nonchalance when his son informs him that he has failed his physical and is being discharged from the military. And, Andy reveals nothing when his son tells him that he has been accepted into the Police Academy and has chosen to be a police officer. Not only was his son's problem minimal, but he wants to be a cop like his Dad! What more could a father wish for?! But Andy masks it all with an indifferent shrug and leaves it to his wife to offer their congratulations. Only in the final moments does Andy break down and show any emotion—he gives his son a pat on the shoulder. This episode was moving and brilliantly acted—without words, Andy's thinly veiled mask allowed us to experience his character's proud, loving core.

MASKING WITH HUMOR

So how do we survive our fear and pain? Through humor. As children, we learn very quickly how to cover up our insecurities.

At age five, when my son confronted an unfamiliar situation, he put on his clown face and made people laugh. A master at hiding his vulnerability with silliness, he was, in reality, afraid of rejection. It starts so young!

As adults, many of us wouldn't dream of walking into a party without being armed with our favorite jokes. The class clown, the life of the party, the wise-cracker all use comedic masks to gain acceptance.

[2] Franz has won the Emmy Award three times for his work in this series.

In the film, *Funny Girl* (written by Isobel Lennart, based on the musical by Jule Styne, Bob Merrill, Lennart; directed by William Wyler), Barbra Streisand[3] plays legendary comedienne, Fanny Brice, a homely, unsophisticated girl from Brooklyn who amazingly ends up in the Ziegfeld Follies. Surrounded by the most beautiful women in the world, Fanny is asked to sing a song about how beautiful she is through the eyes of her beloved.

"I am the beautiful reflection of my love's affection
The walking illustration of his adoration
His love makes me beautiful
So beautiful, so beautiful . . . "

Feeling unworthy of such glowing words, Fanny tries desperately to get out of singing the number. Ziegfeld refuses. Faced with the prospect of having to sing the embarrassing lyric, Fanny has no choice but to perform the song utilizing her own comedic interpretation. She stuffs a pillow up her dress, revealing a hugely pregnant Fanny; she turns a lovely, romantic song into a hilarious moment of love's consequences. She masked her insecurities with humor.

THE VULNERABLE MOMENT

An interesting conflict can arise between the actor and his character with regard to vulnerability. Many of you go into your auditions eager to impress the casting director with your full range of emotions. You plan to cry at a certain point in the scene, then pray for the tears to fall. Your character, however, moves through their world hoping to hide that same vulnerability. The character will do anything in their power to avoid revealing their inner pain. It is a fine line you must tread between your wish to expose your feelings and the character's need to conceal them. But as you sift through the layers of core and masking in a scene, an opportunity may emerge during which the two intersect. I call this the "Vulnerable Moment"—that very instant when a flash of raw feeling shines through and your character exposes their true feelings. The Vulnerable Moment provides a fleeting glimpse into your character's fears, at once exposed, then hurriedly covered up.

Thelma & Louise

Following is a scene in which Thelma lets us see behind her mask. Uncertain about Louise's convictions, Thelma is pushed to reveal a deeper side of herself that we haven't seen before. In addition, her candor comes as a surprise to Louise. See if you can find Thelma's Vulnerable Moment in the following scene.

---

[3]   Streisand won the Academy™ Award for her performance.

p. 114

EXT. PAY PHONE - DAY

ANGLE ON Thelma. She has her finger on the lever.

>   THELMA
>   Come on, Louise. Don't blow it.
>   Let's go.

She walks away towards the car. Louise is still
standing there holding the phone. Thelma stops and
looks at her.

>   THELMA (cont'd)

Louise doesn't move.

>   THELMA (cont'd)
>   Louise?

>   LOUISE
>   Yes, Thelma?

>   THELMA
>   You're not gonna give up on me,
>   are ya?

>   LOUISE
>   What do you mean?

>   THELMA
>   You're not gonna make some deal
>   with that guy, are you? I mean,
>   I just wanna know.

>   LOUISE
>   No, Thelma. I'm not gonna make
>   any deals.

>   THELMA
>   I can understand if you're
>   thinkin' about it. I mean, in a
>   way, you've got something to go
>   back for. I mean Jimmy and
>   everything.

Louise is surprised to be hearing this from Thelma.

>   LOUISE
> Thelma, don't worry.

>   THELMA
> But I don't. I don't have
> something to go back for. And
> now, I don't know...
> something's crossed over in me
> and I can't go back. I mean, I
> just couldn't live...

>   LOUISE
> I know. I know what you mean. I
> don't think Jimmy would even
> marry me for real now. You
> think he's gonna consent to
> some kinda death row wedding? I
> don't wanna end up on the damn
> Geraldo show.

They are both quiet for a moment.

>   LOUISE (cont'd)
> He said they're gonna charge us
> with murder.

>   THELMA
>   (making a face)
> Eeuww.

>   LOUISE
> And we have to decide whether
> we want to come out of this
> dead or alive.

>   THELMA
>   (exasperated)
> Gosh, didn't he say anything
> positive at all?

Louise STARTS the car. They lurch into reverse then
SCREECH forward as they tear off down the road.

Thelma starts out the scene with strength and determination, adamantly pushing Louise to continue on their journey. In the middle of the scene, however, we recognize what is beneath Thelma's insistence. (Her core bleeds through when she says, "I don't have something to go back for. And now, I don't know . . . something's crossed over in me and I can't go back. I mean, I just couldn't live . . . ") Behind those words lie Thelma's real fears. Notice that the vulnerability lasts only for that moment, then they get right back on track with the business of deciding their fate.

From the Studio

In the Academy Award™-winning film, *Ordinary People* (written by Alvin Sargent, based on the novel by Judith Guest; directed by Robert Redford), Conrad (played by Timothy Hutton) meets his friend Karen (Dinah Manoff) at a coffee shop. The two met as patients at the mental hospital and this is the first time they've seen each other in the months after their release. Each is having a difficult time adjusting to life outside the hospital. Susan and Robert have just completed the scene in class.

```
INT. SODA FOUNTAIN - CONRAD & KAREN
In a small booth. She is bright and warm. She smiles
at him, but it is apparent she is nervous. There is an
awkward silence.

                KAREN
      When did you come home?

                CONRAD
      End of August!
          (pause)
      It's great to see you.

                KAREN
      You too.
          (looks at watch)
      I'm sorry I can't stay long.
      I've got a meeting at school.
      Our drama club is doing 'A
      Thousand Clowns'—do you know
      it? We're going wild tryin' to
      get it together. I'm secretary
      this year, that's probably why
      we're so disorganized...
```

                    CONRAD
        Don't let me hold you up, then.

                    KAREN
        No, it's okay. I really wanted
        to see you. Although I was sort
        of afraid. You seemed so down,
        over the phone.

                    CONRAD
                (quickly)
        Yeah, well, that was just a
        grey day. Actually,
        everything's going great. I'm
        back in school, and I'm
        swimming...

                    KAREN
        Oh, really? I'm glad.

                    CONRAD
        Well, we haven't had any meets
        yet. I could end up on the
        bench all year.

                    KAREN
        Oh, no, you'll do fine, I'm
        sure. And your folks'll be
        proud, too.

The counterman appears with their drinks. He puts the
cokes down, walks away. Conrad watches him, then leans
in to Karen.

                    CONRAD
                (re: counterman)
        Definitely a low self-image
        day.

Karen giggles. Conrad smiles at her. Then he drinks
his drink. Studies her.

                    CONRAD
        You look beautiful.

                    KAREN
You do, too.

                    CONRAD
You miss it?

                    KAREN
Miss what?

                    CONRAD
The hospital?

                    KAREN
No!

                    CONRAD
Not even Mr. Minnow's goldfish
trick?

                    KAREN
      (laughs)
Oh, God!

                    CONRAD
You were brilliant that day.
You told everybody off. Even
the judge.

                    KAREN
I can't believe I ever did
that.

                    CONRAD
You did it, all right. I'll
never forget it. And then we
sneaked into the kitchen and
talked all night, remember?

                    KAREN
Yeah...Wow...

                    CONRAD
Yeah...

>   KAREN
>   So what's going on? Are you
>   seeing a doctor?

>   CONRAD
>   Yeah. I see a real cracker. How
>   about you?

>   KAREN
>   Dr. Crawford gave me a name,
>   and I went for a while, but
>   then, I don't know. Finally I
>   decided it wasn't doing me any
>   good. He wasn't telling me
>   anything I couldn't figure out
>   for myself. Anyway, that's what
>   Dad says, and Dad has
>   confidence in me and I know
>   he's right. The only one who
>   can really help us is
>   ourselves. And this guy was
>   over in Elk Grove Village and
>   expensive as hell. I don't mean
>   that there isn't any value in
>   it, if you need it. I mean, for
>   some people it could be just
>   the right thing. If it's
>   working for you, Conrad, that's
>   what counts.

>   CONRAD
>   Well, actually, I don't know
>   how long I'll keep it up. I got
>   shoved into it, sort of...My
>   father...

Silence. Finally:

>   KAREN
>   Your hair grew in.

>   CONRAD
>   You still painting?

                         KAREN
              No, I quit that. They were so
              weird, those paintings.

                         CONRAD
              You can't give that up. You
              taught me everything I know.
              You got me to stop drawing
              straight lines. You taught me
              to draw with ketchup.

She laughs.

                         CONRAD
                    (continuing)
              Remember? If we can't sell 'em
              we'll eat 'em.

More laughter. Then silence.

                         KAREN
              How's your mother?

                         CONRAD
              My mother? Good. Real good.

                         KAREN
              That's good.

                         CONRAD
              Yeah.
                    (pause)
              So you don't draw with ketchup
              anymore, huh?

                         KAREN
              No, but I'm in the church
              choir.

                         CONRAD
              Hey! Me too, at school. It's
              great, isn't it?

                         KAREN
              Yeah. It's great.

                    CONRAD
                (sings)
            'I've got a mule and his name
            is Sal. Fifteen miles on the
            Erie Canal.' I'm a tenor.

                    KAREN
            Sounds good.

Pause. She reaches into her glass to pick up some ice.
Conrad watches her. She starts to chew on the ice.

                    KAREN
            They're right, you know?

                    CONRAD
            Who?

                    KAREN
            Our parents. They know
            something we don't know.

                    CONRAD
            What?

                    KAREN
            Oh...how to meet obstacles and
            how to be popular, I guess.

                    CONRAD
            Like 'The Waltons', huh?

She chews the ice.

                    CONRAD
            You still like ice.

                    KAREN
            Oh, God, I'm sorry, it's a
            terrible habit.

                    CONRAD
            Hey, it's okay. I don't mind. I
            like it. It reminds me of you.

Pause. She chews real hard and the ice makes a lot of
noise and they both laugh again.

                    CONRAD
        I don't know, I miss it
        sometimes. The hospital.

                    KAREN
        I know, Connie, but things have
        to change.

                    CONRAD
        But in the hospital, that's
        where we had the laughs.

                    KAREN
        But we aren't there now. It has
        to be different now. That
        wasn't real life back there.

                    CONRAD
        Yeah...I guess you're right.

She looks at her watch.

                    KAREN
        I've really got to go. I've got
        a meeting at school. Our drama
        club is doing 'A Thousand
        Clowns.'

                    CONRAD
        I know, you told me.

                    KAREN
        Oh. Did I...Well, I'd better
        hurry.

                    CONRAD
        Yeah, well, thanks for seeing
        me, Karen.

                    KAREN
        Connie...let's have the most
        wonderful Christmas of our
        lives. We can, you know. We can
        have a wonderful year. It can
        be the best year ever.

>   CONRAD
>   Yeah, okay.
>
>   KAREN
>   (getting up)
>   And will you call me again? I'd
>   like to see you. Really, I mean
>   it. Will you?
>
>   CONRAD
>   Sure I will.

Karen gathers her coat about her shoulders. She's
awkward.

>   KAREN
>   I wish I could stay longer.
>   It's really good to see you,
>   Con, it really is.
>
>   CONRAD
>   You too.
>
>   KAREN
>   'Bye.
>
>   CONRAD
>   'Bye.

Karen turns, leaves without a backward glance. Conrad
sits there, palming the empty Coke glass back and
forth between his hands; he looks disappointed.

Margie: Both characters have similar cores. They are terrified of the
world and are afraid to live in it. Their masks, however, are very different. This scene is a good example of how some masks are thicker
than others. Let's talk about the feelings that are exposed in the opening beat.

Susan: Karen is really nervous and uptight.

Margie: True, but does Conrad recognize her behavior as fear?

Robert: I think Conrad feels badly because Karen seems so happy and excited about her new life.

Margie: Right. What feelings does Conrad bring with him into the scene?

Robert: Before Karen arrives, we notice that he's very anxious to see her. His fear of rejection bleeds through the whole scene. Conrad is not very good at hiding his core. His mask is much more transparent.

Margie: Excellent. What about Karen's mask?

Susan: It's thick. She acts so excited for Conrad and for herself, especially at the end, when she says, "Let's have a great Christmas. Let's have a great year. Let's have the best year of our whole lives."

Margie: Yes, Karen's bravado is very strong.

Susan: She needs to make Conrad believe that everything in her life is great. Maybe she's also trying to convince herself.

Margie: You portrayed Karen's mask well, but you need to do more work on highlighting her core. When Conrad says he misses the hospital, you could allow more of your impatience and irritability to be seen as her veneer begins to crack.

                    CONRAD
        I don't know, I miss it
        sometimes, the hospital. I
        really do.

                    KAREN
        Things have to change, you
        know.

                    CONRAD
        But that's where we had the
        laughs.

                    KAREN
        But that was the hospital. This
        is the real world.

```
        CONRAD
Yeah...yeah...I guess you're
right.

[silence]

        KAREN
I really have to go. I'm sorry,
I have a meeting over at the
school. A drama club meeting.
We're doing A Thousand Clowns.
    (starts to put on coat).

        CONRAD
I know, you told me.
```

Margie: In the previous unit, Conrad has a Vulnerable Moment when he talks about missing the hospital. He puts himself on the line when he shares his loneliness. What you missed, Susan, is how disarming Conrad's honesty is for Karen. She wasn't prepared to confront those memories. We become aware of her discomfort, not only in the lines, but during their silence. In the last unit, you could have been more flustered when Karen manically repeats herself, "I have a meeting over at the school. A drama club meeting. We're doing A Thousand Clowns." Otherwise, I thought you and Robert captured the awkwardness of their meeting.

TIPS

- Don't fall into the trap of believing that every moment is important and vulnerable. Pick and choose your Vulnerable Moment carefully. The less you expose, the more interesting the work.

- It is important to note that not every scene contains a Vulnerable Moment but it is your job to look for one.

- The character tries to cover up his sadness, hoping that the other characters won't see it. Meanwhile, the actor prays that he will be able to cry on cue. Be the character!

- Remember, anger is the mask, not the core. Discover what is underneath your character's anger.

QUICK TAKE

CORE AND MASKING: *What are the character's true feelings? Which are exposed vs. concealed?*

- What is the CORE, or the center of my character?
- How does my character MASK, or cover up, their true feelings?
- What is the VULNERABLE MOMENT in the scene—the moment when my character's true core is revealed?

—

SENSE OF HUMOR

Where is the lightness in the scene?

TONY ROBERTS / *Annie Hall, Stardust Memories*

This has to do with an audition I gave while I was still in college which turned out to be a blessing in disguise. I was to audition for the biggest college show in America—the Waa-Mu Show. It's been in existence for about fifty years and it costs about $50,000 to produce; it is a huge musical done every year on campus in a giant auditorium.

At any rate, I was a lowly sophomore at the time and went to audition as a singer. I found myself in a room on the wrong day and at the wrong time being lined up with a bunch of guys who had these great physiques and were being told to do some steps across the floor. Rather than admit that I had made a mistake and gone to the wrong audition (like Shelley Berman not wanting to say he thought the propeller of the plane was on fire because he'd rather die than make a fool of himself), I proceeded to dance as directed and, in fact, was cast as a dancer. (I had meant to go to the singing auditions.) The good part of the story is that having appeared in the show as a dancer, I learned to look at the other dancers a little bit and try something I'd never dreamt in a million years I'd be doing. I was in good stead for my career on Broadway which later led to a Tony nomination for Best Performance in a Musical in "How Now Dow Jones" in 1967 which called for me to do quite a bit of dancing. And I couldn't have done it without the Waa-Mu Show!

TONY ROBERTS

You go to a party where you are introduced to a handsome man. You begin a conversation, hoping for a flirtatious moment or two only to find you're losing concentration. Your eyes begin to wander. You scan the room furiously looking for someone to save you from this fate worse than death—BOREDOM. Each joke you make falls flat. He just doesn't get it—the man has no sense of humor!

We are always drawn to people who make us laugh.

My close friends are those who have an ability to lighten situations that would otherwise seem dark. Think about your own circle of friends. Is there someone who always makes you smile? Is there someone whom you call when you're feeling blue because you know they'll cheer you up?

So, then, when you pick up a script, why do you leave your sense of humor behind? It's true: as actors, we all have a need to be dramatic. Most of us feel that the drama of the scene is the best showcase for our talent so we dig deep for those emotions which reveal our character's pain. However, when you do this, you get so caught up in the conflict and struggle that you may overlook one of life's most important survival elements—your sense of humor. It astonishes me that, sometimes, my most interesting, dynamic clients allow themselves to become washed out during dramatic auditions. They'll focus so intensely on the seriousness of the situation, their personalities go out the window! They'll save their sense of humor for comedy, and yet, the dramas often need comic relief the most.

> In 1974, my father was in the hospital, terminally ill. As I look back on that time, it's not the pain of the situation that I remember most but the closeness I experienced with my sisters as we shared the lighter moments of our youth; it was my father's smile as I stood before him doing the Ed Sullivan impersonation I had been doing since I was five. The room was transformed—it was no longer filled with sadness and despair because my family knew they could rely on me to brighten up this sad situation. I learned that, during the darker, more dramatic moments of our lives, a sense of humor has immeasurable value.

PERSONALITY

Sometimes, no matter how hard you look for the humor in a scene, you can't find it because it's just not funny. That's when your personality comes into play. (I don't mean a theatrical type of personality, such as Bette Midler's character C.C. in *Beaches* or even her larger-than-life protrayal of Mama Rose in *Gypsy,* chewing up the scenery.) I am referring to the essence of your be-ing—your quirks, distinctive qualities, playfulness. Your personality is what makes you special. It's what sets you apart from everyone else. Seamlessly meshing your personality with your character is what the casting director will remember most about your audition.

Occasionally, I'll have work with two or three actors who are preparing to audition for the same role. People will ask me if this is a conflict and I'll always tell them, "No." Even if we break down the scene using the same struc-ture and explore the character's emotional life together, each actor's audi-tion will be completely different. As long as they let their personalities come through, each portrayal will be unique.

> When I moved to Hollywood from New York in the '70s, I befriended Julie Bridges, who was married to Beau Bridges at the time. She invited me to spend the day at their beach home in Malibu. I was charmed by Beau's warmth and playfulness with his child, Casey. That evening, I went as their guest to watch Beau's performance in Cantersville Nine. At one point during the play the audience was laughing and I remember seeing Beau's expression—it was the same look I had witnessed hours before at his home. I whispered to my friend, "You see, that's Beau! That's who he really is." I learned a valuable lesson that night as I watched Beau infuse his personality into his character. As an actor, he under-stood the art of making a character come to life. He was not afraid to bring in his own personality.

BREAKING THE STEREOTYPES

Most of the time when you audition, you're only given a few words of de-scription about your character. The script might call for an "attractive law-yer in her thirties" or a "young doctor" or maybe a "ruthless aging politi-cian." These stereotypes are easy to grasp, but they can also be limiting if you're not careful.

Once, during an exercise in class, I had the actors prepare a closing argu-ment from *The Practice.* Half of the group prepared for the role of the defense attorney; the other half played the prosecuting attorney. In the casting setup, each actor would enter to address an imaginary jury. Many of the actors fell into the trap of "playing" a lawyer: they had an image of what a lawyer should be—serious, professional, persuasive, intellectual. They were so busy play-ing the stereotype, they left out their own personalities. The few actors who introduced their own personalities and found the lightness in their deliver-ies were the only ones to present successful readings.

HUMOR VS. LIGHTNESS

Is there humor in every scene? Of course not. In fact, many scenes are devoid of humor but can be filled with lightness. "Lightness" is an approach to the material that takes in the absurdity of the human condition. It means working against the drama by alleviating the trap of heaviness that is so easy to get caught up in. Instead, you lightly interpret a serious situation. Lightness can be accomplished in many ways: through sarcasm, a mocking laugh or a simple gesture, like a shrug of the shoulder. Whatever genre you're working in—action films, soap operas, hospital or crime dramas, etc.—you must always look for the lightness.

ACTION/ADVENTURE FILMS

There you are, in a darkened theater, hands over your eyes, watching with trepidation as hundreds of slithering snakes crawl up Indiana Jones's legs. Suddenly, Harrison Ford does a double-take and breaks the tension with that devilish look we've come to know so well. It's a necessary release because the audience can't sustain that level of tension for very long. Throughout his work in the *Indiana Jones* and *Star Wars* series, Harrison Ford has led us through perilous situations with a wink and a smile. Through his ability to laugh at himself and at the danger he encounters, we discover our shared humanity. He's not afraid to show us his doubt and fear. He shows us that he is human, too.

Macho heroes like Clint Eastwood and Arnold Schwarzenegger are known for their whimsical remarks in the face of danger. Who can forget such classic Clint lines as, "Go ahead, make my day!" or Arnold's "Hasta la vista, baby!" Here again, the humor provides much-needed comic relief for the tension and violence found in their films. It also adds complexity to their otherwise tough but one-dimensional characters. Certainly, the writers give them these verbal gems to utter but if the humor is not written into the script, you must create it.

Toby, an actor from London, was cast in an independent film and asked me to help him prepare. In this science fiction piece, he played a commander whose ship lands in a futuristic world of robots and androids. When we began, Toby got caught up playing the "responsible soldier" but the scene was boring and his character was one-dimensional. He needed to find humor to liven it up.

In one scene, just before he boards the robot's vehicle, he confers with his crew member and gives him a help signal. The scene, as written, was dry, with only one clue as to the potential for humor. A stage direction for a particular response read, "(sarcastically)." Between the lines, I suggested that Toby find a way to relieve the tension. How would Harrison Ford play this moment? With a twinkle in his eye or a sideways glance that would indicate, "Okay, here goes nothin'!" Because of that suggestion, Toby began to explore another side of the character that he hadn't yet discovered—his sense of humor.

BUDDY FILMS

Buddy films are built on the strong relationships between the main characters. But, often, they get their charm from the actors' humorous takes on sometimes delicate situations. The film classic, *Butch Cassidy and the Sundance Kid*[1] (written by William Goldman; directed by George Roy Hill) is filled with precarious moments that are enjoyable to watch because of the magical way that Paul Newman and Robert Redford play off each other. For example, having been chased by a mysterious posse for days, Butch and Sundance end up at the edge of a steep cliff where they can either die fighting or jump hundreds of feet into the raging waters below. When Butch insists on jumping, Sundance shouts back, "I can't swim!" He then stares stubbornly up and down at his friend, finally giving in with a pathetic shrug. Butch breaks out into hysterical laughter—and so do we—as they jump into the rushing river, screaming, "O-O-O-H, S-H-I-I-I-I-I-T!" It is a tense moment, but because of the humorous way in which they connect, we know they'll be okay.

Thelma & Louise

In the last fifteen minutes of the film, as Thelma and Louise face their most dire consequences, our heroines continue to hold onto the humor despite their desperation. When the tension gets thick, they turn to each other with wit and sarcasm. Although it's not a comedy, and their circumstances aren't funny, the personalities of these two characters help continue the entertaining adventure.

pg. 118

```
                    THELMA
          Well, try to look at the bright
          side. At least you don't have
          to go to work tonight.

     This gets a smile out of Louise.

                    THELMA (cont'd)
          Are you gonna call 'em and tell
          'em you're not coming in?
```

---

[1] *Butch Cassidy and the Sundance Kid* won Academy Awards® for Best Screenplay, Best Cinematography and Best Song and received three additional nominations.

>   LOUISE
>   Can you do that? Call in
>   psychotic? "Hi, it's Louise.
>   I've had a complete mental
>   breakdown. Can you get someone
>   to cover my shift?"

This cracks them up.

>   LOUISE (cont'd)
>   "Hi, Eddie, I'm off on a crime
>   spree will you see if Cheryl
>   wants my section?"

Louise and Thelma both get quiet for a second.

>   LOUISE (cont'd)
>   We'll be drinkin' margaritas by
>   the sea, Mamasita.

>   THELMA
>   We can change our names.

>   LOUISE
>   We can live in a hacienda.

>   THELMA
>   I wanna get a job. I wanna work
>   at Club Med.

>   LOUISE
>   Yes! Yes! Now what kind of deal
>   do you think that cop can come
>   up with to beat that?

>   THELMA
>   It would have to be pretty damn
>   good.

For a moment, Thelma and Louise step out of their grim reality and into a tropical fantasy, experiencing a world they both know is unattainable. Their sense of humor bonds them and keeps them going.

LIKABILITY

Humor also makes a character more likable, which is an important element in movie-making. If the characters are not likable then the audience doesn't care if thet live or die, nor will viewers empathize with that character's journey. Entire careers have been built on the quality of likability, such as those of Jimmy Stewart, Cary Grant, Henry Fonda, Katherine Hepburn, Donna Reed and Doris Day. Why are these legends so likable? They each have a sense of humor. Today, stars like Robin Williams, Harrison Ford and Meg Ryan continue that tradition.

Philadelphia (written by Ron Nyswaner; directed by Jonathan Demme) was the first studio film to tackle the sensitive subject of AIDS. Although the producers could have cast many actors for the lead role, they needed someone immensely likable who could make the audience feel compassion. Who better than Tom Hanks[2] to play the AIDS-stricken lawyer? Tom is an Everyman; he has an almost childlike quality which draws us to him. In the film, he had the ability to make the audience feel comfortable in an uncomfortable situation.

DAYTIME DRAMAS (SOAPS)

Drama! Drama! Drama! There's nothing more boring than watching an actor get stuck in the gut-wrenching drama of a scene. And there's no genre more abused in this manner than the soap opera.

> *I have worked with some brilliant actors in daytime series, including Terry Lester (Jack) and Eileen Davidson (Ashley) in* Young and the Restless *and Lisa Rinna and Michael Easton in* Days of Our Lives. *Each has a unique ability to take the verbose, overly dramatic material and bring it to life using personality and humor.*

Most soap opera actors fall into the trap of focusing on the drama. But, the drama is already built in, so why sink deeper into the pain and trauma? As an audience, we are grateful when actors work against the material. Let's go to the studio and I'll show you what I mean.

---

[2] Tom Hanks won the Oscar® for his portrayal of Andrew Beckett.

From the Studio

In the scene from *Young and the Restless*, Eric and Ashley have been having an affair but Eric must leave Genoa City and return home. He is in conflict—he has fallen deeply in love with Ashley but he is committed to another woman.

> **Margie:** Jason, I saw how much your character, Eric, cared for Ashley, but I think you fell into a trap. You were busy playing at the sexuality of the scene.

> **Jason:** I knew that they were attracted to each other. And soap operas are all about sex . . .

> **Margie:** Yes, but when you play it like Mae West, it becomes predictable and boring. It's much sexier to bring out the attraction with your personality and lightness, which, unfortunately, was missing in your scene. Sex can also be fun!

> **Jason:** But the scene didn't seem very funny.

> **Margie:** Eric is attractive but he doesn't need to flaunt it. He is charming and witty and wants an honest reply from Ashley. There's a sexy, boyish quality about him when he says, "I'm not against sex" and "I'm not the celibate type." That's where the lightness comes in. Another trap you fell into was playing the sadness of leaving rather than the playfulness of the game.

Whether you are given the opportunity to perform classic Tennessee Williams or you have the challenge of working through lengthy, dry soap opera material, you will brighten up your work if you use your personality and sense of humor.

Mary Wilson, of The Supremes, was one of my best friends back in the '60s and '70s. In the group, she was always the one with the personality that lit up the stage. As a singer, she was never afraid to fill the stage with her presence. Years later, when Mary came to study acting with me, I had to remind her to bring that personality into her acting. Each of us is special in our own way. It is important to let your personality come through in your work.

TIPS

- Remember to bring your own quirkiness and specialness to your work, as long as it's appropriate to your character.

- Always work against the drama.

- Your sense of humor can help make your character likable.

- Stop trying to be sexy. Rely on your personality.

QUICK TAKE

SENSE OF HUMOR: *Where is the lightness in the scene?*

- Look for the lighter moments in the scene.

- Are there places where your personality can shine through?

—

MOMENT TO MOMENT

Now that you've done the work, trust it!

ROBERT NEWMAN / *The Guiding Light*

"Let it go, let it go, let it go." This is my fondest memory of working with Margie. She used to say this with arms up and hands sweeping outward, releasing whatever needed to be released. My wife and I still use this all the time. It comes in very handy when you're at an audition and are asked to do a 180 degree change from what you had so carefully planned, or perhaps for those times when you've just given what you think is the worst audition of your life and have another one across town in thirty minutes.

They say many casting decisions are made within a few seconds of the actor walking in the door. It becomes our job [as an actor] to either support their thoughts about you, "Yes, I think he's right for the role," or change their mind, "No, he's not right." There was only one nightmare audition I remember where I felt it was a lost cause from the get-go. I walked in the door and a very worn and tired female casting director looked up at me and with disgust in her voice informed me that I reminded her of her "son of a bitch ex-husband" before I had even spoken a word. During the entire reading, she gave me nothing but nasty attitude. I did the best I could, but the role would never be mine. I walked out, took a deep breath and said to myself, "Let it go, let it go, let it go."

ROBERT NEWMAN

Opportunity knocks: you get a call from your agent to read with the lead actor of a network series. The executives want to see your chemistry. You've already read for the producers a couple times and you're feeling pretty good about your work. You've broken down the scene thoroughly—you have a specific relationship and a strong intention; you've layered in your history and personalization; you have a good opening beat; you're coming from the character's point of view; you've boxed your units and know exactly where the transitions should be; the core and masking are there; you've even found some lightness.

The casting director introduces you to the handsome star and asks you to get started. All's going well until he throws you a curve: his interpretation of the scene is completely different from yours and his transitions are in different places. You try desperately to stick to your plan, but what you've rehearsed is no longer appropriate.

Remember, in Chapter 7, when I asked you to use pencil to mark your units? That was a reminder that nothing is permanent. Now—you need to let go of your choices and go with the moment.

"Moment to Moment" means being completely present so that you're able to ride whatever wave comes at you. (For example, you may think the scene is going to go one way but then it shifts and you have to adjust. So, go with the flow.) It doesn't mean abandoning your preparation altogether, nor does it mean that your preparation was in vain. It just means that you should be available to change.

Moment to moment means having the guts to freefall off the edge of a precipice trusting that you'll land safely on your two feet. It's a matter of trust.

TENNIS, ANYONE?

Working "moment to moment" is a lot like playing tennis. You can spend hours or days practicing your strokes, working on your grip or analyzing your game strategy but once the ball is in play, it's time to quit thinking and swing! You don't have time to worry about whether you've followed through on your last forehand or if you should be facing the net on that lob. Once you've practiced your game, you have to trust that your strokes will be there when you need them.

I see this happen in my classes all the time: an actor is in the middle of a scene but he doesn't feel connected to what he is saying. He'll usually stop, go back to the beginning of the line and start over again, hoping to be more connected the next time. No! Continuing the tennis analogy—the ball is already over the net! You can't go back and retrieve it. In the audition, the moment is gone. Forget about whether you've achieved exactly what you had hoped for. Move on to the next moment and leave your judgments behind.

THE COVERUP

You're in the middle of a dramatic moment and suddenly, the wrong words come out of your mouth. You panic, wondering if anyone noticed your *horrendous* mistake. You withdraw, pulling into yourself—the coverup begins. You shut down and pretend the mistake never happened. The casting people may not have noticed your mistake, but you can bet they noticed the coverup—because you called attention to it! It's not the mistake that's the problem, but the coverup.

When you pull back or pretend that nothing happened, you lose the truth of the moment. By accepting your mistake and going with it, you stay present in the scene. Just think, you could end up on a new road you haven't traveled before that just might be full of wonderful surprises. I give you permission to turn your mistakes into gifts.

> *In my previous career as a speech therapist, my specialty was working with children who stutter. Ironically, the more one tries to avoid stuttering, the more severe the stuttering becomes. As part of my work, I gave the children permission to stutter. The block was removed, so they could learn to talk with ease. Covering up your mistakes in an audition has the same effect: the harder you try to cover them up, the worse they get.*

MISTAKES ARE YOUR FRIENDS

Wonderful surprises can happen from mistakes. Mistakes take you out of your prepared state and bring you into a world of spontaneous moments; they keep you off-balance and make you alert; they also allow you to be vulnerable because you are forced to respond instantly to a stimulus that you might otherwise have overlooked.

> *Actress Serena Scott Thomas auditioned for the series* Nash Bridges *starring Don Johnson. Chemistry was necessary between the two. She and I were working on her audition scene when, in the middle of it, she broke character and, in her very English manner, began to giggle. As she pulled out of the scene, I said, "No! Stay with it! Use that wonderful quality of yours!" Then she whined, "But I made a mistake!" I said again, "Use it!" She did and the relationship became instantly more alive. She booked the series.*

Mistakes are a natural occurrence. We make mistakes in our everyday life so why feel you have to be perfect when you audition? Characters are flawed and so are we. That's what makes it interesting. So, don't try to smooth out the edges. Keep those bumps and cracks. It's okay to be human.

CRAZY THINGS THAT THROW YOU

As many of you have come to know, some pretty bizarre things can happen when you're in the middle of a reading. Some actors ignore these, hoping they'll go away while more creative actors may use them to their benefit. All actors have been thrown for a loop at one time or another. Here are some of the more interesting audition stories I've heard:

LAR PARK LINCOLN / *Knot's Landing*

I went to the network to audition for a very popular show. I was prepared and excited. I walked in, sat down and began to read. As I was doing the scene, I began to notice many pairs of eyes staring at me—from high, low, everywhere. This producer was a game hunter and taxidermied animals were in lifelike positions all around me. As I got used to that—one of them suddenly jumped up and came towards me!!! I guess it hadn't been stuffed yet!!!

. . . .

MARGA GOMEZ / *Sphere*

I got an audition with Ellen Chenoweth who was casting *Sphere* for Barry Levinson. I was up for the role of Jane Edmunds, military computer techno whiz. As the date approached, I thought of bailing out because, in real life I'm cyber-challenged—I wipe out when I surf the Web and, most of all, I didn't believe I could pass for someone named Edmunds or Jane.

Instead of giving up, I went shopping . . . and found a soft, but scientific, WASP-y, roll-up-the-sleeves, light rose blouse. When I walked into Ms. Chenoweth's office, I kept thinking to myself, "I'm Edmunds. I'm Edmunds . . ." She invited me to sit and have a chat. Ms. Chenoweth is one of the warmest casting directors you'll ever meet and I would have greatly enjoyed talking to her if there wasn't this voice in my head saying, "I lost my character. I'll never get the part now. Never!"

She had me read two or three times with a couple adjustments each time. I was thinking, "I'm SO not Edmunds. I'm wasting her time." Then she had me do my last two lines down into the lens of the camera which was propped on her desk. It took effort to keep my eyes focused there because I had been told by several people never to look directly into the lens.

My impulse was to apologize to Ms. Chenoweth. Fortunately, I stifled it. I thanked her, shook her hand, wished her success and fled. I immediately told my manager that I blew it. Later that afternoon, my manager and my agent called me with news that I got the part without even a callback. I still believe it was because of that blouse.

. . . .

CHERYL RICHARDSON / *General Hospital, Nightmare on Elm St. IV*

I was in a reading with a major casting director whom I had not met before. We were on page 2 of a 6-page scene when suddenly her phone began ringing. I got a bit unnerved but maintained my focus and we continued reading. As the phone continued to ring, unanswered, 20-plus times, I began thinking of everything else but the scene we were reading. My mind suddenly remembered something we always talked about in class, "It's your audition, take control of it!" Before I could think of anything else, I reached across her desk abruptly, picked up the telephone receiver and screamed, "Casting!!" I couldn't blame the caller for hanging up, but at least I got a well-deserved apology from the casting director. (I would have preferred to get the job!)

. . . .

DON McMILLAN / *"I Love You, Man!" Budweiser national campaign*

Death by Accent: I was lucky enough to have a pre-read for a lead in a new sitcom that was being cast by the people who cast *Seinfeld, Friends*, and *3rd Rock from the Sun*. For anonymity's sake, let's call them "Manfeld Casting." The reading was with one of the two owner/agents named "Mark." The role was described as the co-host of a popular radio talk show about cars. He was 35-45. Blue-collar. With a Wisconsin accent. Wisconsin accent? What exactly is that? I figured I could do a Chicago accent. That should be close enough. So, I enthusiastically prepared for my BIG audition with a Chicago drawl that would have made "da Bears" proud.

The audition began well enough. Mark told me he had heard about me. (Yes!) Then, he asked me if I had any questions about the scene. Without thinking, I said, "Yeah. It says, Wisconsin accent. I do more of a Chicago thing. That's okay, right?"

He immediately said, "No! Definitely NOT Chicago. A Wisconsin accent is similar to Chicago, but it's more Nordic."

"Okay," I thought, "I can make that adjustment. Chicago with a touch of Nordic—piece of cake!"

He had the first line, which he delivered in a perfect L.A. accent. My first line was supposed to be, "Cripes—will you look at that." The words came out fine, but the accent missed by about a continent. Apparently, in my verbal arithmetic, Chicago plus Nordic equaled Tanzania. I could not believe what I heard come out of my mouth! I sounded like I was on a safari.

Mark, to his credit, bravely delivered his next line. I don't know what he said, I had stopped listening to him. All I could think was, "What was that?! That was NOT Wisconsin! What am I going to do?! This is Manfeld!" Then the solution became clear to me—Add Swedish! And that's how my next line came out—in a Swedish accent. Two lines, two accents. I was on a roll. Mark gave me his next line which AGAIN I didn't hear because all I could think was, "That was Swedish! I sounded like the chef from the Muppets! How can I fix it? I know . . . Add more inflection!"

As my next line came out of my mouth, I learned something— Swedish minus the rhythm plus more inflection gives you . . . Chinese. Mandarin to be exact.

The rest of the audition continued in the same way. Each one of my lines brought a new accent. 13 lines, 13 accents. It was as if Sybil was auditioning. My performance had NO intention, NO stakes, NO emotion (other than my own panic) and NO basis in reality. It totally sucked! I didn't get a callback. Manfeld Casting didn't bring me back in for over a year. And I didn't get my own series on NBC between Seinfeld and ER. Can you believe it!!!

What I did get was a good story, enough angst for five good therapy sessions and some important lessons:

1) Do what you prepared. If the casting director wants to make adjustments after you've read, he can. If it's a difficult adjustment, ask for more time to prepare.

2) If you MUST use an accent, DO NOT try an accent you have not worked on extensively.

3) The scene is about your relationships, your intentions and your stakes—NOT how you sound.

. . . .

TIM QUILL / ER, *The Quick and the Dead*

My big break was a meeting and reading for Oliver Stone, who had just won an Oscar for *Platoon*. I was reading for a part in *The Doors*, as one of the band members, and I was really nervous. I arrived right on time and was escorted in by the casting director, Billy Hopkins, only to meet Mr. Stone as he was heading out to the restroom. After a very uncomfortable five minutes, with Mr. Hopkins and I having nothing to talk about, Mr. Stone returned to the room with a bottle of mouthwash in one hand and the wet, cold cap in the other. And the cap was between our hands during the handshake! After a brief chat, I started my reading for my "big break." A few lines into it, I heard the sound of gargling and as I read, I watched him spit mouthwash into and empty metal trash can. Needless to say, that didn't turn out to be my "big break."

. . . .

KEITH ALEXANDER / *Party of Five*

I went in to audition for a film where I was paired up with an older woman (around sixty) who was to play my grandmother. In the scene, grandma and grandson argue about her granddaughter, who's a hooker. My partner and I quickly worked it through before we went into the room. Once we entered, we met the director and casting director. Then, this sixty-year-old woman asked the director, "I know you're casting for the hooker and I wasn't sure how old you would go for the role." I looked at her like she was crazy. The director said, so as not to insult her, "Well, we're going a little younger." The woman then said, "That's all right, I came prepared to show you my body anyway." And before the director could say anything, the woman unbuttoned her blouse and unzipped her dress. We were all in shock. Even the director. Before I knew it, my "grandmother" was standing next to me in a thong bikini! And right before lunch, no less.

So the director muttered, "Thank you, uh . . . let's read the scene." I could not focus on this woman for the life of me. I certainly couldn't think of her as my "grandmother" and I'm sure I gave a bad read. She could have warned me! It definitely threw me off.

I walked out, thinking about my real grandma walking around the Jewish home in a thong and laughed all the way back to my car.

. . . .

JAMES HARRISON LURIE / *Buffy the Vampire Slayer*

Auditions for David Mamet's *Oleanna* were being held in a large rehearsal studio on Seventh Avenue in New York. My turn to read for the Professor finally arrived and I was introduced to the room. Precisely as I delivered my first line, dance auditions for a production of West Side Story began in the next room, with a deafening roar! Between the music and twenty pairs of women's dance shoes thundering through the walls, there was no chance of us to continue.

The director stopped the proceedings and we all went to look for another room. Nothing was available. Out of sheer frustration, he said, "Hell, let's just do it in the stairwell. At least it will be quiet." So we perched ourselves on various stairs and began again. Several lines into it, the door opened and a young woman began threading her way between us whispering, "Sorry. Sorry. Excuse me. I'm sorry." All the way down. So we started up a third time. Then, two people marched through us, speaking at full volume as if we didn't even exist.

The director apologized and said, "Look, let's just try it once more. If we can't get through it I'm afraid I'll have to ask you to come back tomorrow before callbacks." We launched into it a fourth time and we were a good three-quarters of the way through when, naturally, the door opened again. I was so angry, I raised my voice to be sure these two people knew something important was going on here. Well, it didn't stop them—they inched their way through in complete silence, trying to be as invisible as possible. As for me, I kept right on going with the scene. I just wanted to get through the damned thing once!

Needless to say, I left the audition feeling completely frustrated, that the entire thing had been a joke. I was amazed, therefore, when I got a callback and even more amazed when I got the part. The director told me later that my flash of anger on the stairs and the effect it had on those people walking through was a critical quality he was looking for in the Professor. Thank God I was the only actor lucky enough to be forced to read in the stairwell!

THE CALLBACK SYNDROME

You go into your first read and you do a great job. The casting director says, "Don't change anything! Bring it back exactly the way you did it!" Your callback is five days later and you practice over and over again, trying to remember exactly what you did so right the first time. You go in for the callback and you desperately try to repeat your performance. You realize halfway through that you're not listening to one line the casting director is saying. You're on automatic pilot and the plane's about to crash! What happened to the spontaneous magic of the first read? How can you recapture that freshness?

I have a name for this: the Callback Syndrome. You believe the casting director expects a repeat performance and you panic—how do you duplicate your first successful audition? The answer is: You don't! You can't possibly recreate every nuance that just happened to work for you last Monday at 4:27 p.m.

But, you must keep your reading spontaneous and fresh. One way to do this is to let your senses work for you. Let the character's environment feed you. Learn to rely on your senses and images instead of your thoughts and the lines (which keep you stuck in your head). And don't think that the exact same images or thoughts will work for you every time. You may need to change them ever so slightly to keep them new.

Actor Stephen Collins told me about how exciting and challenging it was to work opposite Diane Keaton in the movie, The First Wives Club *(written by Robert Harling, based on the novel by Olivia Goldsmith; directed by Hugh Wilson). Stephen, a veteran of television and current star of TV's 7th Heaven, is more familiar with the fast pace of television so he is consistent with each take and tends to match his performances skillfully. However, working in the film medium and with such a seasoned actress as Diane Keaton, he saw that no take was ever the same. He was fascinated by her freedom to take chances, which made both of their performances more spontaneous.*

From the Studio

Lisa was to read a scene from *The Goodbye Girl*. Two other actresses were absent the day of that workshop, so Lisa had to do the scene three times, with three different actors. The first time, her performance was excellent. Her relationship was strong, her intention was clear and her history was full. With the second actor, she tried to repeat that performance but it wasn't working. So, I took her aside, whispering, "Look at Michael's muscles; they're huge! Look at his long, blond hair; it's prettier than yours! She laughed and I said, "Take him in, Lisa. Watch his unique style." When she repeated the scene with Michael, Lisa started laughing in the middle of it, causing him to break away from his planned reactions. He began to join her in laughter. They were still in character, but they allowed themselves to go with the moment. What I explained to them, and what they certainly felt, was that for the first time, they were able to come out of the haze that prevents actors from being truly "present." Working Moment to Moment really woke them up.

MAKING ADJUSTMENTS

Directors want to know if actors can take direction. If given direction, can you incorporate it immediately into your work. Sometimes adjustments can be relatively minor; "I'd like to see it again, but this time throw it away more." Other times, the director might ask for a major adjustment that changes the nature of the relationship, "You're not in love with this person anymore and you want out of the relationship." And there are the often frustrating general adjustments that leave actors struggling to interpret lines (such as, "More energy, please!" or "Do it again with more feeling!").

Remember, movie-making is a collaborative art. Don't be too rigid with your choices. Go in with a strong choice, but be flexible. There's usually more than one way to play a scene, so always try to go in with a few options. And if something isn't working, don't be afraid to let go of an old choice and try something new.

Some actors go overboard. Instead of making a specific adjustment, they'll toss out everything, including their good choices.

Faith called me frantically one day: she had been called back to read, but with certain changes. Usually, when she's given an adjustment, she is so busy focusing on it that when she steps into the audition room, that's all she can think about. We talked about her problem, and I suggested that she make the adjustment and forget about it. In taking my advice, Faith went into the room and couldn't remember a thing about

> *the scene. Later, she sighed and asked, "What was the problem?" I explained that she had left out a very important step—she still needed to enter the audition owning the character. Faith had swung from one end of the pendulum to another. Either she was too obsessed with getting the adjustment or she went in empty.*

How do you find the middle ground? Start off by working from the character's point of view. Make sure you have a strong opening beat to launch you into the scene, connect with your environment to ground you, and most important of all, trust the work and see where it takes you.

TIPS

- Use what the casting director is *not* giving you to affect the moment.

- Listening keeps you in the present. Don't forget to listen to what the other character is saying.

- Leave your homework outside the door.

- Trust your preparation and go with what is happening at the moment.

- Remember, it's a reading, not a performance. You don't have to be perfect.

QUICK TAKE

MOMENT-TO-MOMENT: *Now that you've done the work, trust it!*

- It's time to throw all of your preparation away and allow your choices to be affected by the moment.

- Be present and available to change.

—

SAMPLE SCENE BREAKDOWN

TRAYLOR HOWARD / *Two Guys and a Girl, Boston Commons*

I'd just been doing commercials. It was my second pilot season and I had tested a lot before, but I had no experience. I got close, but wasn't getting the parts, because I just hadn't done anything.

So I got to test for *Boston Commons*. It was between me and another girl. It was kind of unusual since they had to bring us into the room separately four different times, which is a lot for a test.

The director, Jamie Widdows, asked to speak with me. He was actually in *Animal House* and all I could think about was, "You were in *Animal House*." I could barely hear what he was telling me. But he gave me a note and I went in and I did it. And I ended up getting the job.

The next day, the producer, Max Smudgenick (*Will and Grace*) said, "I have to tell you . . . you were so calm that it made me slightly paranoid." He said, "I was wondering if you knew something that we didn't know." They weren't sure if I could be funny, because sometimes, depending on my mood, I like to just go in and do the work and do what I have to do. Sometimes I chat and sometimes I don't, and in that instance, I just had to stay focused. He said, "You really, really threw us."

But I got the lead, which was the beginning.

TRAYLOR HOWARD

MEETING GENE HACKMAN

As I worked on this book, I took a retreat to Santa Barbara's El Encanto, a beautiful, historic hotel tucked away in the hills. I spent the afternoon breaking down a scene from *I Never Sang For My Father* and, as I worked, images of the classic film with Gene Hackman, Melvyn Douglas and Estelle Parsons (written by Robert W. Anderson, based on his play; directed by Gilbert Cates) ran through my head.

Coincidentally, later that night I found myself seated across from Gene Hackman. I told him I thought he was one of the finest actors and that I loved his work, for which he thanked me graciously. Then I asked him if he had had to audition for the role of Gene. He admitted that he couldn't remember, but he did tell me that he used to love to audition during his early years—auditioning was his only chance to really act.

I nodded in agreement and told him that I encourage my students to approach each audition as a chance to express their talent. Off he went, with that devilish smirk we all know so well.

Yes, it's been years since Gene Hackman has had to audition, but when he did, he *enjoyed* the process.

Now that I've taken you through all the steps of breaking down a scene, let's put these steps into action. Here is a scene from the classic film, *I Never Sang For My Father*[1]. It is a confrontational scene between a brother and sister who love each other dearly, but who have passionately opposing views on how to take care of their recently widowed father. It is an emotional piece, layered in pain and resentment. As you read through the scene, search for hints in both dialogue and stage directions that will help you uncover your character's innermost needs.

When you begin your breakdown, remember: always come from the character's point of view. In answering the breakdown questions later in this chapter, answer them as if you were the character (Gene or Alice). Try to get out of your head and into your body and emotions as quickly as you can so you stop intellectualizing the information. How much time you have to prepare will determine how much depth your analysis will have. If you only have a few minutes, at least be clear on *who* you are and *what* you want from the other character.

---

[1] The 1970 film was nominated for three Academy Awards™: Best Actor (Douglas); Best Supporting Actor (Hackman); Best Adapted Screenplay

                    GENE
You can go with a clear
conscience. I'm doing this
because I want to.

                    ALICE
You're doing it because you
can't help yourself.

                    GENE
Look, when I want to be
analyzed, I'll pay for it.

                    ALICE
Didn't you see yourself there,
when he started to rage? You
shrank.

                    GENE
I shrank at the ugliness of
what was happening.

                    ALICE
You're staying because you
can't stand his wrath the day
you say, "Dad, I'm leaving."
... You've never been able to
stand up to his anger.

                    GENE
Look, Alice...

                    ALICE
He'll call you ungrateful...
and you'll believe him.

                    GENE
    (Lashing out)
What do you want us to do?
Shall we get out a white paper?
Let it be known that we...
Alice and Gene, have done all
that we can to make this old
man happy in his old age...
without inconveniencing
ourselves, of course... And he

has refused our help. So, if he
falls and hits his head and
lies there until he rots, it is
not our fault.

          ALICE
I don't think anyone expects
either of us to ruin our lives
over an unreasonable old man.

          GENE
It is not going to ruin my
life.

          ALICE
It is!

          GENE
A few weeks... a month.

          ALICE
Forever!

          GENE
Alice, let's stop this. I know
what I'm going to do. I just
can't do anything else. Maybe
there isn't the same thing
between a Mother and
Daughter... but the "old man"
in me feels something very
deep... wants to extend some
kind of mercy to that old
man...I never had a father... I
ran away from him... He ran
away from me... Maybe he's
right. Maybe it's time we found
each other.

          ALICE
Excuse me for saying so, but I
find that a lot of sentimental
crap!...What do you think
you'll find?

                    GENE
I don't know.

                    ALICE
You hope to find love. Couldn't
you tell from what he just said
what you're going to find?

                    GENE
Don't give me the textbooks,
Alice.

                    ALICE
He wants your balls...and he's
had them!!
        (Gene starts to leave)
I'm sorry. I want to shock you.
When has he ever regarded you
as a man, an equal, a male?
When you were a Marine...and
you only did that for him. You
didn't want to be a Marine.
"Now Poppa, will you love me?"
When has he ever been proud of
the things you do...the things
you value? When did he ever
mention your teaching, or your
books, except in scorn?

                    GENE
I just don't want to let my
father die a stranger.

                    ALICE
You're looking for something
that isn't there, Gene. You're
looking for a Mother's love in
a Father... Mothers are soft
and yielding. Fathers are hard
and rough, to teach us the way
of the world, which is rough,
which is mean, which is selfish
and prejudiced. I've always
been grateful for what he did
to me, kicking me out. He
taught me a marvelous lesson

and has made me able to face a
lot. And there has been a lot
to face... and I'm grateful as
Hell to him. Because if I
couldn't get understanding and
compassion from a Father, who
could I get it from? So I
learned, and didn't expect it,
and I've found very little, and
so I'm grateful to him. I'm
grateful as hell to him. (The
growing intensity ends in tears)

      GENE
   (He moves to her and
   touches her)
I'll stay Alice...for a while,
at least... for whatever
reasons. Let's not argue
anymore.

      ALICE
And Peggy?

      GENE
We'll see. She'll be here in a
week for a meeting.

      ALICE
Don't lose her, Gene. Maybe I'm
still fouled up on myself, but
I think I've spoken near the
truth about you. Suddenly, I
miss Mother so...

FIRST READ

1. Relationship

- *What's going on for my character in relation to the scene?*

(Gene) I feel guilty. I have so much conflict regarding my father. I hate him, and yet, I want him to love me. If I'm not there for him, who will be? I want to protect my dad out of guilt. This scene is about my struggle between love and hate, between caring and resenting.

(Alice) Once again, I must witness the same unfair, cruel behavior of my father towards my brother; it's what I ran away from years ago. It makes me sick inside to see Gene put up with this crap. I wish my brother could see how much our father is destroying his life.

In this scene, both characters are faced with looking at the truth about themselves. For Gene, it is his fear of never really knowing his father. For Alice, the scene exposes her old wounds.

- *What is my relationship with the other main character and how do I feel about him/her?*

(Gene's relationship to Alice) She's a wonderful woman and I love her very much but she is self-righteous and so full of anger. She would have me dump my father, but I can't leave knowing that he needs me.

(Alice's relationship to Gene) I love Gene, but I can't stand watching him throw away his life taking care of that unappreciative, selfish old man. Gene is sweet and kind and deserves more.

- *Are there other characters mentioned in the scene and how do I feel about them?*

(Gene's relationship to his father) This is the most complex relationship of all. My father has never told me that he loves me. All I have ever wanted is for us to love and understand one another. I hate the way I feel about myself when I'm with him. I cower to him and lose my own identity.

(Gene's relationship to his mother) I loved my mom. I knew she always wanted the best for me even though she could never support me around my father. My mother lost all of her power when it came to him. Didn't we all?

(Gene's relationship to Peggy) Peggy is like a breath of fresh air to me. She represents the possibility of future happiness. I could see spending the rest of my life with her, but it would mean moving away and I don't know if I can leave my father alone.

(Alice's relationship to her father) I despise him! I have not spoken to him in years. He's a selfish, unfeeling man who only makes me feel rage when I am in his presence.

(Alice's relationship to her mother) I loved my mother. I always felt sorry for her because she got so little love from the old man. Now that she's gone, I regret my lost time with her.

- *Where am I? Where does the scene take place?*
  We are in my father's house, where we grew up. It brings back every painful memory of our childhood—like it was yesterday.

SECOND READ

2. **Intention**

- *What is my overall intention in the scene?*

  (Gene) To stop my sister from interfering in my life.

  (Alice) To make Gene leave this horrible prison.

- *What do I want from the other character? What is my action verb? What are my opposing adjectives?*

  (Gene) I want to push away my caring, but interfering sister.

  (Alice) I want to shake my loving, but weak brother into realizing that he has to move on with his life.

- *What are my obstacles in the scene?*

  (Gene) One obstacle is my love for Alice, which makes it more difficult for me to shut her out. The other obstacle is my father who sits in the other room. I don't want him to overhear our conversation.

  (Alice) My love for Gene makes it hard for me to stay angry with him.

- *What is my key phrase?*

  (Gene) "I just do not want to let my father die a stranger."

  (Alice) "Suddenly I miss Mother so."

3. History

- ### *What is my character's background?*

    (Gene) I grew up wealthy, with everything a child could want except the love of a father. Although my dad was one of the most important men in town, I grew up feeling inferior. Later, I watched my wife die a slow, painful death. I have just returned from California where I met a wonderful woman doctor whom I wish to marry.

    (Alice) I grew up the same as my brother, but I felt even lonelier. I had very little self-confidence and was extremely insecure.

- ### *What is the history of my relationships?*

    (Gene) No matter how hard I've tried to please my father, it's never been enough. From my earliest memories, he's never seemed proud of me. My mother was an island of warmth and security. I took refuge in her love. I always looked up to my older sister and I missed her terribly when she left.

    (Alice) My father threw me out of the house when I wanted to marry a Jew. He's never accepted me. My mother stood by and allowed it to happen. I love my brother. He needs me so I've returned for his sake. I can't wait to get back to my safe home.

- ### *What is the history of the times?*
    This story takes place in the '60s, when certain prejudices were more strongly felt. Today, Alice's father probably wouldn't have reacted negatively to her marrying a Jew. Also, family life has changed since then—it is not uncommon for children to live 3,000 miles from their parents. Gene moving to California today might not be such a big deal, and he also might not feel such a strong sense of responsibility to care for his elderly father.

    As you elaborate on your character's history, remember that if it's not written in the script, you must use your imagination to create it. But please make sure that it's appropriate to the material.

4. Personalization
History and personalization go hand-in-hand. Once again, depending on time, expound on your character's history by using images and sensory work.

- **If I were the character in this situation, how would I feel?**

  (Gene) If I were Gene and I just returned from my mother's funeral, I would be devastated over the loss of my mother, who was always there for me.

  (Alice) If I were Alice and I just came back from the funeral, I would shut down any feelings of sadness or pain. And, I would feel empty.

- **What images and sensory work can I use to connect me to my character's feelings?**
  I suggest recreating the burial service because of its strong emotional content.

  (Gene) I can smell the dampness in the air. A chill races through my body. I can feel the dirt in my hand as I toss a handful of it on my mother's casket. I can see my father standing stoically before the crowd. I hear the muffled cries of the mourners. A salty tear drips down my cheek as I say good-bye to my mom.

  (Alice) I can feel the muscles in my back and shoulders tense up and I can taste the awful dryness in my throat. My father's aftershave reeks as I watch him casually greet his old pals as if he were at a party. I hear my brother's strangled sobs as I touch his ice-cold hand, then pull away.

- **How can I, the actor, relate to my character's situation?**
  Here's where you must step out of the character's point of view and use your own personal experiences so that you fuse yourself with your character.

  (Gene) I can connect to Gene's love for his mother and how terribly sad he is. However, I would be much more distraught and would have to be careful not to connect too deeply to that part of me that is not appropriate to Gene's reaction.

  (Alice) It's harder for me to connect to Alice's detachment, but she does love her brother and I can relate to that part of her. Though I understand Alice's distance from her father, I would react differently: I would comfort my father and brother. Alice would never do that. She would be afraid to let go and feel her pain.

- ***What feeling or event from my own life can I substitute for my character's?***
  If you get stuck and cannot connect to your character's feelings or situation, you can substitute an incident or feeling from your own life—but during preparation only. Don't rely on substitution during your actual audition. Here's an example:

  (Margie) Although my mother is still alive, my father died about 15 years ago and I recall how I felt during that period. I can substitute the imagery of my father's burial to help me connect to my character. Again, I only use what feeds me in the work and helps me jump start into the character's emotions.

- ***If I have more time, what imaginary incidents can I create through my senses to help complete my character's history?***
  Both Gene and Alice have such a strong negative history with their father, it's important to have that emotional juice churning during their conversation. Therefore, you really need to develop those early memories. Here's an example of an imaginary incident:

  (Gene) I can smell the dusty air at home plate as I nervously kick up clouds of dust. I can feel the sweat pouring down my face as I wait with bat in hand for my father to throw the ball. My heart pounds with fear at the thought that I'll miss the pitch. I can see my father's face filled with disappointment and disgust when I do miss. There's a metallic taste in my mouth as my dad approaches.

  (Alice) I can smell my Mother's pot roast cooking as my father screams at me for wanting to marry a Jew. I can taste the sour juices as my stomach turns, listening to him bellow. I can feel the heat from the kitchen as my mother wipes her brow with her apron, avoiding their confrontation.

5. **V.I.P.S. (Values, Intellect, Physical traits, Social status)**

- ***What are the similarities and differences between me and my character?***

GENE'S V.I.P.S.
(Values, Intellect, Physical Traits, Social Status)

	– SIMILARITIES –	– DIFFERENCES –	
		GENE	ME
VALUES/ MORALS	caring kind gentle loving honest	feels like victim sacrifices for parents	powerful take care of self
INTELLECT	smart well-educated both teachers	more scholarly serious	intuitive lighter
EMOTIONAL	strong need for acceptance large capacity for love close to Mom in touch w/own pain	more depressed holds resentment	happier communicate my feeling
PHYSICAL TRAITS	same age same aches & pains	slower more deliberate more cautious hesitates	quicker walk & talk faster more confident make a bold entrance
SOCIAL STATUS	comes from $ loves teaching	stops himself afraid to take risks works for others drives older Volvo saves money	push to succeed risk-taker self-employed drive sports car spend money

ALICE'S V.I.P.S.
(Values, Intellect, Physical Traits, Social Status)

	– SIMILARITIES –	*– DIFFERENCES –*	
		ALICE	*ME*
VALUES/ MORALS	honest care about our children love our siblings strong-willed	tough hates father painfully aware of the world's cruelty	gentle love my father look at world thru rose- colored glasses
INTELLECT	bright well-educated speak well	more intellectual book smart serious	more worldly intuitive humorous
EMOTIONAL	afraid of being hurt express anger	protected shuts down rarely cries	freely express love available cry easily
PHYSICAL TRAITS	walk w/ confidence similar in age	stiff, controlled talks slower more precise '60s attire, dresses plain	loose talk fast casual dresser attractive put together
SOCIAL STATUS	come from $	dutiful wife homemaker drives a Toyota convertible	more independent very ambitious drive a Saab

6.   Opening Beat

- ***What occurs the moment before the scene begins? What physical life can I bring into it?***

(Gene) My father and sister have just gotten into their usual fight. I can't leave if it means I'm going to hurt the old man. And Alice just doesn't understand that. She had no right to speak for me. It only upset everyone. The moment before the scene, I'm thinking, "I can't take this anymore. I've got to get out of here!" I leave the room to escape their arguing.

(Alice) I just witnessed my father repeat the same destructive behavior with my brother that he used with me. I can't stand the way he treats Gene, who has just left the room; I'm following him. For me, the moment before the scene is the image of my brother seething in silence as my father talks down to him.

THIRD READ

7.   Units and Transitions

- ***Where, in the scene, do the changes occur that cause the focus to shift?*** Mark off the unit blocks in pencil.

- ***Are there any baby beats?*** Note them as "bb" and don't forget that baby beats are subjective and may change from moment to moment.

- ***What different tactics can I use to get my intention met?*** Label your character's adjustments by units. Remember, the same tactic may be used for more than one unit, or different tactics may be used for the same unit.

                    GENE
        You can go with a clear
        conscience. I'm doing this
        because I want to.

                    ALICE
        You're doing it because you
        can't help yourself.

(dismissingly)   GENE   **(angrily)**
        Look, when I want to be
        analyzed, I'll pay for it.

                    ALICE
        Didn't you see yourself there,
        when he started to rage? You
        shrank.

                    GENE
        I shrank at the ugliness of
        what was happening.

                    ALICE
        You're staying because you
        can't stand his wrath the day
        you say, "Dad, I'm leaving."
        ... You've never been able to
        stand up to his anger.

                    GENE
        Look, Alice...

                    ALICE
        He'll call you ungrateful...
        and you'll believe him.

Gene's Adjustments		Alice's Adjustments
	GENE (Lashing out) What do you want us to do? Shall we get out a white paper? Let it be known that we... Alice and Gene, have done all that we can to make this old	
(angrily)	man happy in his old age... without inconveniencing ourselves, of course... And he has refused our help. So, if he falls and hits his head and lies there until he rots, it is not our fault.	**(resentfully)**
	ALICE I don't think anyone expects either of us to ruin our lives over an unreasonable old man.	
(defiantly)	**GENE** It is not going to ruin my life.	
	ALICE It is!	
	GENE A few weeks... a month.	
	ALICE Forever!	
(compassionately)	**GENE** Alice, let's stop this. I know what I'm going to do. I just can't do anything else. Maybe there isn't the same thing between a Mother and Daughter... but the "old man" in me feels something very deep... wants to extend some kind of mercy to that old man...I never had a father...	

Gene's
Adjustments

I ran away from him... He ran
away from me... Maybe he's
right. Maybe it's time we found
each other.

                    ALICE   Alice's
                                               Adjustments
Excuse me for saying so, but I   **(emphatically)**
find that a lot of sentimental
crap!...What do you think
you'll find?

                    GENE
I don't know.

                    ALICE
You hope to find love. Couldn't
you tell from what he just said
what you're going to find?

                    GENE
Don't give me the textbooks,
Alice.

                    ALICE
He wants your balls...and he's
had them!!

          (Gene starts to leave)   **(persuasively)**
I'm sorry. I want to shock you.
When has he ever regarded you
as a man, an equal, a male?
When you were a Marine...and
you only did that for him. You
didn't want to be a Marine.
"Now Poppa, will you love me?"
When has he ever been proud of
the things you do...the things
you value? When did he ever
mention your teaching, or your
books, except in scorn?

Key Phrase   GENE
(sadly)
I just don't want to let my
father die a stranger.

ALICE
You're looking for something
that isn't there, Gene. You're
looking for a Mother's love in
a Father... Mothers are soft
and yielding. Fathers are hard
and rough, to teach us the way
of the world, which is rough,
which is mean, which is selfish
and prejudiced. I've always
been grateful for what he did
to me, kicking me out. He
taught me a marvelous lesson
and has made me able to face a
lot. And there has been a lot
to face... and I'm grateful as
Hell to him. Because if I
couldn't get understanding and
compassion from a Father, who
could I get it from? So I
learned, and didn't expect it,
and I've found very little, and
so I'm grateful to him. I'm
grateful as hell to him. (The
growing intensity ends in
tears)

(painfully)

(lovingly)

GENE
(He moves to her and
touches her)
I'll stay Alice...for a while,
at least... for whatever
reasons. Let's not argue
anymore.

ALICE
And Peggy?

(lovingly)

GENE
We'll see. She'll be here in a
week for a meeting.

Gene's Adjustments

Alice's Adjustments

```
                ALICE
Don't lose her, Gene. Maybe I'm
still fouled up on myself, but
I think I've spoken near the
truth about you. Suddenly, I
miss Mother so...
```

Key Phrase (sadly)

8. Core and Masking

- *What are my character's true feelings? In what ways does my character mask their core?*

  (Gene) My core is the fear of losing my father's love. I am also filled with guilt. I'm afraid of being a bad person or a bad son. I mask my fear with indifference as well as anger.

  (Alice) My deepest core feeling is the pain of abandonment. All through my life I have felt unloved and I am terrified to feel that pain. My mask of anger begins to crumble when I talk about the prejudice I had to face. Now the facade isn't working so well.

- *What is my vulnerable moment?*

  (Gene) My vulnerable moment happens to be my key phrase, "I just do not want to let my father die a stranger." This is the reason for my behavior, the reason why I can't go on with my life, the reason why I'm willing to live with my father and sacrifice my relationship with Peggy.

  (Alice) My vulnerable moment is also my key phrase, "Suddenly, I miss Mother so . . . " By the end of the scene, I am in touch with my pain as well as the loss of my mother's love. My expression of anger has taken me on a journey that ends in sad longing.

9. Humor

- *Where is the lightness in the scene?*
  Remember, it's not about being funny—it's about letting your personality shine through in a light moment or a sarcastic reaction. It's not always easy to find the lightness but you must look for it.

(Gene) It was difficult to find a light moment for Gene but he does give way to sarcasm in his line, "Let it be known that we . . . Alice and Gene, have done all that we can to make this old man happy in his old age . . . without inconveniencing ourselves, of course . . . "

(Alice) Alice's ironic statement could be considered her light moment, "Maybe I'm still fouled up on myself, but I think I've spoken near the truth about you."

10. Moment to Moment

- ***You've done all the work, now trust it.*** Be present in the reading. Don't try to replicate your homework. Be in the "now" and allow yourself to go moment to moment.

PART 3
THE HABER PHRASE TECHNIQUE®

—

READING IN PHRASES

I've got rhythm, I've got music . . .

CREE SUMMER / *Sweet Justice, A Different World*

When I first came to Margie's class, I was eighteen and had never studied acting. I was very unhappy about taking the class—it was something my manager was forcing on me. Needless to say, it was an exceptional experience and I gained confidence.

When I got an audition for *A Different World,* I had the sides in advance and I knew them inside out. I was really confident about going in, only to arrive at the audition and discover I had the wrong sides. They wanted me to go in within the next five minutes and read something from *A Raisin in the Sun.* Then they said, "Make it funny!" Well, I thought, *A Raisin in the Sun* is about as funny as a hernia or a root canal with no anesthesia. So I was looking at the sides and I was really scared and then my name was called.

I was tested on the spot with my knowledge of cold reading. Margie tells you to set up the scene in advance, so I danced around and did some funny things and used my technique and they adored it! It worked and it got me the job. So I really have to give credit to her technique for getting me that job. If I didn't know how to use the technique and if I wasn't confident about it, I would have been afraid of the lines and I wouldn't have been able to include my interpretation.

CREE SUMMER

Actress Heather Medway, our "network queen," had gone to the net-works at least five times in one season, but she hadn't yet booked a show. The input on her had always been, "Heather was fantastic! We loved her but we just decided to go with a different look." She then had an audition for Viper. Heather did her usual wonderful reading but, this time, one of the producers said, "We love it, but we'd like you to read a different scene. I'm having it faxed over."

Meanwhile, Heather could hear the two other actresses who were auditioning for the same role, in the waiting room, beginning to panic as they overheard the conversation. The producer handed Heather the scene and said, "Look it over quickly and do the best you can with it." Most actors would have been extremely intimidated, but Heather took the scene with confidence and, using my Phrase Technique, she not only nailed the audition, she booked the series.

Whether you are asked to do a cold reading on the spot like Heather, or you have days to prepare, the phrase technique I've developed will give you the freedom to use the paper, rather than make excuses for it. My technique gives you permission to stay on the page longer than you think you can without having to memorize the whole scene.

THE TRAP OF MEMORIZING

Many actors believe that if they memorize the scene, they'll have more control over the audition. Actually, the opposite is true.

Actor Brandon Hooper came to me for a private session to work on an audition for a new film. He was distraught because he had not done well on his last few auditions. He admitted he had gone back to his old habit of memorizing—during an important audition, he had tried to memorize the whole piece. He was doing well, but, right in the middle of an emotional moment, he had forgotten his lines and couldn't find his place in the script. It threw him and he was never able to recover.

As you can tell from Brandon's experience, memorizing can get you into trouble. Here are some good reasons *not* to memorize:

1. **You spend too much time memorizing the lines rather than breaking down the scene and doing the real work.**
   One of the primary differences between auditioning and performing is time. For an audition, you are only given a short time to work on a piece, whereas for the actual shoot, you may have had weeks or even months to prepare. Don't waste your valuable time trying to memorize the scene. You'll be lulled into a false sense of security, thinking you know your

lines well. But, you'll lose them if you get nervous. When that happens, you'll stop connecting to the *life* of the character and your focus will shift to worrying about the forgotten words. In such a short time, you can't possibly *own* the words. Concentrate on breaking down the scene and using your precious time wisely.

2. **When you forget your lines, it registers in your eyes that you have forgotten the words and this will take away from the reading.**
Don't think for a moment that the casting director doesn't notice the sudden flash of panic in your eyes as you blank out on the words! It's as disruptive for them as it is for you and it pulls both of you out of the reading. Your character vanishes as you sift through your memory and desperately try to remember the correct line.

3. **If you don't say the words as written, it could have a negative effect on the auditioners.**
It's not uncommon when memorizing to make up words. Actors often concentrate on the *sense* of what's being said and thereby sacrifice the written word. It's important to realize that the casting people (the director, the casting director, the producer) have heard the scene many times before and can probably recite the lines verbatim. When you ad lib, it throws them off and they lose their concentration.

If you veer from the script, you'll really be in trouble if the writer is sitting in the room. This is especially true of comedy, where there is a certain rhythm to the words. For example, Neil Simon has talked about the musical flow of his dialogue. In his play, *The Prisoner of Second Avenue,* Simon writes the following dialogue exchange: "When you came back into the building, did you notice anyone suspicious looking?" "Everyone in this building is suspicious looking!" It's not as funny if you were to alter it by saying, "When you came back into the building, did you notice anyone suspicious looking?" "Everyone is suspicious!" You lose the rhythm of the exchange. In rehearsal, when actors have commented to Simon that a certain line isn't funny, his reply has been, "You're not saying it right." Writers spend countless hours making sure each word and punctuation mark is perfect. As an actor, you should respect this effort.

4. **You are at a psychological disadvantage if you go into a reading with a memorized performance.**
Think about it. Two actors come in to read for the same part. The first actor has spent the previous three days carefully memorizing the whole scene. He comes in with a full-blown performance. He does a good job, but you ask yourself, "Is that the best he can do?" The second actor doesn't have the scene memorized. He freely uses the paper for a terrific

read. You are equally impressed, but you can't help wondering how much better the second actor might be with more preparation.

It's an audition, not a performance. You are allowed to use the paper. Psychologically, it gives you the advantage by reminding the casting people that there is room for improvement.

DEVELOPING THE PHRASE TECHNIQUE

In the 1970s, I taught speech and cold reading at the Strasberg Institute in Los Angeles. It was like teaching at the United Nations! We had actors from all over the world—France, Germany, Spain, South America—who spoke different languages and with different accents. One of my jobs was to help the actors eliminate their thick accents. Most of the students mistakenly believed that the best way to lose an accent was to over-enunciate each word separately. You can imagine how choppy their speech sounded—it was staccato and artificial, with no natural flow.

During my time at the Strasberg Institute, I thought back to my years as a speech therapist in the Culver City School District, where I worked on articulation with first and second graders. I taught them to speak in phrases, linking the end sound of one word to the beginning sound of the next. While teaching them how to pronounce the "Z" sound, for example, words like "His ball" became "hizball" and "hands off" became "handzoff." I thought this same phrasing technique might help my foreign students at Strasberg.

Rather than teaching them one word at a time, I began teaching them how to speak in groups of words. As American English speakers, we link the small words and emphasize the more important ones. Articles such as "the," "a;" prepositions such as "in," "of," "on," "around," "in-between;" and conjunctions such as "and," "or," "but" should be linked to the nouns. Small, unimportant words need not be emphasized at all, such as the small words in the following phrases (in which the more important words are underlined): "into the <u>house</u>," "over the <u>bridge</u>," "under a <u>chair</u>."

I realized that I could apply the same phrase technique to cold reading.

THE HABER PHRASE TECHNIQUE®

Musicians learn to see ahead, in groups of notes, rather than one note at a time. Similarly, typists type in groups of words, not letter by letter. Actors, dealing with a cumbersome script in hand, should use a similar approach when auditioning. The Haber Phrase Technique® is a rhythmic method that allows you the luxury of staying on the paper in groups of words, or "phrases." It lets you keep your eyes down on the page for two or three phrases at a time, rather than bobbing them up and down every two or three words.

The Haber Phrase Technique® is a three-step process that works unit by unit:

1. **Eyes are up for the opening phrase(s) in the beginning of each new unit.**

   When you start a new unit, look down on the page to pick up the first phrase or two. Then, look up and come from a thought before speaking. Always start with a thought.

2. **Eyes go down on the page for the next group of phrases, then back up to connect with your partner for a few phrases, returning down to the paper to repeat the cycle.**

   When your eyes go down on the page, your intention must be just as strong as when your eyes are up. It is your need to connect to your partner that draws your eyes off the page. Make sure that you come up for at least three or four words.

   When you're up for a group of phrases, always finish the last word of the phrase before going back down to the paper. I call it "landing," which establishes a touch point with your partner and completes the communication. Landing is a commitment of your intention to the relationship. By landing, you are investing what you want with the other person; you are making a commitment to communicating that thought.

3. **Eyes up at the end of the unit, for the resolution.**

   When you complete a unit, there is a moment of consideration that I call a "resolution." A resolution occurs at the end of each unit. It is a part of the closing beat that contains a thought and supports the actor being present. More than a landing, it is a check in time when you ask yourself, "Did I succeed or fail in my communication?" Having your eyes off the paper at the end of the unit gives you time to take in the other person; it also gives you time to gather your own thoughts and emotions.

PUTTING THE TECHNIQUE INTO PRACTICE—*L.A. LAW* CLOSING ARGUMENT

Now let's put the technique into practice. As you begin to familiarize yourself with the concept of reading in phrases, don't get bogged down with the technicalities. It may seem technical at first, but once you've learned the technique, you'll throw it away and learn to trust the rhythm of the piece, coming off the paper when you feel you should.

Below is a closing argument from the television series, *L.A. Law*. For now, we are not going to break down the scene. Its insertion here is strictly for the purpose of practicing the Haber Phrase Technique®. I have broken down the argument into units, as you already would have done in your ten-step scene breakdown.

Normally, you would never indicate whether your eyes are up or down on the page, but for teaching purposes, I have underlined those phrases where your eyes may be *down on the paper*.

This is an example of only one possible way of phrasing the piece. If you are good at remembering lines, you may be able to stay up longer for six or seven phrases, then your eyes will go down for three or four phrases. But remember, once your eyes go down on the page, they must stay down for at least a phrase or more, not just a word or two. And, don't forget, your eyes are always up in the beginning of a unit as well as at the end of the unit for the resolution.

Kuzak sits down. Mathers rises slowly.

                 MATHERS
To paraphrase a great American patriot—<u>I may not agree with a single word of what Mr. Kuzak says, but I would</u> defend to my death his right to say it. <u>And in the end, isn't that what this case</u> is really about— freedom. <u>Those precious rights, guaranteed under the Constitution,</u> to every American citizen <u>to express himself as he chooses</u> in thought, speech and action

---

... You've heard a lot of conflicting testimony here— <u>maybe smoking is dangerous—</u> maybe it isn't. <u>But if smoking is dangerous, so is flying in an airplane. Or skiing down a mountain.</u> Or even crossing the street. <u>All of us, everyday, measure risks and make choices.</u> That's exactly what Mr. O'Brien did. <u>Only now he's asking to have it both ways. He wants the freedom to do what he wants. But he also wants someone else to take the responsibility</u> if he doesn't like the outcome.

```
As much compassion as we may
feel for Mr. O'Brien, that does
not entitle him to seek out
scapegoats and financial
windfalls.
```

```
Ladies and gentlemen, in the
furtherance of your oath as
jurors, I ask you to set
aside your emotions and draw
that important distinction.
Thank you.
```

Read the speech a few times and practice the eye technique until it starts to flow naturally. Notice how the lengths of the phrases vary to avoid predictability.

- Are you surprised about how long you can stay down on the page? As long as your intention remains strong, your reading will not be affected when you look down on the paper.

- Did you find that you phrased differently each time? This is normal. The technique is not something that should ever be set or planned. Just keep the three basic steps in mind:
  1. Eyes up in the beginning of the unit;
  2. Eyes down in the middle for a group of phrases; then
  3. Eyes up at the end for the resolution.

PUT YOUR THUMB INTO ACTION

It's easy during a cold reading to get lost when your eyes return to the page—you're in the middle of an emotional moment and you go down for a line and words are swimming everywhere! You start to panic because you can't find your place. Here's where your thumb comes in handy! Whichever hand is holding the paper, follow your lines in the script by using your thumb, which becomes your marker. As you complete one set of lines, briefly grab the paper with your other hand, moving your thumb to the next set. Keep practicing this technique until your thumb seamlessly moves along with you.

"THAT DARN PAPER"

Most actors hold their scripts at their sides, trying to pretend they're not really doing a reading. Then, when they need a line, they cheat a look, momentarily distorting their face as they frantically sneak their eyes down to the "forbidden" page. They think of the paper as a foreign object that should be quickly discarded so they can get down to the business of acting ("If only I didn't have this stupid piece of paper in my hand, then I could really act!").

Don't be afraid of the paper. It is connected to your feelings and carries an emotion—for example, if you're angry, hold the paper with anger. You should include the script as a part of your physical life—the paper should not be held like a tray on which to serve food, nor should it be held so low that you have to dive down to the page to get your lines; it should not be curled up between your legs or lay helplessly on your lap; it should not be hidden in the fold of your arms or held far off to your side.

The paper should be held out in front of you with a bent arm, your elbow tucked in at your side. Your arm should be loose enough so that the paper can breathe in and out with you; it should always stay in the same plane as your body. Don't let that arm drop! Whichever way you turn, the paper should go with you. Treat it as an extension of you.

From the Studio

Each month, I introduce the phrase technique to a fresh group of actors in my eight session "boot camp." Some are afraid to let go of their old habits, clinging to every one they ever learned. But, as I've said, the technique involves trust and a willingness to change. Some pick it up quickly, others take longer to own it. At the end of class, once every actor has practiced the technique individually, I ask two students to use it in a scene, in this case, Jack and Hannah. At first, they were having difficulty knowing when to come up and go down for their lines.

Margie: Jack, you need to stay down on the paper longer. Your eyes were bobbing up and down. Not every sentence you say is important.

Jack: I thought I had to come up after every sentence.

Margie: No, you can join sentences when you're down on the page. Ignore the punctuation and then come up after a few phrases.

Hannah: Even if it's a question mark?

Margie: Yes, as long as you keep your intention strong when your eyes are down. Let's try it again.

Jack and Hannah ran through the scene again to give the class an idea of what the technique looks like in action. Here are some of the student reactions:

- "It looked so easy and effortless."
- "They were listening so much more."
- "It never bothered me that their eyes were on the paper."
- "It looked so natural."
- "I never even noticed them going down on the page."
- "It flowed. It didn't drag. They really kept the scene going."
- "It looked like they had worked on it for weeks."

I asked Jack and Hannah how they felt using this new technique.

Jack: I usually try to memorize my scene. It was such a relief not to have to worry about the lines.

Hannah: Once I got the hang of it, stopped thinking about it and trusted my intent, it flowed automatically. It didn't feel technical, it just felt right.

COMMONLY ASKED QUESTIONS REGARDING THE TECHNIQUE

- **How do I keep the phrase technique from getting too technical?**
  While learning this technique, some of my clients get too caught up in the technical aspects of the process. They concentrate on going up and down with their eyes and are afraid to stay on the page. If you *trust* the phrase technique to work, then you will focus on what really counts— who you are and what you want in the scene. Let the technique help you achieve your intention, rather than let it get in your way.

- **How do I know when to come off the paper?**
  You will automatically come off the paper when you *need* to connect to your partner. When you stop thinking about when to come up, it becomes an emotional decision. That's why I discourage you from marking your ups and downs in the script. These will change with each reading, based on your needs at that moment.

- **Why are landings so important?**
  Landings force you to make a commitment to your choice. There's no going back after you land. When you are making a point and your eyes land on the other person, you complete the connection and therefore you risk being seen.

- **What's the difference between a landing and a resolution?**
  Though they both deliver a message to the other character, a resolution also includes the act of receiving your partner's message and having thoughts about that communication. That takes time.

- **Why do some casting directors ask us to memorize the scene?**
  They may be tired of actors forgetting their lines, bobbing their eyes up and down on the paper (which is always distracting) or losing their intent when their eyes hit the page. Every once in awhile, you'll meet a casting person who prefers memorization; in that case, you have no choice but to do so. But most casting directors are against memorization. If you own the Haber Phrase Technique, these casting directors won't care if your eyes are on or off the paper.

TIPS

- *Don't* memorize the entire scene. *Do* memorize your first line and other key phrases.

- Make sure you come off the page with a group of words, not just one.

- Don't lose your life as your eyes go down to the page. Your intention should remain just as strong on as off the paper.

- Make sure your hand holding the paper stays active and alive. Think of it as an extension of what you are feeling.

- Don't worry about when to land. If your intention is clear, you will naturally land to complete your thought.

—

USING THE HABER PHRASE TECHNIQUE® IN A SCENE

"Shall We Dance?"

LISA RINNA / Melrose Place, Days of Our Lives

I'm reading for *The Hogan Family* on NBC. They've seen 200 girls. I've gotten through the whole process, so I go in to screen test with Jason Bateman to play his girlfriend. (He's never had a girlfriend on the show.)

In the scene, the girl's room is a mess. It's a college dorm and there's stuff everywhere. So I go in for the screen test, and there are about twenty people in this small office at NBC. I take the pillows off the couch. They have a dish of M&Ms and they've got stuff on a little coffee table. I take everything, and I throw it all over the floor. I throw the M&Ms all over the room so that when the scene starts, I pick up all the stuff and, of course, I have to eat a few M&Ms, to make it very physical . So then, during the scene, I decide to kiss Jason Bateman. (And there's no kiss in the scene.) I give him a big smooch and I get the part.

It's really about M&Ms. I think the M&Ms were the key. Because I threw the M&Ms all over the floor and then I started eating them, for some reason, I think that's what got me the job. And then the kiss . . .

LISA RINNA

MICHAEL EASTON / *Total Recall, Ally McBeal*

I remember being in beginning class with John Corbett. At first, John and I were so bad at learning the technique that we would always have to go last and be paired together so Margie could let the rest of the class go home early. She would keep John and me late working hard, but somehow the two of us must have learned something because we both went on to do a little bit of work.

You've heard the phrase, "It takes two to tango." In the tango, two dancers glide together in a sensual rhythm, punctuated with quick, percussive steps. One person leads, the other follows. Two bodies move across the floor as one, in sync with the music. They do not stop to think about the steps and they must forget about the mechanics of the dance, letting the music guide them, otherwise they would lose the fluidity of their performance.

Working with a partner in an audition is very much like dancing the tango. You take your cues from the other person. If your eyes are down on the paper at the wrong time, how can you receive those cues and go moment to moment? You can't. It's impossible. Even if you're working opposite a casting director and he is giving you very little, you still must work off him. The Haber Phrase Technique allows you to be available and alert for the audition's unexpected changes. The flirtatious twinkle in your partner's eye can stir you to new heights for your next line, but only if you're present in the moment to observe it. Just as you trust the music of the dance, you must learn to trust the rhythm of the technique and let it lead you.

THERE'S NO SUCH THING AS A MONOLOGUE

Remember back in high school, when you had to audition for *Twelfth Night* by reciting a Shakespearean monologue? Do you recall how silly you felt talking to yourself for hours in the mirror with no one talking back? Or how about flipping though those awful, generic monologue books, desperately trying to find a good audition piece for an agent? In my estimation, there is no such thing as a monologue. In life, there's always someone talking and someone listening. Even in a soliloquy, when there's no one else around and you're talking to yourself, you usually answer your own questions.

In the previous chapter, when we worked on the closing argument from *L.A. Law*, most of you probably viewed it as a monologue. Actually, it is a dialogue between the attorney and everyone present in the courtroom. There are times when the attorney directs his lines to the jury, the defendant, the judge or the opposing counsel. If you assume the role of the attorney, just as you would use your imagination to place these other characters in your environment, you must also check in with them and experience their reactions. If you land on the end of the phrase, "defend to my death his right to say it," you are making a powerful point that needs to be received by a juror. Again using your imagination, you must make a specific choice as to whether that juror is skeptical or receptive. Your next line will be affected by the imaginary response that you receive.

Go back to the closing argument in the last chapter and spend some time giving life to the other characters in the scene. Use the Haber Phrase Technique® to enhance the dialogue between you and your imaginary courtroom.

WORKING WITH A PARTNER

Normally in an audition, you read with a casting director or a reader. Sometimes, you'll be paired with another actor. In both cases, you'll want to develop a relationship with the other person. Remember in Part 2, we talked about the importance of having a strong relationship. Learning to use the Haber Phrase Technique® correctly in a scene will only strengthen that connection. In fact, it enhances all of the work you've done previously when breaking down the scene. If the goal in acting is to create the illusion of real life, then the aim in an audition is to present a piece of that life. In some very practical ways, the Haber Phrase Technique® helps you turn an unnatural situation into a seamless slice of life.

We've talked about phrasing. Now, the question is: How do you apply the Haber Phrase Technique® when working with a partner? Let's go over some fundamentals of using the Haber Phrase Technique® in a scene.

LANDINGS

My acting students will tell you that the landing makes all the difference in the world! It reinforces your commitment to involve your partner; it makes a strong statement of what your character feels and needs. The landing is one of the most effective ways to cement your relationship to the other character, freeing you to go back down to the page.

In the *L.A. Law* closing argument, Mathers says, "And in the end, isn't that what this case is really about—freedom." Mathers needs to land emphatically with his eyes so he can bring home the power of that statement. If Mathers' eyes return to the paper *before* completing the word "freedom," he loses the case. He must make sure the jury gets his message.

RESOLUTIONS

A resolution is similar to a landing in its need to communicate the phrase and its completion of the message, but, because of when it is used—at the end of the unit, when your eyes are off the paper—it is even more powerful. A resolution gives you the time to experience how your message has affected the listener. This precious moment keeps your work alive and fresh, leaving room for unpredictable reactions.

When Mathers completes the following unit, "Those precious rights, guaranteed under the Constitution, to every American citizen to express himself as he chooses in thought, speech and action . . . " he can now take the time to consider what he has just said and its impact on the listener. For example, Mathers could be thinking, "I've got them now," or "This juror is not buying this. How can I get through to him?" That thought will affect his next unit and could change his whole approach.

Actors are afraid to take time for the resolution, and yet, it is the heart of spontaneous acting, the key to Moment to Moment work. It's easy to get caught up in preparation, your choices and the way you envision the scene to flow. But, being available to the changes that may occur during the resolution, you stay present and open to surprise. The resolution feeds you into the next unit.

COMEDY RESOLUTIONS

In comedy, a resolution can directly affect the punch line. In his hilarious play *Thieves*, Herb Gardner writes a perfect comedy setup requiring a clear resolution. Sally has been talking on the phone to what the audience thinks is a baby while her husband Martin listens impatiently. She then hands the phone over to Martin, giving him what he sees as the unpleasant task of talking to a dog. This excerpt shows you that it's all about timing.

```
                MARTIN
Sally, stop it! For Chrissakes,
we've got more important...(she
holds the phone out to him.)
Sally, we're right in the
middle of a very
important...(Grabs phone.)
Okay, Okay, if you'll
stop...(Into phone, quickly.)
Hello, Barry, gotta go now;
'bye.(hangs up.) I can't tell
you how much that depresses me.
```

The unit ends with, "if you'll stop..." But, Martin must complete a strong resolution to set up the comedy punch line, "Hello, Barry, gotta go now; 'bye." So, after Martin says, "Okay. Okay, if you'll stop . . . " he needs a specific thought before talking to the dog, which begins his new unit.

Martin's could be thinking, "She's driving me crazy! Just play along . . . " before he utters, "Hello, Barry, gotta go now; 'bye." Setups must have time to sink in before the payoff is delivered.

WHEN DO YOU GET YOUR NEXT LINE?

We've all witnessed dancing partners who make the tango look easy—how do they do it? Similarly, how do you stay connected to your partner in a scene if you don't know your next line? Following are some simple rules using excerpts from, *I Never Sang For My Father*.

- If your partner has a short line, then you must stay with her until she finishes it. Then <u>look down</u> in the beginning of your own line, staying down for a few words and coming up to land.

>   ALICE
>   You're doing it because you
>   can't help yourself.
>
>   GENE
>   <u>Look, when I want to be</u>
>   <u>analyzed</u>, I'll pay for it.

Gene needs to wait for Alice to complete her line, then go down and stay down for the first part of his line, "Look, when I want to be analyzed," coming up for, "I'll pay for it."

- If your partner has many lines, you may go down in the middle of his speech to get your phrase as long as you come up before he finishes. When you are both off the paper at the same time, you are able to take in the other character and be available for that moment.

>   GENE
>   What do you want us to do?
>   Shall we get out a white paper?
>   Let it be known that we, Alice
>   and Gene, have done all that we
>   can to make this old man happy
>   in his old age, without
>   inconveniencing ourselves of
>   course, and he has refused our

```
help. So, if he falls and hits
his head and lies there until
he rots, it is not our fault.

        ALICE
I don't think anyone expects
either of us to ruin our lives
over an unreasonable old man.
```

Somewhere in the middle of Gene's lines, Alice must look down to get her cue line, "it is not our fault" as well as her first phrase, "I don't think anyone . . ." and be up and ready by the time Gene completes his speech.

WHEN TO TURN THE PAGE

You've come to a dramatic moment in the scene. For example, you're right in the middle of telling off the other character when, all of a sudden, there is a page turn and a big, unnecessary pause occurs just after your partner says his line. You can't spit out your next line fast enough because you're stuck trying to turn the page. How do you avoid this temporary lapse of unwanted time?

- **If your partner has the last line** on the page, don't wait until he's finished to turn the paper—it will be too late! When you complete your last line on the page, turn the page, so you are prepared for your next line.

- **If you have the last line** on the page, make sure you keep your intention strong as you turn the page so the process of turning the page doesn't look mechanical, therefore pulling everyone out of the scene.

- **If you have the *first* line on the *next* page**, try writing it in on the bottom of the *previous* page so you have it during the page turn.

You'd be surprised how these simple suggestions can help the flow of the scene and make your job easier.

REPETITIVE PHRASES

There are times when memorization is necessary. For instance, your first line in the opening beat of the scene; when uttering small words like "thank you," "okay," "hello," "good-bye," etc. (which help the rhythm of the piece); or when using repetitive phrases. "Repetitive phrases" occur when the writer uses the same line for your character that was immediately said by the previous character. As you can see from the following excerpt from *The Prisoner of Second Avenue*, Neil Simon likes to use repetitive phrases.

>   MEL
> Alright, sit there. I'll get a
> drink.
>
>   EDNA
> I don't want a drink.
>
>   MEL
> A little scotch. It'll calm you
> down.
>
>   EDNA
> It won't calm me down because
> there's no scotch. They took
> the scotch too.
>
>   MEL
> All the scotch?
>
>   EDNA
> All the scotch.
>
>   MEL
> The Chivas Regal too?

Notice the repetitive phrases, "All the scotch?" "All the scotch." When auditioning, you should not take the time to look down at your script between these two lines—it will wreck the comedic timing. Lines that directly echo one another should be memorized to maintain the scene's pacing.

EYE-STARING CONTEST

As a kid, do you remember having contests to see who could stare at the other for the longest period of time without blinking? Believe it or not, there are acting coaches who encourage actors to say all of their lines to the other person, without ever looking down on the page! I feel that staring at your partner is extremely unnatural. Think about it—in life, we frequently look away. In fact, looking away is a natural part of our physical behavior that occurs during communication: we look away to make a point, to complete a thought, to cover our true feelings. Rarely, if ever, do we openly stare at the person we're talking to.

THROW IT AWAY!

This may surprise some of you, but guess what? Not everything you say is important! Feel free to place less emphasis on the insignificant lines (throwing them away) so when you have a point to make, that point will stand out.

JOINING SENTENCES

Another way to avoid making every line sound like the *Declaration of Independence* is to practice the art of joining sentences. When your eyes are on the paper, you may be able to combine two sentences into one without pausing for punctuation. Just because there is a comma, an exclamation mark or a period doesn't mean you must automatically pause or that your eyes should immediately come off the page. There are times when even a question can be asked with your eyes down, as long as you keep your intention strong. Following is an example (underlined phrases indicate eyes down on the page):

```
                    GENE
          What do you want us to do?
          Shall we get out a white paper?
          Let it be known that we, Alice
          and Gene, have done all that we
          can to make this old man happy
          in his old age, without
          inconveniencing ourselves of
          course, and he has refused our
          help. So, if he falls and hits
          his head and lies there until
          he rots, it is not our fault.
```

The strength of Gene's conviction is propelled by the added momentum of the lines running together. By joining the sentences, " . . . and he has refused our help." and "So, if he falls and hits his head . . . " you help shape the arc of the unit. Staying down on the paper gives you the fuel to come off the page. Even though your eyes are on the paper, there is an urgency that sustains Gene's intensity.

PUTTING IT TOGETHER—*I NEVER SANG FOR MY FATHER*

Once again, here's the first page of the scene from *I Never Sang For My Father*. For teaching purposes only, I have diagramed some of the more technical aspects of the Haber Phrase Technique® that were already discussed. Your eyes should be down on the page for the underlined phrases. *Please note that, for an audition, you would never mark up your page with these technical items or worry about where your eyes should be.*

                    GENE
You can go with a clear   *1st line up*
conscience. I'm doing this
because I want to.

                    ALICE
You're doing it because you   *1st line up*
can't help yourself.

                    GENE
Look, when I want to be
analyzed, I'll pay for it.

                    ALICE
Didn't you see yourself there,
when he started to rage? You
shrank.

                    GENE
I shrank at the ugliness of
what was happening.

                    ALICE
You're staying because you
can't stand his wrath the day
you say, "Dad, I'm leaving."
... You've never been able to
stand up to his anger.

                    GENE
Look, Alice...

                    ALICE
He'll call you ungrateful...
and you'll believe him.
     [Resolution]

```
              GENE
           (Lashing out)
     What do you want us to do?
     Shall we get out a white paper?
     Let it be known that we...
     Alice and Gene, have done all
     that we can to make this old
     man happy in his old age...
     without inconveniencing
     ourselves, of course... And he
     has refused our help. So, if he
     falls and hits his head and
     lies there until he rots, it is
     not our fault.

              ALICE
     I don't think anyone expects
     either of us to ruin our lives
     over an unreasonable old man.

              GENE
     It is not going to ruin my
     life.

              ALICE
     It is!
           [Repetitive Phrase]

              GENE
     A few weeks... a month.

              ALICE
     Forever.
           [Resolution]
```

In the unit above, when Alice confronts Gene, their pain and frustration are experienced regardless where their eyes fall.

DON'T LOSE YOUR LIFE!

The truth is, no one will care where your eyes are as long as you continue your life (which means, you must maintain whatever feelings your character is experiencing at that moment). So, no matter what happens—even if you get completely lost on the page—DON'T LOSE YOUR LIFE!

If your character is having a fit of anger, you must maintain that rage; if your character is afraid, stay with the fear; if your character is in the middle of a love scene, continue that sensuality whether your eyes are on or off the paper.

Keeping your life means keeping your intention strong throughout. The paper will seem to vanish if your life is full.

SILENCE IS GOLDEN

Don't be afraid of silence. Silence can provide some of the most interesting moments in acting and can give the audience a chance to catch up to their emotions. Silence occurs during transitions. Typically, actors like to rush through these changes, afraid of the audience getting bored. Also, they don't feel justified taking the time to experience those images and allowing their senses to affect them. In order to create tension in a dramatic piece, you need to give yourself the luxury of staying with your thoughts. There is a big difference between a pause and a transition. When an actor pauses, he has no thoughts. It is an empty void that causes the scene to drag and can negatively affect your intention. But a transition that is filled with struggle and emotions only adds depth to your reading.

From the Studio

News Flash: There is Life After Your Lines!

Breck and Randy were reading a scene from *Man of Steel*, in which two strangers are sitting at a bar getting to know each other. At first, the actors were having tremendous difficulty because they kept worrying about their next lines. It was particularly frustrating to watch because every time they finished their lines, they would immediately go down to the page and cut off their emotional connection.

Margie: Breck, don't look down after you speak to get your next lines. We lose you.

Breck: But I'm scared that I won't know what comes next.

Margie: The lines are the last thing you should be worrying about. The most important thing is to continue the life of your character. In real life, we don't worry about what we're going to say next. We listen to the other person talking and then we respond. Try it again and when you finish your lines, see if you can stay with the character's thoughts rather than return to the page.

Breck and Randy went through the scene a second time, trusting the Haber Phrase Technique®. They did not continually search for their next lines—the difference was astounding!

Margie: Did that feel any different?

Randy: Unbelievable! I have never felt so free in a reading. I wasn't worried about what came next. I stopped concentrating on my fears and started thinking more as the character.

Breck: It felt so empowering. I was really listening. I didn't have time to think about being right or wrong. I just responded.

Margie (to class): What was it like watching the scene for the second time?

Comment: I never saw them scrambling to get their lines. They weren't rushing anymore. It was like they had all the time in the world.

THE STATE OF CONFUSION

Right now, you're probably feeling confused, maybe even afraid, of all this new information being thrown at you. Be patient and kind to yourself—many people are afraid of this state of confusion because they wonder if they'll ever get out of it. The good news is that when you are confused, you are learning and beginning to understand the method, even though you may still have some doubts. Your mind is busy sorting out all the new information.

It's okay to be confused. You *should* be confused at first. Don't push yourself too quickly. Give yourself time to experience the uncertainty. Allow yourself the freedom to explore the Haber Phrase Technique® and let it work for you. Once you own it, it's yours.

THE TEN COMMANDMENTS OF THE HABER PHRASE TECHNIQUE®

1. Thou shalt not memorize except for your first line, key phrases or repetitive phrases.
2. Thou shalt not eye bob.
3. Thou shalt not make up your own dialogue.
4. Thou shalt remember to keep your paper up and follow along with your thumb.
5. Thou shalt not waste time turning the page when you should be saying your lines.

6. Thou shalt not look down right after you finish speaking to get your next lines.

7. Thou shalt honor your partner by always having your eyes off the paper when he finishes speaking.

8. Thou shalt allow yourself to land and connect to your partner by completing your phrase before returning to your paper.

9. Thou shalt always have your eyes off the paper for the beginning of the unit as well as at the end for the resolution.

10. Thou shalt not lose your life when you go down for a phrase.

 TIPS See the Ten Commandments above.

PART 4
WORDS FROM THE PROS

"It takes a very special person like Margie to show you what to focus on, what to pay attention to during your preparation. It makes all the difference in getting the job. Meeting Margie, the influence of the Haber technique, and Margie's wisdom about performing are with me always.
I never leave home without it."
—MICHELLE SHAY
(One True Thing, Seven Guitars—Tony nomination)

"I send all of my clients to Margie because she's the audition guru. Don't miss out on her wit and wisdom."
—VINCE CIRRINCIONE, Manager

"Margie's workshop was really helpful because of the confidence it gave me, the support that I got there and mostly because of the tangible message that I got. It is something that I can hold on to and take with me. Margie's technique made it possible for me to work as opposed to just worrying about the circumstances and who I was auditioning for."
—ROSALYN COLEMAN (Music From the Heart, Seven Guitars)

"Margie Haber's workshop provides a rare opportunity to examine your audition technique in a direct and focused way."
—LAURA INNES
(E.R.—Emmy nomination)

"Margie's insight, intuition, and experience make her able to see what an individual actor needs at that moment. I've worked with Margie and she has an uncanny ability to see you the way producers and casting people will see you and to get you to move through things that are often unconsciously holding you back from getting the roles you want and deserve."
—STEPHEN COLLINS (7th Heaven, First Wives Club)

"In this business, actors must constantly be able to adjust, even when the adjustment makes no sense at all. If you've truly learned Margie's technique, you can make whatever adjustments are necessary at a moment's notice."
—ROBERT NEWMAN (The Guiding Light)

"Before *Chicago Hope*, I would sneak into Margie's class whenever I was in between jobs just to soak up some of her magic. It never failed to recharge my battery. She's the best!"
—VONDIE CURTIS-HALL (Chicago Hope, Die Hard 3, Passion Fish)

"When I worked with Margie on the movie, *Touch,* I was all over the place until she centered my attention on the other character and VOOM! I was suddenly focused. She's got the magic touch and nice tits."
—TOM ARNOLD (*True Lies, Touch, Nine Months*)

"After Margie's second class I got *Days of Our Lives.* It's a testament to what she teaches. I really believe that she helped me get this job. Her technique brought my confidence up. It's concise, it's specific and I had a lot of fun."
—LISA RINNA (*Melrose Place, Days of Our Lives*)

"I find my sessions with Margie absolutely essential to making my contribution to the number one daytime show on television for over one decade and counting. Without Margie, Esther would never have grown."
—KATE LINDER ("*Esther Valentine*" on *The Young and the Restless*)

—

MEET THE PROS SEMINAR

GARRETT WANG / *Star Trek: Voyager*

I had gone in on my fourth audition for *Voyager*, and at that point each producer seemed to have a different vision of how the character should be played. I tried incorporating all the differing suggestions and notes into my fifth call back. The result was, predictably, a very confused and diluted reading.

On the sixth callback, I made the difficult decision to focus on playing the scene the way I believed it should be played. I felt that the only way to make the character believable was to make it believable to myself. With this renewed clarity of mind and the utilization of Margie's specific audition techniques, I strode confidently onto the Paramount lot and got the part. Always trust your gut instinct and let your training be on autopilot.

GARRETT WANG

This chapter is transcribed from an actual seminar held at the Howard Fine Acting Studio. We invited working actors from Howard's studio and from my own to participate. I moderated a panel that included the following top industry professionals, for this inside look at the audition process.

PANELISTS:

JEFF WITJAS, Agent, William Morris Agency

AL ONORATO, Manager; former Vice President of Casting at Columbia Pictures Television

FERN CHAMPION, Casting Director—*The Mask, Mortal Combat, Beverly Hills 90210*

SAM WEISMAN, Producer/Director. Began his career as an actor, then directed episodic television, such as *Family Ties, Moonlighting, L.A. Law, The Single Guy*. Produced and directed the series, *Brooklyn Bridge* and such features as *The Out-of-Towners, George of the Jungle, D2: The Mighty Ducks* and *Bye Bye, Love.*

MH: **We're going to start from the beginning of the audition process— with preparation. Sam, you get the script first among us. How do you begin your audition process? Do you have specific actors in mind?**

SW: In television, for example, in pilots, there is a lot of list-making that goes on about who the network is interested in, who your casting person is pushing and then, of course, who you want. Unfortunately for actors, as a director, I try to see as few people as possible. For me, it wears me down to see a lot of people, so I really put a lot of pressure on the casting people I work with to screen and set the reality for me.

MH: **What is your first conversation with the casting director like?**

SW: We talk about the qualities we're looking for in the roles, using examples of, "If we could get so-and-so" or "a blend between so-and-so and so-and-so." Then you usually have lists of people that you'll never get. But the lists are made anyway.

MH: **The wish list.**

SW: Exactly.

MH: **Do you attend the first reading as well as the callbacks?**

SW: I'm going to be there for anybody that we're really interested in seeing. Frankly, I don't put a lot of weight on callbacks. Instead, I react instinctively. Many of the people I cast are among the first people I see. And if the casting director's doing a great job, then that's possible.

MH: Fern Champion is the next person in this journey. The producer calls you and wants you to cast his project. Where do you go from there?

FC: First I read the script and make sure it's something that I believe in, that I feel comfortable doing and that would be fun for me to do. At that point, we do make lists of people. Personally, I like casting for films better. Film casting enables me to see more of the actor; it gives me a little bit more leeway to gamble. Television, for me, has always been somewhat pre-set—it's a good guy, a bad guy, a blond girl, a dark-haired girl.

MH: And how much do you rely on managers and agents?

FC: With two of them sitting on my left, I rely on them quite a bit.

AO: And we rely on you.

FC: You begin to learn who you can and who you should not trust. I want an agent that has one, maybe two (actors) who can do it. I don't really want to see an enormous amount of actors in the same role from one agent.

MH: How do you feel about general interviews?

FC: I'm not a fan of the general interview. I understand that it should be done when an actor is in town for a little while, but basically, I feel that you, the actor, want to do your job. You want to come in with material and you want to show me that you know what you're doing. For me to ask you, "Hi, where're you from? How's everything? How's your mother? How's your father?"—I mean, it's nice to sit across the desk from each other, but you're there to show me that you know how to act. Generals really don't mean anything to either one of us, I don't think.

MH: How much do you rely on pictures and resumés for casting?

FC: I rely on them enormously. And I'll be the first one to look at a picture; if it doesn't look like someone, I'll tell you.

MH: What impresses you about a picture?

FC: That it looks like a person. I really want a shot just of you. That's all I want. I don't want an angle. I don't want something overly dramatic. I really don't need a color picture. A black and white is really fine.

JW: As an agent, I like to have two or three pictures. I like to have the ammunition for the type of role I'm sending my clients for. Maybe one should show more of a smile, a little bit lighter for the comedy or light-drama and one more serious. As far as the resumé, your name on top . . . You may think it's not important, but your name should be very large up there. Your name should stand out.

MH: How much do you rely on the breakdowns?

JW: It is only something that we look at to help the bids, because the breakdowns are misleading. They do not give you the true sense of the role.

MH: Anything you want to say about that, Al?

AO: I rely on the breakdowns because that's the bread and butter for some of the clients. You want to know as much ahead of time as you possibly can in a situation.

MH: What is your role in the audition process? Do you give tips to your actors before they read?

AO: I do. Only because I feel as though I have some feel for the drama or the comedy of the situation. When I work with somebody on a piece, it's because that is how I interpret [that piece] and how I impart the interpretation to the client that I'm dealing with.

MH: When are the scripts usually available?

FC: Scripts have to be available. It was a ruling that was passed the last time the Screen Actors Guild went on strike. A script is always available in the casting director's office. And as far as Jeff and Al helping, they can help to a certain point but then it's up to you folks [the actors] to help yourselves. Go to the office, pick up the material and ask the questions that you're unsure about. Get it one-on-one.

AO: Let me add one more thing. Actors, unfortunately, are lazy. You want everything spoon- fed to you. I can't tell you the number of times [an actor will] say, "Well, I can't get there 'til such-and-such. I'll just go in a little bit early." If it's available to you, avail yourself of it. You've got to be on top of things.

Question: If somebody comes in and he's a little off the mark, but is the right type, how do you take it from there?

SW: Something that's right in an actor's quality is almost more important than how perfect his reading is. I had a situation when we [cast] the *Brooklyn Bridge* series. Marion Ross came in to read for the part of the grandmother and everyone thought it was complete nonsense except for me. Her reading was horrible—it was awful! But there was something about her that I felt was the woman. We brought her back three more times, we hired a dialect coach for her, we screen tested her twice and she ended up playing the part and being nominated for two Emmys. So those situations can turn around.

FC: I definitely agree. There are also times where someone is totally the wrong type but does a brilliant reading. And I'm all for bringing that person in, too. I mean, why not?

SW: You know, I find what's really interesting lately is I've seen more unprepared auditions than I could possibly even imagine. And that's really a big change for me. People come in to read for leads in pilots [or series] and they haven't completely read the script. That's the one thing that turns me off. The other thing I've come across a lot in the last couple years . . . Actors now tend to leave the written word more. Nothing offends a writer more. And since television now is completely run by writer/producers, the biggest advice I can give to you is—don't change the words in an audition! That's one of the things that I think turns off people in a room quicker than anything else.

MH: **We're into the second stage of the journey, so this is for you, Fern. The actor walks in the room, what do you look for in the first audition?**

FC: A cold read is tough. Walking into us is sometimes a very uncomfortable situation but you gotta make the best of it. Try to be as prepared as you can, starting with the script and knowing your material. Don't walk in saying, "I'm really sorry. I didn't read the script. I have four other appointments today." You're there to do your job.

MH: **What would make you want to call an actor back to read for the producer?**

FC: If I liked his work. If it's something so unique and so different, but yet is so entertaining. I do take that gamble. Maybe that's what I look for . . . something that's a little different.

JW: Here's where we have a little fun. Once in awhile, the casting director doesn't see eye-to-eye with the agent. And the casting director will say, "No, I don't see your client as right for the role." Well, an agent can't take "No" for an answer. We don't have it in our vocabulary. And I think a manager's pretty much the same way. We have to find a way of getting to the next level . . . whomever can help push buttons, we try to get you back in.

AO: You have to have the wherewithal to be able to deal with somebody who says, "No, I don't think he or she is right."

MH: **Let's go on to the topic of memorization. As my students know, I don't believe in memorization. What are your feelings about memorizing the first reading?**

FC: I'm totally against it. You're nervous enough and if you're trying to remember those lines, you're going to lose the performance. Invariably, you lose. That doesn't mean you shouldn't be familiar with the material. But I might want to change something you're doing and if you're stuck in a certain mode of the way you've memorized it, and your nerves are taking over, it's very difficult to turn your performance around. So I'm in 100 percent agreement with you on that.

SW: I agree, too. I tend to think when people come in to an audition and have it memorized, there's nothing more for them to show me.

MH: **That brings us to another question that my clients always ask me. What about physical behavior and props?**

SW: Don't touch anybody!

MH: **Let's say, for example, there's a kiss in the scene. Obviously, you can't suck the mouth of the casting director.**

FC: Don't like props. Don't kiss the casting director.

SW: Hate props. Kiss me, I'll kill ya!

MH: **That certainly summed up that issue!**

SW: I hate props and I hate costumes!

AO: And, I think, so often you rely on stage directions for your interpretation rather than on your [own] interpretation. Don't be encumbered by the stage directions.

SW: The most you can do is make a choice about the scene and about the character and just play that choice to the hilt. One choice. And, you know, as a director, I'll admire the actor that makes the choice and who plays the choice no matter what happens. I can always give the actor another choice.

JW: Sam, you're actually an exception to that. Because I find that the feedback may be, "Well, the energy's too low, the energy's too high, he did this, her interpretation of the role is that." I've often wondered why more directors would not say something to the actor, "Well, do it again. Raise the energy."

FC: Sitting in a room [casting] a television situation with the director is a fast pace and they want to see it! The director wants to know the actor can do it and that's it. Beginning, middle and end. If you're wrong, we'll turn you around. But if you're coming in from the left and the right and you're up and you're down . . . it's a mishmash.

SW: The problem is, the situation of auditioning is unnatural. So I think the more natural you can make it as an actor coming in the room, and the more comfortable you can make everyone—that's the biggest leg up you have. Likewise, I think part of it is recognizing you shouldn't be there if you're totally not right for the part. Nothing turns me off more than an actor who somehow has gotten in the room and they haven't even come close and they're totally wrong for the part.

MH: **This brings me to what I call the "Coverup." An actor blows a reading during the middle of an audition. Should they start over or just pretend that nothing happened? What do you do when you make a mistake?**

FC: Well, I think most of you know when you're into about the second line if you're off on the wrong foot. Stop it! Past the second line, you're committed. I will absolutely let you begin again if you say, "You know something. I started off on the wrong foot." But not into your fifth or sixth line. That's really unacceptable. Or at the end, "If you have a minute, I'd like to be able to try it this way." There are those times. [You shouldn't do it] every time, but there are certain auditions when a character can be played an entirely different way. Unless you are going to show me something entirely different, don't do it.

AO: I think you've got to be careful, too. [If you're] already thinking about how you want to do it a different way, your focus is already gone. I think you've gotta go in and be committed.

JW: Also, if you are confused when you're reading the script as to how to go in, don't be afraid to ask your agent or manager. We will talk to the casting director and try to get you some tips.

MH: **I would like to hear your no-no's for an actor in an audition situation. What are some common mistakes that actors make?**

SW: Don't come in and immediately start making excuses. Boy, nothing turns people off more. "There was so much traffic," or any of that stuff. Just stick to business. I also have a personal peeve: The moment before an actor is about to read, I hate it when they say, "Is there anything you want to tell me?" I find that to be really annoying. My feeling is, if you've made the choice, you don't have to ask that question.

FC: I agree with Sam. The other thing is, [on a callback] doing something entirely different than what you did for me. All of the sudden you had this brainstorm and you walk in and you're this whole other character! What happened here? If you are called back, there's a reason. There is absolutely a reason in that first reading why you're being called back. Don't decide to do something entirely different.

SW: I once had a very well-known actor audition for me. It was one of these situations where he was really wrong for the part. He did the reading. He obviously had great commitment and really loved the role and then he said instantly upon finishing, "I just want to try it another way. May I?" He went on to do it and it was exactly the same. I mean, not an iota different. And that so turned me off this guy. There's almost nothing that you could do to convince me to bring him in for something again.

FC: Another thing that could annoy a casting director or producer/director is when you're telling him, "Can I just try this other part? I really think I could do this other role very well." That's really a no-no.

SW: I have a good no-no. And this is for women. It could be for men, too. A woman should not dress absolutely so suggestively, provocatively that it will distract people from the reading.

JW: Men, too. There's one other thing: As I said before, a lot of this is a mind game. People are sitting out there for an hour, an hour and a half sometimes, waiting for their reading. And they're fuming, "How dare they do this to me! My reading's at 3:00 and it's 4:30!" Well, you've got to calm yourself down and do one or two things in my opinion. You could call your agent and have the meeting rescheduled because you're not prepared at that time or you could go in. But I would not bring it up as soon as you walk in the room by saying, "How dare you keep me waiting out there for that time!" Because it won't work.

AO: Also, because walls are thin, sometimes you have a tendency to hear the readings that are going on inside the room, which sometimes triggers something up here with you guys. "Maybe I should change my whole concept and go with the way that person's doing it, because they've been in there for a longer time." And it just screws everything up terribly.

MH: Let's talk about the actor's behavior when they enter the room. Should they say, "Hi! How are you?" or should they stay in character?

FC: I think it's up to the individual. Most of us are here to do a job. We're here to read, so, let's read! "Hi! My name is . . . " and then, let's read. If you have a question about pronunciation or if you have certain questions you need answered, that's another thing . . .

SW: Pronunciation. That's a good point. I've had situations where actor after actor would come in, pronouncing the name of a character wrong. It really throws you as a listener. If you don't know, you should really ask beforehand.

MH: **So, now the actor leaves the audition and he wants to throw up because he feels like he's done the worst job in the world. How about feedback?**

JW: I think it's "Agenting 101" to get feedback on a client. The call should be made the same day. Now, you may not get the answer the same day because the casting director may be in sessions until the end of the day, but surely the first thing the next morning, the agent must get the feedback, whether it's positive or negative.

AO: I had a client the other day who went in for a reading and when he left, he thought that everyone loved him. What he neglected to tell me was that as he was going in, he had this bird he decided to bring with him because he thought it was cute. And not five minutes after he left the room, I got a call from the casting person saying, "Is this actor crazy, thinking we like to have birds visiting us?" So, I get feedback all the time, too. And in those situations, don't bring extraneous objects or things with you.

QUESTION: **This all sounds really terrific, but it seems to me that, with the exception of the top leading roles, I have lost so many roles where they have said, "Well, we really loved your read but we had to give the part to someone who was a friend of the producer." This immense nepotism . . . what can we do to combat that?**

FC: I don't think nepotism will die. I think it's here to stay. There's nothing we can do about it. We should all have those friends!

JW: As far as producers and their relationships, we hope that, as agents and managers, we do have great relationships out there and sometimes if it's between you and someone else, we can tilt the scale a little bit. But very rarely, I think, will a producer or director cast someone just because he wants to cast a friend in a role. The project's too important.

AO: I agree. It's not as prevalent as you all have heard it to be. It's a myth that exists in this town.

SW: I avoid bringing friends in because: A) I don't want to disappoint them, and B) I've had the painful experience in the past of trying to do a favor—casting friends—and it hasn't worked out. And that's really not a way to keep a friend or a lover, lemme tell ya.

JW: In fact, we don't even send clients in on roles where there's an offer out to someone. We let that offer play itself out with that specific actor and then, when it's free, we start sending people in again.

SW: I think what it all boils down to, for me, is that you have to come in and do your work for yourself. You can't do it for the people you're auditioning for. And if somehow you can get to the place where, when you do your work you're doing it because you believe in yourself as an actor, that will be the path that guides you. If you're in the room to please somebody, it's not going to work. And that's the biggest issue about callbacks, too. I see people undo themselves in front of, let's say, the network or if they have to come in and read for a studio. All of a sudden, they're trying to duplicate what they think they did the first time or what they think they did that got them there, as opposed to going back to the wellspring, which is, "What's the choice that I made? Who am I? Who am I regarding this character?" That's what you have to hang onto.

QUESTION: Is it true that, a lot of times as a casting director or director, you don't know what you specifically want, so maybe we shouldn't focus on that so much?

FC: That absolutely can happen. You know, there are more developments for some characters than others. It really depends on the script you're reading.

SW: The last project I did, a pilot, for one of the roles, I ended up having a specific notion in mind as to who the character was and I'd steer the casting director that way. I'd say, "She sort of needs to be like Bebe Neuwirth in *Cheers*. That's her function." And we ended up casting an Asian actress who was sort of dizzy and all over the place. It was completely different, you know. And it was to the credit of the casting person that she kept hunting.

JW: That's why it's also not as important to get in at the very early stages of the casting process. Wait until the project settles a little bit and then start pushing.

MH: Let's go on to callbacks. I say callbacks, because many of my clients have told me they don't go to just one callback. Sometimes there are two or even three callbacks. I tell my clients to take the input that was given to them by the casting director and just enhance that. Stay with what you were given the first time and don't try to change it. How do you feel, Fern?

FC: What Margie is saying is absolutely correct. You are more than welcome to ask for feedback from your agent and/or manager, but if there is a callback, I have to believe that what you've done for me or another casting person was right. The reason you're being called back is because you're on the right track.

MH: Who is at the callback?

SW: Well, it really depends on the "auspices," as I say. I think you'll find that the higher the level of the project, the fewer people making the decision. So, in other words, the more control a director or producer has, the fewer people need to affirm what he wants. The one situation that's very hard to avoid is the whole network thing in television. That is an unreal situation that almost no one can avoid.

MH: What's the difference between auditioning for the network and auditioning for the producer or director?

SW: You gotta know when you go in for the network, there ain't gonna be a lot of yucks, a lot of laughs. And the reason for that is, by the way, people's insecurity about their jobs. And that's what you have to understand—everyone has somebody to answer to. So it's not that people don't want to be nice to actors. Everyone's worried about what everyone else is thinking and that makes for a tense room.

JW: Let's take a pilot situation, for example. You can pretty much figure that you're going to go in for four or five readings for the same role. If you're talking about the casting director, the next level would probably be for the producer and director, so that's maybe two readings there. There is a studio reading before you get to the network. The studio is a test—a lot of times the agent has to negotiate a deal at the studio level before you even read for the studio people. And that could be for naught. In fact, sadly, most cases are for naught. But then, if you get through the studio, you go on to the network. So it's five readings at least before you get a home run.

AO: I think that's one of the hardest situations. You're going to the studio and the deal's been ascertained, including how many years you're going to do it, what amount of money you're going to get, and then suddenly the studio says, "No. We don't want them to go any further." That's one of the hardest things for me, when I have to call a client and say, "You're not going to the network. The studio has turned you down."

SW: Also, that goes back to the auspices situation. Any writer, any producer worth his salt, is not going to bring to the studio a choice of theirs and have the studio say, "No. We're not going to bring that person to the network." That means, basically, they're letting the studio push them around, which is not going to make for a good show.

MH: **As far as the difference between the first reading and the callback . . . I don't think we discussed wardrobe.**

FC: Personally, I'm very clothes-conscious and talking with my actresses, I am very helpful in that area. If you are unsure and it has not been discussed with me in the first read, then have your agent or manager call and ask, "Anything you want to say about clothes?" That's the way it's handled.

JW: It's not always as clear as that. A lot of times, the network may have a vision for the role. They may want hot, sexy, good-looking. The studio and, at times, the producer or director may want something suitable for the character. Now, obviously, you can't satisfy both a lot of times with the same actor. So it is sometimes a crap shoot when you go in because it's going to be a political battle between the studio/producer/ director and the network as to who gets the role. So even if you do a great reading, it doesn't mean you're going to get the role.

MH: **What are the differences between a screen test and a callback, especially with regard to memorization and other points?**

SW: A lot of it is semantic. I mean, in the case of television, the test very often is not a test but is simply a reading. It's just a way of referring to a negotiation. In other words, when there are choices being made for a pilot, a test deal is negotiated simply so that once the studio decides who they want, the agent can't hold them up for more money. Most situations now in television don't actually do testing. They're mostly just readings. For a movie screen test (or if there is a screen test for television), the one thing I would suggest strongly is for the agent or your manager to push very strongly to control the circumstances, especially when it comes to women. You don't want to be put on tape or film unless there's some sort of lighting, unless there's makeup and hair. I find that a bad-looking test can really be held against the actor or actress.

MH: **So do they memorize? Do they bring props? What should they expect when they have to do an actual soap screen test, for example?**

AO: That's a real rehearsal. The director will go through the rehearsal with you. Yes, you should have it memorized, because you are probably going to be doing it with the star of the show. And you are pretty much going to interact with that person.

FC: With a film test, that's absolutely right. I mean, on *The Mask*, the ladies who were up for the role will have tested with Jim Carrey. As far as daytime serials—I think that's full-blown hair and makeup as well.

MH: **Are there any other questions or comments regarding callbacks?**

FC: Sometimes, there are a lot of us in the room. It's not necessary to shake 12 hands. It breaks everybody's momentum. A lot of people are leery about touching people and they just don't want to start shaking every person's hand. A casual hello to the room is really fine; then, sit down and begin. Don't think you're going to remember everybody's name because there's nothing more embarrassing than, "Oh, oh, I'm sorry, Bill, no you're . . . " Don't even try. Just say hi.

MH: **When you go into a callback and it's a very emotional part, do they expect you to say hello and carry on a conversation?**

FC: No. You're there to read. So, read. Hello and goodbye.

MH: **I believe there's an inner circle of space that is needed and I'm sure that for callbacks, there needs to be some space. If there's no table there, what do you do?**

SW: Sometimes, in Hollywood, the spaces aren't exactly the most advantageous. The offices are usually not huge. Don't stand behind furniture. I always look for that—I get the sense that people are hiding when they stand behind a table or a chair. Just get out in the open. Get completely "naked." Present yourself. The other thing is, don't back up against the wall. If you feel yourself backing up against a wall, just move to a space where you feel like you're in the room, you own the room. Take a deep breath. Imagine the people in the room sitting on the toilet—and, start. I hate it when actors get crammed up in a corner.

MH: **Anything else you want to tell us about things you hate?**

SW: I hate it when people lie on their resumés. It's a pet peeve of mine because I was an actor. It's just one of the most embarrassing things I can imagine. And it's really bad if you get caught. I actually have had actors come in with my name on their resumés and I've never laid eyes on the people!

JW: My pet peeve? Once in awhile, an actor goes in and thinks he did a fabulous, fabulous job on his reading. You check in and the feedback is terrible! You tell the client that the reading was not very good and the client blames me for that. He can't understand how it changed from the reading to the feedback, so he thinks the agent did something to kill the role for him.

MH: **We've covered the callback part. Let's ask some questions from the audience about callbacks and screen tests and networks and then, when we finish that, we'll just open up for general questions.**

QUESTION: What's the difference between a casting director, associate and an assistant?

FC: I know that my assistant will help me with lists, help me set up appointments, help me to get scripts out. An associate that works with me usually is someone that has done shows on their own and is past the assistant level; they can do pre-reads. Usually, before I hire associates and let them go on their own, I will sit in that room because they're representing me.

SW: A casting director's job is one of the most difficult jobs there is. And the people who do it well, like Fern does, I mean, really deserve medals repeatedly, because very often they're dealing with a lot of stupid people.

AO: For the most part, everybody has insecurities on the network level, on the producer's level, on the casting person's level. But in that situation, Fern's there to help you. She's not there to hurt you. So don't go in as an adversary. Go in with the attitude, "This person wants me to get the job and he or she is gonna help me, not hinder me."

MH: What should an actor do when they go in for a read with someone who never looks at them? For example, "They didn't care about me. I only saw the top of their head. They didn't pay attention to me."

JW: You're playing mind games with yourself. You've gotta block that stuff out. This is not an easy career you have entered. It's going to be a roller coaster, but when you're in the reading—focus. Have tunnel vision on the role and what you're there to do. Forget about the personalities of the other people in the room. You're going to read over and over again for different projects. You're going to have to deal with many different personalities. A lot of the people you're going to read for are very nice people. They're going to give you some feedback in the room, some vibes. If they don't, so be it. Continue your reading.

QUESTION: This last season, I was in the position where I almost had two pilots and was second choice for second person. In that case, I was struggling very hard not to take it personally. One person said, "Well, if she doesn't sign her contract, then it's yours." Or, "This person has a higher TVQ. She's been seen on TV more. She's more recognizable." What do you think if you're getting that close . . .

FC: You're up at bat. You're there. It's higher than a lot of folks get in this town. You're at a level where you're close. It's a numbers game.

QUESTION: But that TVQ thing is my question . . .

FC: One of these days, the TVQ will be yours.

JW: If you look at most series on television today—look at *ER* and some of those shows—there are fabulous actors there. They blend together extremely well, but George Clooney, who is a client at William Morris, wasn't really well-known before he entered that series. That whole cast really was not well-known.

SW: Yeah, George Clooney did about fifteen failed pilots.

FC: That's what he was known for.

JW: He just stayed in there.

SW: George Clooney was known as the guy you took when you couldn't get the other fifty guys you wanted. It's true. Now look at him. The guy is huge. So you never know. It's a marriage of an actor and a part. The way I used to make myself feel better when I was an actor . . . and actually, it's the thing that led me into directing, was that, in a fit of absolute depression once, I went through my appointment books for a few years. I looked at the number of pilots I had read for or tested for and I counted the number of those pilots that succeeded as a series. And do you know how many there were? One. One in the space of about six years. So, those are the odds right there. So, I'm gonna knock myself out because I'm not getting a pilot that everybody wants to forget?!

JW: And what happens today more than ever is, you get a pilot, you're excited, it's great. They shoot it and then the pilot is picked up. But, it's no guarantee you're going to be in the series. They may rewrite it, add new roles or they knock your role out.

AO: Actors worry about getting tied into a series for seven years! You all worry about these contract situations.

MH: From your mouth to God's ears—it should happen to you.

AO: You can count them on your hand, probably, the number of TV series that have lasted more than three or four years that you watch regularly. It doesn't happen any longer. You don't have a *M*A*S*H* on television—a show that runs nine, ten or eleven years.

QUESTION: Sam and Fern, what's a good way to say good-bye without having another no-no? What are the no-no's at the end of the audition?

FC: It should be as light as your hello. "Nice meeting all of you." "It's a pleasure meeting you." "Thank you." And, out. And try not to forget your keys or your book. Try to make sure everything is together right by you, or leave it outside. Because, invariably, we'll hear a knock:

"Excuse me, I just forgot something inside." Really, try to make sure that all of your belongings leave with you.

QUESTION: What are some of the signs for the actor to see whether the audition has gone well or not?

SW: Everyone in the room is cross-eyed, that's a bad sign. In the feedback area, when you have an agent like Jeff—who's a real agent—the relationship between him and his client or between Al and his client—those are substantial relationships . . . You trust that feedback. I find, being on the other end, that very often there is a lot of miscommunication that goes on. That's where it's important that you are in touch with the people who represent you, because you don't want these cross-communications. You know, like people who come in with the wrong script. Or, they'll come in and say, "Oh, so-and-so said I should dress this way." You've just gotta get this stuff straight. And that's your responsibility.

JW: There are a lot of casting directors and producers who really won't tell you that much in the room. I mean, unless they put a contract right there and say, "Sign it!" I don't think you're really going to know how well you did or how badly you did. There are times when they say, "Good reading, nice reading, well done . . . " and how do you interpret that? You really can't until you get back and call your agent and then find out the real story.

MH: Isn't it simply that you have to do the best you can do and move on?

SW: And then forget about it.

JW: It's not only about good readings. Remember that. It isn't. You could nail it in the room. I've had a casting director and producer call me, crying about how well an actor did, but this actor did not fit into the chemistry of the cast. No matter how much they could have changed the role, it didn't work. And he gave a great, great reading.

SW: I had that in the pilot I directed. We had a guy who was clearly the first choice for the part going into the network. And something just clicked in the room for the other actor. A conversation ensued where everyone said, "Well, wouldn't it be great if we had this kind of energy in the show instead of what was written." And the guy, literally, was blown out of the water in a two-minute reading.

JW: There are times when they are the only actor going into the room but I won't tell them that. First of all, the pressure is intense and second, the network and the producer can see another reading in the room and maybe it just doesn't work. How devastating it is to the actor to know they were the only one and they still didn't get it. So, it isn't smart to tell the actor that.

QUESTION: I know we actors, or at least for myself, seem to be a little neurotic. This is in reference to preparation. How much mercy can you have on us?

SW: Sports analogy . . . you're in the batter's box, the pitcher's in his motion, you can't go out. You have to take the pitch or swing at it. That's all there is to it. You can't then say to the ump on the called strike, "Oh, I'm sorry. Could I try that again?" That's just the way it is. It's a competitive field.

QUESTION: But you're not going to get the best of us . . .

SW: Okay, here's my answer to that. If the part needs to be solved by an audition in the first place, that's unfortunately the way it has to be. Many parts are cast without auditions, so you circumvent this process completely. If it has to be an audition-rated process, then everything is up for grabs. I would prefer to cast no parts with auditions, but unfortunately, this is the way it is.

FC: You really gotta let it go. You've gotta get a life.

SW: Should I tell him the John Kimball story?

FC: Absolutely.

SW: When I was an actor in the early part of my career, looking for the perfect agent, I met a wonderful agent still very prominent in the William Morris Agency, John Kimball. Except this was years ago. It was in New York and I was whining about something, you know, somebody threw me off, or the sun got in my eyes, or I should've gotten this, you know. He said, "You know what? This is an easy conversation to have. Who asked you to be an actor?" That really shut me up and it sent me into directing!

MH: **What's different about the audition is that it's a craft unto itself. It is not, "Here I am this wonderful actor. If you give me six days, a week, two weeks, three weeks, I can do a fantastic job on this. And when you get me on the set, I'm so fabulous!" That's not what it's about here. It has to do with having a very short period of time to prepare in an artificial situation. That's the way it is. And it isn't yours to change. You have to accept those things. You have to go in there and do the best you can. You have to be as professional and friendly as you can be and you have to know that that's where you're at. And you can't start over and over again. You can't make it perfect and** you know what, they don't really want to know that you're the most talented person. They don't really care that you're the most talented person. They want that role to be filled.

SW: And, by the way, the way to not worry about it is to realize that the whole audition process is really more about who doesn't get the part, as opposed to who does get the part. So, who cares?

QUESTION: This a question for Sam and Fern. You said something before about sending a demo tape somewhere if there's no possibility for a reading. I watch my demo tape and think there's nothing on it which can be compared to the character they are looking for. Do you think I'm doing myself a favor by sending my demo tape in, even though it has something completely different on it?

JW: I don't think you should send in a comedy tape for a dramatic role. Do not assume they can see you're right for the role from the wrong piece of material.

QUESTION: What do you think are the chances of European actors here in this town?

FC: I think, more than ever. I think it's absolutely more international now.

SW: I had an actor once get a part. He had acted very little in English. He was Danish, actually, and he was having a real problem, but he actually got the part because I asked him to switch instantly into Danish. He was perfect speaking in his native language. So when we sent the tape into the studio, he was the choice for the part, but they had to approve it. We sent only his Danish performance, not his English performance at all.

JW: I think as far as television, it's very difficult, because you're really playing to a Midwestern audience that wants to hear very clear English. Now after saying that, there are many more co-productions being done with foreign markets, whether it's syndication, like *Voyager* on UPN, or cable, like Showtime. There are other avenues. But television, as a whole, is not an international medium yet for actors. Features are more so.

AO: I think daytime television may be more agreeable to it. I think it's better than it has been. It may never get to be as prolific as you'd like it to be, but I think it's like casting women in roles—for many years, you'd never think of casting a woman in certain roles, but now, roles like judges are portrayed by women. So I think it's a lot better than it was.

QUESTION: I have an agenting question. What's a positive way to say to your agent, "Look, you're really not seeing me right," or, "I'm not going out right," or, "Something isn't working about our relationship."

JW: I think you have to sit down with your agent and formulate a game plan. See if his game plan is in sync with where you want to go with your career. If it's not, and he doesn't have any creative thoughts, then I think maybe you have to leave your agent. If you want to give him an opportunity to change more to your thinking, then you've got to be firm in expressing to him or her what type of roles and projects you'd like to go out for. You have to be very clear. Don't leave anything in-between the cracks. It's your life and your career. Don't waste time.

AO: That might be one of those times when you ask, "When do you get a manager?" You might suggest to the agent, "Do you think we need somebody else on our team to help with my career?" or "Is there something I can do?" In other words, don't make it so much like you're blaming him or her, but more, "What can I do to augment what we do together?"

QUESTION: This actually ties in mostly for Al and Jeff in terms of taking on new clients. What do you guys look for? Is it strictly credits? Do you actually look at pictures and resumés when they come in?

JW: I don't look at pictures and resumés that much, honestly. Because, number one, I don't look at them when they're blanketed across town. I just throw those out. What I would do? Two things really: I would come out and see a play or if Margie called me and said she was having a special workshop and she'd like for me to see some of it, I would come out. The second thing, if there's anything on tape . . . Also, sitting in an office and just chatting for a little while gives me a little bit of a feel. And I've been doing it long enough that I have a little bit of an instinct as to the look and the feel of the person and what the buyer is looking for, but I prefer and I will take the time to come out and see a play.

QUESTION: Or comics?

JW: Comics are a lot easier to see. I represent alot of comedians.

QUESTION: I know you do. The thing is, a lot of times you'll call for industry showcases, but to actually get the agent to come out is a little more difficult than you make it sound.

JW: It depends who you call.

QUESTION: What about managers?

AO: It's the same thing. It's a difficult situation. You try as much as possible. I mean, I spend a lot of nights out. I work with a group called the Actor's Gym, a repertory group that we work with every Thursday. It's a place to expand your craft. I also try to get to the theater as much as possible, to the clubs to see stand-up comedy. Budd Friedman is a friend of ours and every so often he or Mark will call us to go down to the Improv. So, you try as much as possible to get to those places. It's impossible to see as many actors as everyone would like and you can't take on everybody who wants to be part of it. It's not a situation where I can keep the doors open by having a lot of, if you'll excuse the expression, wannabes. You need people who are also going to be producing.

JW: That's a good point. Don't have people come out unless you're absolutely ready. You've gotta be smart about this. If it takes you another six months to be seen by a top-notch agency, then wait. Because you have one shot and then . . . it doesn't mean the door's closed forever, but we're human. We're not going to spend the time and rush out again for awhile. So be smart about it.

MH: Is there a difference in auditioning in New York vs. Hollywood?

SW: I think there are fewer actors in New York.

FC: And fewer projects.

SW: I find when I read people in New York, I tend to see a lot more people who aren't right for the parts. I don't know why that is.

JW: Maybe because there are not that many projects so everybody's rushing in to see what's there.

SW: I think also, sometimes the actors in New York aren't as well-prepared. I guess the actors in New York don't get wrought up about it as much as the actors here do.

MH: Is there a difference between auditioning for theater, film and TV?

FC: Absolutely.

MH: Let's just talk about that for a second, because a lot of people come from the theater and all of a sudden they're faced with film and TV.

SW: There's an enormous difference.

FC: A play is large and television is a very small medium that picks up everything you do.

SW: I think when you audition actors for a play, one of the first things you're looking for is stage presence and whether or not they're right for the space the play is in. I mean, if you're auditioning people for a large space and they don't have a lot of stage and vocal presence, then you eliminate them instantly.

FC: I think your mannerisms are much larger, everything you're doing is that much larger for theater. I've read many stage people. They are wonderful actors but sometimes they have difficulty being brought down to the small medium of television or film, where the camera picks up every little turn of an eye. So there's definitely a difference. Less is more for film and television.

QUESTION: When you're auditioning for a role that requires a specific accent . . .

FC: Like the one you're talking with?

QUESTION: Yes, ma'am. Are you better off trying to fake the accent or are you better off going with something that's natural for you?

FC: I think natural. Whatever feels more natural for someone, because it's such an unnatural situation. I mean, the elements are basically against you. So anything more that's going to be against you is not going to behoove you in your reading.

QUESTION: When you're auditioning for television and every move you make is captured by the camera, but you're trying out in a room full of people and you're far away from them, should you make an adjustment for that?

FC: We don't usually have the luxury of rooms that are large enough. So that's probably not going to happen that often. But if you are, move your chair closer.

MH: This is a tough business. If you're not going to enjoy the process, if you're not going to have fun, if you're not going to enjoy laughing and loving and the things that are important in life—become a mechanic! Don't get into this business unless you enjoy it. And that's the difference—when you walk in and you're happy and enjoying the experience, they feel that. But when you walk in with all your baggage, they experience that, too.

I hope the most important thing you've gotten out of this is to really enjoy yourself and to own the work as best you can. Good luck!

—

DO'S AND DON'TS

EDAFE BLACKMAN / For Your Love, . . . and the Band Played On

I'd been in Los Angeles about a month, maybe six weeks and I wake up one Saturday and I hear music playing. So I get up and walk out and there's a parade going on—Black History Parade in Pasadena. Debbie Allen's the grand marshall. And I think, "Oh, shit!" 'Cause this is when *A Different World* was the #2 show.

So I start running down the street 'cause she's way down at the front of the motorcade. I finally get there and I say, "Miss Allen, I'm doing this play right up the street at the park." And she said, "When?" I said, "Tonight." And she said, "I can't make it tonight." I said, "Well, tonight's the last night." And she said, "Oh, I'm sorry, I can't make it." I said, "Miss Allen, I'm the best actor in North America!" And she said, "Really?" And I said, "Yes!" Then she said, "Well, in that case, you should come audition for my show." I told her, "But I just got to town. I don't have an agent or anything." So she said, "Let me give you the number to the production office."

So I run into a barber shop to borrow a pen. She gives me her phone number. I write it down on a dollar bill. (I would pay money for that dollar bill!)

So I call and leave a message and the following week, somebody calls me. They've got a role on the show that they want me to play. So I get on the bus to Studio City, pick up the sides, go back home, sleep with them all night, and memorize the whole thing.

On Wednesday, I go down to audition and everybody there is a star. I'm talking a line of 50 or 60 guys, because there weren't that many black shows on. It was *A Different World* and *Cosby*. That was it. So I go in and I read. This is my very first audition in

EDAFE BLACKMAN

Los Angeles and I'm so nervous that I can't even feel my feet. I remember just standing there in the middle of the room with all the producers and writers. And so I say, "You know what? I can't feel my feet." And everyone starts laughing and then I knew it was gonna be okay.

So I read. And on my way out, they say, "Can you hang around for a couple minutes?" and I say, "Okay, sure." And a few more guys go in and they say, "Come read again." So I go in. I read again. It gets a little bit better. I'm relaxing. I'm on my way out, "Hang out a couple of minutes." I end up reading and the line is getting smaller and smaller.

It came down to me and one other guy. Kadim Hardison was supposed to direct the show that week. (That was his directorial debut.) And he comes out and starts talking to the other guy. And I think, "Oh, I didn't get it. " And they're talking and laughing. And then he comes up to me and says, "You ready to work?" I couldn't believe it!

So I do the show. Jada's on the show and she says, "I really like your work. Who's your agent?" And I said, "Yo, I just got to town. I don't have an agent." She said, "What? You've got to meet my agent." So the following week, I met with Jada's agent, who was Nancy Rainford, and she repped both of us for awhile back in '92, '93. And that's how I got my foot in the door.

PICTURES AND RESUMÉS

- **DON'T** bring in a picture that doesn't look like you. **DO** stick with a natural shot, no dramatic angles, dogs, cats, trees, etc.—just you.
- **DON'T** print your agent's name bigger than yours on your resumé. **DO** make sure your name stands out.
- **DON'T** lie on your resumé—it's really embarrassing. **DO** stick with the truth—it's easier in the long run.

AGENTS AND MANAGERS

- **DON'T** ask an agent or manager to come out and see your work unless you're absolutely ready. **DO** wait the extra six months if you think it will make a difference.
- **DON'T** take on a manager if your agent doesn't get along with them. **DO** talk to your agent to see what they recommend .
- **DON'T** expect your agent or manager to babysit you. **DO** go to the casting director's office and ask the questions that you need to know.

GETTING IN THE DOOR

- **DON'T** think it's critical to get in at the very early stages of the casting process. **DO** wait until the project settles a bit and then start pushing.
- **DON'T** send in your comedy reel if you're up for a dramatic part (you can't assume that the auditioners will see that you're right for the role from inappropriate material). **DO** submit your tape if it shows something representative, but try to audition in person if possible.
- **DON'T** talk your way into an audition if you know that you're totally wrong for the part. **DO** recognize that you shouldn't be there if you're not suitable for the part.

PREPARATION

- **DON'T** be one of those actors who says, "I'll wait. I'll just go in early to look at the script." **DO** get to the casting director's office and get the sides so you're prepared.
- **DON'T** memorize the script for your audition. **DO** be familiar with the material.
- **DON'T** let yourself be affected by another person's reading that you happen to hear through the door. **DO** concentrate on your own work or remove yourself to the hall until it's your turn.
- **DON'T** get angry with the casting people if the sessions run late. **DO** try to remain calm or reschedule your appointment.
- **DON'T** go into an audition thinking, "How can I do this differently next time?" **DO** focus on the current read.
- **DON'T** second-guess anybody. **DO** go in with your own interpretation of the part.

- **DON'T** approach every audition as life or death. **DO** remember to have some fun in the process.

THE AUDITION

- **DON'T** walk in saying, "I'm really sorry, but I didn't read the script. I have four appointments today." **DO** make it your business to be prepared or keep your mouth shut.
- **DON'T** immediately start making excuses: "Oh, sorry I'm late. There's so much traffic, etc." **DO** stick to business.
- **DON'T** ask the casting person or director or producer just before the read, "Is there anything you want to tell me?" **DO** follow through with the choice you've made.
- **DON'T** just go in and wing it if the character has been revamped or the script has changed. **DO** ask for a few minutes to read over the new material and prepare yourself.
- **DON'T** try to play your character ten different ways during the same scene. **DO** make one choice and commit yourself to it (if you're off, the director can always give you another choice).
- **DON'T** use props or costumes. **DO** dress appropriately for the character.
- **DON'T** dress so suggestively that it detracts from the reading (and, it's unprofessional). **DO** realize that your auditioners are human.
- **DON'T** touch the casting director. **DO** allow yourself to feel any physical effects the other character might have on you. (For example, if John supposedly just kissed you, feel the kiss, even though the casting director is ten feet away.)
- **DON'T** change the scripted words during your audition. **DO** have the courtesy and professionalism to say the words that the writer has written.
- **DON'T** drop the paper to your side (the minute you lower your arm, you'll go up on the lines). **DO** use the sides.
- **DON'T** be encumbered by superfluous stage directions. **DO** take cues from the stage directions about the emotional life of your character. (For example, if the script says, "Paula moves toward the open window in tears," then you know that she is upset. You may not choose to cry at that particular moment, but you've taken in the information.)
- **DON'T** just wing pronunciations that you're unsure of. **DO** ask beforehand if you're uncertain how to pronounce a name or word.
- **DON'T** stand behind furniture or back yourself up against a wall. **DO** take a deep breath, step out in the open and present yourself.
- **DON'T** bring extraneous objects with you to the audition, especially birds or other animals. **DO** try to act professional at all times.

- **DON'T** ask the casting director or producer/director if you can try out for another part. **DO** trust their judgment.
- **DON'T** leave your keys or any other personal items in the room. **DO** try to make sure that all of your belongings leave with you.

CALLBACKS

- **DON'T** go into a callback with a hundred questions (callbacks are strictly to do your work) **DO** have your agent or manager call beforehand if something is unclear.
- **DON'T** think it's necessary to shake all twelve sets of hands in a callback situation. **DO** say a casual hello to the room and begin.
- **DON'T** completely change your reading for the callback. **DO** stick with your original choices unless you have been told otherwise.

SCREEN TESTS

- **DON'T** allow yourself to be put on film or tape in a test situation unless there's some sort of lighting, makeup and hair (especially for the women). **DO** have your agent or manager push strongly to control those circumstances.

FEEDBACK

- **DON'T** blame your manager or agent for a role you didn't get. **DO** ask them to get feedback from the casting person about your audition.

AFTERWORD

ED ASNER / "Lou Grant" on *The Mary Tyler Moore Show*

I met with Ed Asner early one morning; the meeting was arranged by Ed's daughter, Kate, who studies with me. I brought a long list of questions, ranging from SAG union issues to how the business has changed since he was out pounding the pavement. But what I really wanted to hear about was Ed's career-making audition for the role Lou Grant.

AN INTERVIEW WITH ED ASNER

MH: What was the most memorable film or TV audition that you've had?

EA: For *The Mary Tyler Moore Show.* I had had my two worst years in L.A. I was on the brink of disaster in my mind. A wife, three kids . . . I was in dire circumstances. Then I had my best year, thanks to Wally Grummell. And the following year, I was called in to audition for Mary, thanks to Ethel Winant and Grant Tinker who called Brooks and Burns[1]. Ethel Winant said I could do anything.

I came in and read for the part. I had stayed away from comedy in L.A. because the way to be discovered was guest-starring on dramas. And I was also afraid of comedy. Even though I could do an occasional funny appearance, I never did. Although on the stage, I had been good, I couldn't do it the same every night. I fluctuated wildly, which made me afraid.

So I went in, wanting to take advantage of every chance I got. And I read this great script they had written and this great character and I auditioned for the two men. And they muttered, "Um

---

[1] James L. Brooks and Allan Burns created *The Mary Tyler Moore Show*

ED ASNER

hum, um hum. That's a very intelligent reading." No laughs. They said, "When we have you back to read for Mary, we want you to do it wild, wiggy, all stops out, crazily." I didn't know what the hell they were talking about. So I said, "Listen. The few times in my life I've really aced a job was when I acted free and unfettered and unchained to the business or to the job. I'm not sure I know what to do. So rather than have me come back later, why don't you see if I can do it that way now? And if I can't, don't have me back." They were kind of taken aback by that and they said, "Well, we do have another appointment, but, okay. Go ahead and read."

It's all manner and attitude. It's a chemistry that you have to try to make it and I wasn't trying to make it. That probably was the main thing. I was free. And I think being free is more important than trying to do anything. So I read it crazily, out of control, a real meshuganah. I think Jim Brooks was the big laugher. I think he forced all kinds of laughs. I have no idea what they had meant. I think they wanted to see how much I was willing to abase myself in terms of the character, in terms of being a total jerk and flake and not being hide-bound, throwing caution to the wind. When I finished, they said, "Read it just that way when you come back to read with Mary." And I kept thinking, "What the f**k did I do?" I don't know what I did! I said, "Maaaary!" a certain way.

So a week or two later, I came back to read with Mary. She was lovely and sweet, open and generous, and I tried to read it the same way with her then again. And Jim laughed loudly again. Years later, I found out that after I left, Mary turned to them and said, "Are you sure?" And they said, "That's your Lou Grant."

MH: **When you started to audition for Lou Grant, you didn't have any character choices at that moment. Did they just develop as you went along?**

EA: That and I certainly did not do it that crazily. They gave me the spark of manicness which I used. We also did an audition scene, which was shown to advertisers, I believe, and Jay Sandrich directed that. Jay, of course, directed 99 percent of our shows. And we were working in a low-ceilinged studio, a tight set, and Jay, as usual, was a pain in the ass, but I felt secure there because, I said, "I got this job. I don't know who this little shit is. I'll listen to his carping and harping and this and that, but . . . I'll do it as best I can my way and try to accommodate him, but he's such a pest. Once we start the series, I'll have some clout and I'll see that he's not brought back."

MH: **Psychological aspects . . . how do you turn them around?**

EA: Well, you're not really asking the right person. I remember there was a guy who directed *Save the Tiger*. I came in and I was already big on *Mary Tyler Moore* but the director didn't know who I was. "I'm coming in to read for you, you son of a bitch, the least you could do . . . " I didn't like the character I read. It was the one who has the heart attack and is with the prostitute. I didn't give a very inspired reading. Norman Burton ended up doing it, but my resentment and me feeling offended created big stumbling blocks. I'm not saying I would have gotten the part. I think I stopped trying.

MH: **Do you remember your worst audition?**

EA: Well, it was a series of three. During that two-year period that my career had started going in the toilet, Larry Tucker and Paul Mazursky [had written] *I Love You, Alice B. Toklas*. Larry Tucker liked me a lot. So they brought me in to read the first time just for and Paul. I didn't know Paul. And I came in, and the way Larry was responding to me, I figured I had this goddamned job nailed!

That, to me has always been a big stumbling block. Never think you've got a job nailed. To me, it's been the most destructive attitude and has cost me a number of jobs. Even though they tell you you've got the job, you don't have it till you get the check. I've even found that when, consciously, I was telling myself not to count on this, unconsciously, I let the feeling enter in and I'm afraid it affected me.

So anyway, I came in to read for Larry so Paul could hear me. Let's say I started out at a ninety-five. When I left the room, because of the sour, acid look Paul always has on his face, I left feeling no higher than a ninety. Then they had me back again. I guess this implied Paul had doubts. In the meantime, we're preparing to move into a new house. We haven't sold the first house and I'm not working and I go in to read again. Paul's sour look has not improved. So if I went in at a ninety the second time; I left at an eighty-five or eighty, maybe even lower. Then they got a very well-known director and I came in again. I suppose they were going to vote by this time. Paul was against me and they were going to see if the director wanted me, as well, with Larry, in which case it'd be a go. I read again and I think by the time I walked into that room, I was kissing the job good-bye already. I read, I left and whenever I got the eventual phone call I was not surprised that they had cast somebody else.

The last day, I have to go down and pay the money on the new house—which I had to borrow from my agent. I'm driving on Sunset to get this $10,000 and I see a movie company out there. I see two guys walking out of the building with the glass elevator. As I get closer, I realize it's Peter Sellers and Herb Edelman doing my role in a scene that would have negated this trip down Sunset to borrow the $10,000 from my agent. I thought, "How ironic!"

MH: **Do you still have to audition for parts?**

EA: No, I don't remember when I read the last time.

MH: **What are some tips that you think might help actors going into an audition?**

EA: Try to put a cap on your presence there, without overstaying your leave. They may like you very much but you want to make your exit with them wanting more. I've made the mistake of trying to show them in the interview how brilliant I am. I think it's always good to not show them how dumb you are, show them occasional flashes of brilliance, but let yourself be in awe of their brilliance and keep your mouth shut. I have a tendency to talk too much . . .

MH: **Do you believe in memorization? Do you think you should memorize the whole scene before you go in?**

EA: I never have. First of all, I learned a long time ago that if you ground yourself in the role in terms of memorization, it'll make it all the more difficult for the director to adapt you to what he wants. When I was doing *Threepenny Opera* in New York, I'd been doing it about a year and a half, maybe two years—the role of Mr. Peachum. Then I got hold of the *Threepenny* novel, which Brecht had written. I read the novel and I was fascinated by the character of Peachum. I wanted to institute a lot of that into my performance. I went out there the first night after the opening song for the opening monologue. I tried to instill some of that character thought into my opening monologue, missed three or four laughs and by the time I got to halfway down the speech I said, "Ooooh shit! Tracks don't leave me now!" and I jumped back on the tracks and I never looked back.

MH: Your daughter's in the business now. As you follow her career, do you think there are major differences for her auditioning today versus when you were auditioning?

EA: Whatever jungle was out there when I started, it's increased a thousand-fold. The vines are thicker, the snakes are more poisonous and more numerous and the heat has increased. I would be horrified if I took stock of going into the business now as opposed to when I did it. When Ronald Reagan was president of the Screen Actors Guild, there were 18,000 members. And that was only 1960. We're only talking about thirty-five years ago. Now, there are 80,000 members and the jobs have not increased commensurately.

MH: You were president of the Screen Actors Guild in . . .

EA: 1981-85.

MH: What are the struggles that actors face today? There is obviously more competition. What can actors expect for the future?

EA: There's been a lessening of the power of unions to be able to bargain with their members. The union doors are constantly being broken down throughout the country and in our industry. The industry's becoming more and more recognized as being a money-making industry and a possible way to win the lottery, drawing more and more people in it. More and more people are developing that consciousness of winning the lottery in life and therefore are choosing this business, so the arena is filled with volunteers who are ready to die far more and far worse than they did before. So you have to fight all of that non-working competition as well as recognize the fact that the opportunities are certainly no more numerous or hardly more numerous than they were in the old days.

MH: Where are things like cable . . .

EA: Doesn't make a goddamn bit of difference because in the days when there were only three networks, I used to say, "We'd be better off if we just had one." When I was a series performer on CBS, it was the most difficult thing in the world to get a Movie of the Week during my hiatus because they were too busy chasing down the stars of NBC and ABC to appear on the network.

MH: **Fern Champion brought up the idea of having paid readers. Do you think actors should fight for that?**

EA: If it's gonna cost them money, and it is, to have paid readers, I think it's fruitless to try to enlarge the payroll. It's wasted effort.

MH: **Doesn't it affect you when someone's sitting there who doesn't know how to read and he is feeding you monotone lines? When they're not really giving you anything and yet you have to do so much?**

EA: You may have to do that when you're shooting the job, so the thing to do is develop what is necessary for you. The greatest statement I ever heard was from my acting teacher, Mira, who went and saw *The Glass Menagerie* with Lorett Taylor. She was amazed because Mira's technique was doing it. She totally believed in doings. When she saw Lorett Taylor, she said that Taylor was so great, she not only did her own doings, she did Tom's and Laura's. And that's what the actor in the reading will have to learn how to do when presenting his speeches— he must cover not only his own activity but the nerd he's reading with.

MH: **So, you have to respond to what's not given to you as well as what's given to you.**

EA: That's right. Because the producer and director certainly aren't dummies. They're going to see that input added to what the flat, dull voice of the casting person is giving you.

MH: **Is there a difference between auditioning for film and TV?**

EA: Whereas film people were always regarded as low brow by eminent stage people in the past, over the years they have now taken on those trappings of snobbery. They tend to regard TV in the same fashion. And all too often I allowed myself to believe that was fact, when, in actuality, you probably see better acting overall on TV than you do in film. There certainly is no great magic to film acting. If you're a good actor on TV, you certainly would be a good actor in film, but you have to wade through all the mystery and bullshit that they wrap film actors in. A TV actor communes with people on the street, the film actor stays in his ivory tower and preserves his skin. This may sound bitter, but I think there's a great element of truth in what I just said. I don't think there's a difference. I think that if you're a TV actor and you're going in to see film people, you probably have to accord them the worship they demand—until it gets too much to suffer and then you have to make a stand and say, "Who the hell are you talking to?"

MH: Do you have a special way to prepare for an audition?

EA: No, I just try to understand what the scene's about, what the character's about. I never have difficulty getting to the understanding. My problem very often will be not having the outer trappings of accent.

MH: Do you think you should go in there with an accent in the first audition?

EA: If you know the character is from South Carolina, I think it's wonderful.

MH: What if you don't do it well or if you've only had one day to look at it?

EA: I'd probably try to work it up as best I could. Or, you could be bold and brave, I suppose, and say, "I need to do some work on my accent, so I'd prefer to read it straight now and nail the accent later."

MH: I tell my clients to take charge of their audition.

EA: I've never done that though, unfortunately. I can tell you the most amazing thing: I worked up my German accent for *Rich Man, Poor Man*. The first day of work, I went in and David Greene said, "How's your German accent?" I did a little shit-kicking. He said, "Well, you don't have to use it if you don't want to." And I thought, "What? I've worked on it!" How can somebody dispense with something that seems to be such an essential part of the character? How could you do it without an accent? And I said, "Well, I'd like to try it." Thank God I did.

MH: Have you ever been on the other side?

EA: Yeah, and I must say that I'm probably hide-bound. Whereas some people would say, "Oh, how wonderfully free when people leave the script," I would automatically put a black mark down! I don't care how talented you are, if you come in and automatically disregard [the script] . . . I was taught to revere it! That's what Brooks and Burns really were great at, you know. You don't change an "and," "but," or "or."

MH: That's exactly what I say. There's a rhythm to it. Use the words that are written.

EA: And comedy develops that for you much more than drama does. That's why comedy is so helpful to drama, because it teaches you stresses that you might otherwise overlook.

MH: Did you find a difference between the way you audition for a drama or comedy?

EA: My sensitivities are not acute enough to say that they're different. Of course, you want to hear that laugh when you hit an obvious punch line. And another thing: the auditioner should find specific moments where he just shuts up and takes an inordinate pause to look at his fellow reader or to look before answering. Even if you force the other reader to say, "Did you hear me?" or "I said . . . " find a couple lines to give moment to that aren't dictated to in the text.

MH: I tell my clients that silence is their friend. Silent times are the most precious times. Those are times that draw us in, because when you are silent in your thoughts, I want to know what those thoughts are. But if you keep talking, talking, talking, you don't give me a chance to get to know who you are.

EA: In the same vein, from my earliest acting experiences as an amateur, I used to love to turn my back on the audience and try to act with my back. The same should occur in a reading, if possible.

MH: I always say, you don't have to get into an eye-staring contest.

EA: That's right. My lady drives me up the wall. She's gotten out of the habit now, but when she's talking to me—and she does a lot of talking to me—she wants me to look at her. I've delicately tried to say, "I don't look at people when I'm talking to them. I'm looking around. When I feel I want to emphasize, then I come in. Your face is not a kaleido-scope, giving me different shades every minute of the time. I mean, I'm listening to what you're saying, which is more important than the look on your face."

MH: But when you do look, you are there. Any words to end this thing? Any no-no's?

EA: Don't fart. Always remember, the fart you hear will never kill ya. The worse one is the silent one.

EPILOGUE

Well, it's time to say good-bye. It's been wonderful for me to share with you my stories, my technique, my clients' experiences and my love for teaching. There's a lot of information in this book, so remember, give yourself time to integrate it all. Practice as much as possible. If auditioning is something relatively new for you, then go out and audition for everything that you can—showcases, theater, student films, independents, and hopefully TV and features. Just get out there and practice your craft until it becomes second nature.

I end all of my classes with a toast that I would like to pass on to you:

I wish you all great success, but more importantly, I wish you lots of love and laughter. For life is as much a process as the work. Have fun and enjoy it! And don't take this business too seriously or you'll forget why you started acting in the first place!

As Gary Graham (*Alien Nation*), a former student of mine, once said, "If you can teach me to enjoy the process again, it'll make it all worthwhile." Hopefully this book has helped you do just that.

L'Chaim! To Life!

WHAT ACTORS SAY ABOUT MARGIE HABER'S WORKSHOPS . . .

"I had my network reading for the lead in the series, Misguided Angels. They threw three new pages at me, saying, "We know this is really cold, but we need to see another scene." So I had, literally, two minutes to break down the scene and I went into Margie Haber mode: grabbed my relationship, my objectives and my VIPS, used the technique for staying on the page and had a great read. (Probably as good as what I had prepared the week before.) The technique saved me."

—DAVID LIPPER (Misguided Angels)

"I really have to credit Margie's technique with getting me A Different World in the first place. I still use it to this day. It's been invaluable to me."

—CREE SUMMER (Sweet Justice, A Different World)

"Ever since I've been in Los Angeles, I've taken a number of cold reading classes from different instructors, and Margie's class is unique in that it gives one a tangible plan, a set structure to work from which greatly enhances your readings."

—GARRETT WANG (Star Trek: Voyager)

"Learning to 'know thyself' before you walk into an audition room really helps. Through Margie's class, I learned who I was, or at least how I appeared to be."

—BROOKE LANGTON (The Net, Melrose Place)

"The Haber Technique helped me bring more colors to my auditions, ask more questions and use more of me, creating some wonderful, spontaneous moments that happen from having so much information on the character and the scene."

—IONA MORRIS (Slauson Heights, As the World Turns)

"I feel that the nuts and bolts concentration of lifting your eyes at the beginning of the phrase and at the end, allowing yourself to look down and give yourself the time in the middle, holding onto the paper at a certain point with your thumb . . . I know it sounds so mundane, but I like those tasks because it gives me something else to focus on besides myself. It takes away the nervousness and gives me some mechanics to use, so that I don't have to worry about messing up, skipping a word, getting tongue-tied, losing focus and not making eye contact with the casting director. I found those points very, very helpful. Even though they're common sense, we all forget about them and you have to constantly remind yourself, no matter how long you've been doing this. And Margie's very good at it."

—CONSTANCE McCASHEN (Brooklyn Bridge, Knot's Landing)

Margie at the studio with her teachers:
(top row l-r) Crystal Carson, Barbara Gannen, Joe Anthony, Annie Grindlay
(bottom row l-r) Courtney Burr, Margie Haber, Corey Allen

OTHER FILM & ENTERTAINMENT BOOKS FROM LONE EAGLE PUBLISHING. . .

■ SPECIAL FEATURES ■

THE ULTIMATE FILM FESTIVAL SURVIVAL GUIDE
The Essential Companion for Filmmakers and Festival-Goers
by Chris Gore

Learn the secrets of Sundance, Telluride, Slamdance and over 500 film festivals worldwide in this comprehensive and eye-opening guide. Packed with information, this book reveals how to get a film accepted and what to do after acceptance, from putting together a press kit to putting on a great party to actually closing a deal. Includes interviews with festival directors, PR pros, acquisition experts and others. Also contains complete directory listings of hundreds of film festivals plus resource appendices for screening rooms, affordable video dub facilities, and agents for independent filmmakers.

CHRIS GORE has been called everything from "the Gen-X Leonard Maltin" to the "pit bull of journalism." He is the publisher of *Film Threat* magazine and has been a judge at the Florida Film Festival, Athens Film Festival, Slamdance Film Festival and for the American Film Institute.

$14.95 ISBN 1-58065-009-0, original trade paper, 6 x 9, 304 pp, illustrated.

THE HOLLYWOOD JOB-HUNTER'S SURVIVAL GUIDE
An Insider's Winning Strategies For Getting
That (All-Important) First Job...And Keeping It
by Hugh Taylor

Hugh Taylor offers insider's advice on getting that all important first job, Setting up the Office and Getting to Work, the Script and Story Development Process, Production, Information, Putting It all Together, and Issues and Perspectives.

HUGH TAYLOR received his MBA in business from Harvard's School of Business Administration. He has worked as an assistant to one of Hollywood's top producers moving up from the job of "gofer" to Vice President.

$18.95 ISBN 0-943728-51-7, original trade paper, 5.25 x 8, 250 pp, illustrated.

SCHLOCK-O-RAMA
The Films of Al Adamson
by David Konow

The films of Al Adamson captured the '70s drive-in era and reflected the time and culture in all its glory. Often compared to zany director Ed Wood, Adamson gave a twisted version of what was going on in America, told with the wildest characters imaginable. Adamson is the only film director who ever gave Colonel Sanders a part in a movie in exchange for all the chicken the crew could eat. David Konow documents how a maverick filmmaker with a few bucks made a fortune on his own terms. Includes never-before seen photos, insider stories and interviews.

$19.95 ISBN 1-58065-001-5, original trade paper, 8.5 X 11, 160 pp, illustrated.

To order or for more information,
call 1-800-FILMBKS (345-6257) or go to www.loneeagle.com

OTHER FILM & ENTERTAINMENT BOOKS FROM LONE EAGLE PUBLISHING. . .

ACTING

THE ACTOR'S ENCYCLOPEDIA OF CASTING DIRECTORS
Conversations With Over 100 Casting Directors
On How to Get the Job
by Karen Kondazian with Eddie Shapiro, Foreword by Richard Dreyfuss

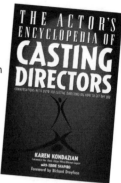

Karen Kondazian has compiled insider information and intimate profiles from talking to the premier casting directors in film, television, and commercials from Los Angeles to New York. Casting directors speak on the record to reflect and convey expert advice on how to get in the door and prepare effectively for readings. Each interview contains a photograph, filmography and personal profile. Find out from Casting Directors what's hot and what's not.

KAREN KONDAZIAN is a feature writer for *Back Stage West/Drama-Logue*. Her column, The Actor's Way, is read by thousands every week. Ms. Kondazian lives in Los Angeles.

$19.95 ISBN 1-58065-013-9, original trade paper, 6 x 9, 480 pp.

MAKING MONEY IN VOICE-OVERS
Winning Strategies to a Successful Career in TV, Commercials, Radio and Animation
by Terri Apple
Foreword by Gary Owens

This book helps the actor, radio DJ, vocal impressionist and amateur cartoon voice succeed in voice-overs, no matter where you live. From assessing one's competitive advantages to creating a demo tape to handling initial sessions, Apple provides a clear guide full of insider tips and strategies helpful to both beginners and experienced professionals.

TERRI APPLE is one of the top paid, award-winning voice-over actresses whose work is heard everyday all across the country. She lives in Los Angeles, California.

$16.95 ISBN 1-58065-011-2, original trade paper, 5.5 x 8.5, 224 pp.

NEXT!
An Actor's Guide to Auditioning
by Ellie Kanner and Paul G. Bens, Jr.

Written by two of Hollywood's hottest casting directors, NEXT! is the definitive insider's guide to successfully navigating the complicated maze of auditions and landing that all-important role in a movie or TV show. NEXT! details the common errors that most inexperienced actors make when auditioning.

ELLIE KANNER cast the TV pilot of *Friends* and *The Drew Carey Show*. **PAUL G. BENS, JR.** is a partner in Melton/Bens Casting.

$19.95 ISBN 0-943728-71-1, original trade paper, 7 x 9, 184 pp.

YOUR KID OUGHT TO BE IN PICTURES
A How-To Guide for Would-Be Child Actors and Their Parents
by Kelly Ford Kidwell and Ruth Devorin

Written by a top talent agent and a stage mom with three children working in film, TV and commercials, YOUR KID OUGHT TO BE IN PICTURES explains what the odds of success are, how to secure an agent, where to go for professional photographs, the auditioning process, lots of photographs, plus much more.

$16.95 ISBN 0-943728-90-8, original trade paper, 9 x 6, 280 pp.

To order or for more information,
call 1-800-FILMBKS (345-6257) or go to www.loneeagle.com

OTHER FILM & ENTERTAINMENT BOOKS FROM LONE EAGLE PUBLISHING. . .

■ SCREENWRITING ■

WRITING GREAT CHARACTERS
The Psychology of Character Development
by Michael Halperin, Ph.D.

This valuable book identifies and solves a major problem for writers, creating characters who are so real they literally jump off the page. Halperin has developed an easy to understand, logical system which gives all screenwriters a foolproof and failproof method of developing great characters. WRITING GREAT CHARACTERS is a book for all writers, from the expert who is looking to polish his techniques to the novice who wants to learn the craft from an expert.

MICHAEL J. HALPERIN, Ph.D., has taught screenwriting at UCLA and currently teaches at Loyola Marymount University in Los Angeles, CA. He has written numerous popular television programs and has authored several bestselling computer based interactive media programs. He has given seminars for executives of television and film. He holds a BA in Communications from USC and a Ph.D. in Film Studies from the Union Institute in Cincinnati, Ohio.

$19.95 ISBN 0-943728-79-7, original trade paper, 6 x 9, 208 pp.

WRITING SHORT FILMS
Structure and Content for Screenwriters
by Linda J. Cowgill

Contrasting and comparing the differences and similarities between feature films and short films, WRITING SHORT FILMS offers readers the essential requirements necessary to make their writing crisp, sharp and compelling. Emphasizing characters, structure, dialogue and story, WRITING SHORT FILMS dispels the "magic formula" concept that screenplays can be constructed by anyone with a word processor and a script formatting program. Writing a good screenplay, short or long, is a difficult job. Citing numerous examples from short films as well as feature films, the author teaches strategies to keep a short film on track and writer's block at bay. Chapter headings include The Three Part Nature of Film Structure, Proper Screenplay Format, and Dialogue–The Search for the Perfect Line.

LINDA J. COWGILL received her Masters in Screenwriting from UCLA, after winning several screenwriting awards and Fellowships. She has taught screenwriting seminars at the Boston Film Institute, the American Film Institute, and the prestigious Kennedy Center in Washington, D.C. Currently Ms. Cowgill teaches screenwriting at Loyola Marymount University in Los Angeles. Ms. Cowgill has written over 12 features and teleplays.

$19.95 ISBN 0-943728-80-0, original trade paper, 6 x 9, approx. 250 pp.

TOP SECRETS: SCREENWRITING
by Jurgen Wolff and Kerry Cox

"TOP SECRETS is an authentic stand-out. The combination of biographies, analyses, interviews and actual script samples is a real winner."
–Professor Richard Walter, UCLA

"TOP SECRETS provides an excellent addition to screenwriting literature. It conveys what it takes to be a screenwriter: the passion, the discipline, the art, the craft, the perseverance."
–Dr. Linda Seger, Author of *Making A Good Script Great*

$21.95 ISBN 0-943728-50-9, original trade paper, 6 x 9, 342 pp.

To order or for more information,
call 1-800-FILMBKS (345-6257) or go to www.loneeagle.com

OTHER FILM & ENTERTAINMENT BOOKS FROM LONE EAGLE PUBLISHING. . .

SCREENWRITING

ELEMENTS OF STYLE FOR SCREENWRITERS
The Essential Manual for Writers of Screenplays
by Paul Argentini

In the grand tradition of Strunk and White's *Elements of Style,* Paul Argentini presents an essential reference masterpiece in the art of clear and concise principles of screenplay formatting, structure and style for screenwriters. Argentini explains how to design and format manuscripts to impress any film school professor, story editor, agent, producer or studio executive. The ultimate quick reference guide to formatting a screenplay—no book in shorter space, with fewer words, will help screenwriters more than this persistent volume. Includes a playwrite chapter for structure and format and an updated list of literary agent contacts.

PAUL ARGENTINI is a screenwriter, playwright and novelist.

$11.95 ISBN 1-58065-003-1, original trade paper, 5.5 x 8.5, 176 pp.

SECRETS OF SCREENPLAY STRUCTURE
by Linda J. Cowgill

In her new book, Linda Cowgill articulates the concepts of successful screenplay structure in a clear language, based on the study of great films from the thirties to present day. SECRETS OF SCREENPLAY STRUCTURE helps writers understand how and why great films work as well as how great form and function can combine to bring a story alive. Cowgill includes many helpful anecdotes, insider strategies, as well as do's and don'ts which will help readers make their writing more professional, and therefore, more marketable.

LINDA J. COWGILL is the author of *Writing Short Films.* She received her Masters in Screenwriting from UCLA after winning several screenwriting awards and fellowships.

$16.95 ISBN 1-58065-004-X, original trade paper, 6 x 9, 336 pp.

GET PUBLISHED! GET PRODUCED!
Tips on how to sell your writing from America's #1 Literary Agent
by Peter Miller

This valuable book tells the reader how to avoid being viewed as a neophyte in a business that is notorious for taking advantage of writers. Drawing on over 20 years experience as a top literary agent, Miller offers advice on how to sell your published fiction, structure a nonfiction book proposal, package your book so that it will become a feature film or TV production, market a screenplay, get an agent, tips on contract negotiation, and more!

PETER MILLER has sold over 800 books on behalf of many best-selling authors, sold book rights for film and TV adaptation and produced several film and TV projects.

$19.95 ISBN 0-943728-92-4, original trade paper, 6 x 9, 336 pp.

HOW TO ENTER SCREENPLAY CONTESTS. . . AND WIN!
An Insider's Guide to Selling Your Screenplay to Hollywood
by Erik Joseph

There are more than 50 legitimate screenwriting competitions across the U.S. Entering such a contest is the best and most affordable way to get your screenplay noticed, optioned, sold, and ultimately produced. Contains comprehensive listings of screenplay contests.

$16.95 ISBN 0-943728-88-6, original trade paper, 6 x 9, 184 pp.

To order or for more information,
call 1-800-FILMBKS (345-6257) or go to www.loneeagle.com

ABOUT THE AUTHORS

MARGIE HABER

Over the past twenty years, Margie Haber has taught many of Hollywood's rising stars and working actors. A highly respected acting coach on both coasts, she began her On-Camera Cold Reading Workshop 15 years ago, specializing in the audition process.

Today, Margie's clients can be seen in hit movies (Brad Pitt in *Seven Years in Tibet* and Kelly Preston in *Jerry Maguire*), heart-throbbing TV shows (Heather Locklear, Lisa Rinna and David Charvet in *Melrose Place*), critically acclaimed episodics (Vondie Curtis-Hall in *Chicago Hope*), sitcoms (Téa Leoni in *The Naked Truth*), cult classics (Garrett Wang in *Star Trek: Voyager*), soap operas (Eileen Davidson in *The Young and the Restless*) and much more.

Born in New York, Margie received her Bachelor's degree in Speech and Drama from Ithaca College and a Master's in Speech Pathology from Brooklyn College. In 1970, she arrived in Los Angeles to embark on a successful acting career. Throughout the '70s and '80s, Margie guest-starred on various films and television series including *The Mod Squad, Barnaby Jones* and *Emergency,* and was the quintessential "Mom" in countless commercials.

From 1974 to 1982, Margie taught at the Lee Strasberg Institute, where she recognized the need and value of a good cold reading technique. She left to found the Performing Arts Corporation (PAC) in 1982. Margie's new facility was the first of its kind, offering a forum for producers, directors and casting directors to share their knowledge in a professional teaching capacity.

The mid-'80s found Margie in back in New York, fine-tuning her technique. As demand grew and word spread about her teaching, Margie settled on Los Angeles as a base of operations, where she is regarded as one of the top cold reading specialists in the country. Margie also teaches on-going workshops in San Francisco and New York, and has expanded her teaching internationally to include Canada, Germany and other European countries.

BARBARA BABCHICK

Originally from Houston, Texas, Barbara Babchick has worked in various areas of the entertainment industry as an actress, singer, songwriter, script supervisor and production coordinator for the last fifteen years. Currently employed as a script supervisor for television and commercials, she works closely with numerous directors, producers and actors.

With a Bachelor of Fine Arts in Theatre from USC, Barbara began her career as an actress, studying with fellow actors Eric Stoltz, Anthony Edwards and Forrest Whittaker. After college, Barbara worked as a production coordinator for Gold Castle Records, an independent record label distributed by Capitol Records, where she assisted on new recordings by legendary performers Peter, Paul & Mary, Joan Baez and Judy Collins. During that time, Barbara wrote over fifty of her own songs, including a European hit single for Olympic track star Carl Lewis.

A writer at heart, Barbara is happy to collaborate on *HOW TO GET THE PART...without falling apart,* combining her acting background with her love for writing.